DATE DUE

2/20/15			
3/18/15			
4/16/15			
			PRINTED IN U.S.A.

The Britannica Guide to
The Atom

PHYSICS EXPLAINED

The Britannica Guide to
The Atom

EDITED BY ERIK GREGERSEN, ASSOCIATE EDITOR,
SCIENCE AND TECHNOLOGY

Britannica
Educational Publishing

IN ASSOCIATION WITH

ROSEN
EDUCATIONAL SERVICES

Published in 2011 by Britannica Educational Publishing
(a trademark of Encyclopædia Britannica, Inc.)
in association with Rosen Educational Services, LLC
29 East 21st Street, New York, NY 10010.

Distributed exclusively by Rosen Educational Services.
For a listing of additional Britannica Educational Publishing titles, call toll free (800) 237-9932.

First Edition

Britannica Educational Publishing
Michael I. Levy: Executive Editor
J.E. Luebering: Senior Manager
Marilyn L. Barton: Senior Coordinator, Production Control
Steven Bosco: Director, Editorial Technologies
Lisa S. Braucher: Senior Producer and Data Editor
Yvette Charboneau: Senior Copy Editor
Kathy Nakamura: Manager, Media Acquisition
Erik Gregersen: Associate Editor, Science and Technology

Rosen Educational Services
Heather M. Moore Niver: Editor
Nelson Sá: Art Director
Cindy Reiman: Photography Manager
Nicole Russo: Designer
Matthew Cauli: Cover Design
Introduction by Erik Gregersen

Library of Congress Cataloging-in-Publication Data

The Britannica guide to the atom / edited by Erik Gregersen.
    p. cm. — (Physics explained)
"In association with Britannica Educational Publishing, Rosen Educational Services."
Includes bibliographical references and index.
ISBN 978-1-61530-319-9 (library binding)
1. Atoms — Popular works. I. Gregersen, Erik. II. Title: Guide to the atom. III. Title: Atom.
QC173.B8514 2010
539.7 — dc22

                                                        2010023231

Manufactured in the United States of America

On the cover, p. iii: The atom is the smallest component of matter that has the characteristic properties of a chemical element. © *www.istockphoto.com/Radu Razvan*

On page xii: Pierre and Marie Curie, shown here on their 1895 honeymoon bicycle trip, discovered radium and polonium. *Photos.com/Jupiterimages*

On page xx: Wavelength spectrometers of the early 1900s were used to explore the chemical nature of material. *SSPL via Getty Images*

On pages 1, 51, 72, 103, 144, 184, 217, 242, 301, 305, 314: The carbon atom is the only element to form extensive networks of covalent bonds with other elements as well as itself. *Don Farrall/Photodisc/Getty Images*

CONTENTS

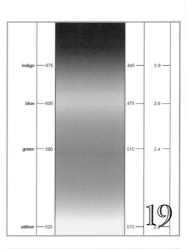

19

32

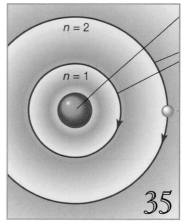

$n = 2$

$n = 1$

35

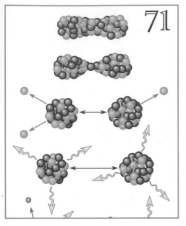

71

74

82

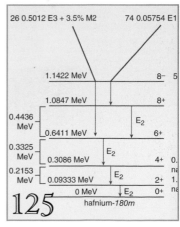

145

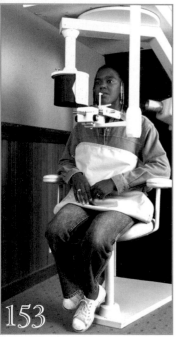

153

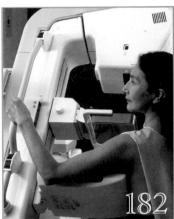

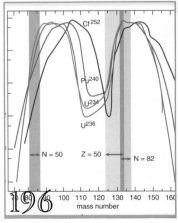

226

232

243

INTRODUCTION

A standard sheet of office paper measures 8.5 inches wide and 11 inches long. If one took that sheet of paper, tore it in half across its width, and threw away the other half, one would be left with a piece of paper 5.5 inches wide and 8.5 inches long. After six tears, the sheet of paper would be a little more than an inch on a side. After seven more tears, that small chit of paper would be about 0.1 inch on a side. It would be difficult to tear that minute piece of paper easily, but perhaps it could be done. However, one would eventually reach the limit of one's manual dexterity and be left with a small speck of paper. Though one could imagine some much smaller creature like an ant continuing the process, there would have to be some point at which the paper could not be torn anymore.

In the 4th century BCE, the Greek philosopher Democritus followed such a speculation to postulate the existence of some indivisible piece of matter. He called these pieces "atomos" (Greek for indivisible), and from atomos comes the modern word, atom. Democritus and other Greek philosophers did not tear scrolls of papyrus into smaller and smaller pieces to find the size of the atom. In ancient times, the atom was a thought experiment, an idea about matter and its properties that was never tested as a scientific theory. But how far would one have to tear the sheet of paper to get down to the atom?

It was not until 1865 that German chemist Joseph Loschmidt, who studied the motion and diffusion of gases, answered this question. The answer was a few billionths of an inch (or one-hundred millionth of a centimetre). Such a minuscule distance would have staggered the ancient Greek philosophers.

This book delves inside the atom to reveal many facets of nuclear physics. The first subject is the history of how humanity began to understand the atom, beginning with the first speculations of Democritus, Leucippus, and Epicurus. In the 18th century, scientists such as John Dalton and Joseph-Louis Gay-Lussac studied how substances combined in chemical reactions and deduced that these substances must be made up of atoms. It was soon realized that atoms differed from each other by weight. For example, hydrogen was much lighter than a metal like cesium. The Russian chemist Dmitry Mendeleyev realized that the elements were arranged in tabular form according to the weight of their individual atoms. This arrangement is known worldwide as the periodic table of the elements. From it, Mendeleyev was able to predict the properties of the elements gallium, scandium, and germanium, which had not yet been discovered.

The 19th century saw tremendous advances in the study of the atom. Atoms were discovered to have electrical properties. The spectral lines of hydrogen were seen to fit a numerical pattern. One of the greatest advances was the discovery that the atom itself contained even smaller particles. In 1897 the English physicist J.J. Thomson discovered the electron. Not only was the electron the carrier of electric charge, but it was also 1/1,836ths as heavy as a hydrogen ion. (The fact that the electron only existed in certain energy levels that corresponded to something like an orbit around the nucleus explained the numerical pattern of the hydrogen spectral lines.)

Another significant advance was the discovery of radioactivity in 1896 by the French physicist Henri Becquerel. This showed that not only did the atom contain small particles, but also that when the atom experienced radioactive decay, it became that of another element. The medieval alchemists had sought the transmutation of elements, in particular, the remunerative changing of lead into gold. Here was such a transmutation, but one that occurred naturally. The discovery of radioactivity led to the discovery that the atom was mostly empty space. Nearly all the mass of an atom save the pittance found in the electrons was concentrated in a central nucleus. These discoveries in turn spurred the development of quantum mechanics, which overthrew commonsense notions of the universe by explaining physical phenomena in terms of probabilities.

The development of quantum mechanics led to an accurate description of the atom and its properties. The atom is made up of a nucleus of positively charged protons and the neutrons, which have no electric charge. These two particles are much heavier than the electron. Every atom has an atomic number, which is the number of protons in the nucleus. Hydrogen, the lightest element, has an atomic number of 1. The heaviest element thus far discovered, ununoctium (of which only a few atoms have been produced), has an atomic number of 118.

Some atoms have the same atomic number but have differing number of neutrons and thus different masses. These atoms with different masses are called isotopes. For example, hydrogen has isotopes with zero, one, or two neutrons. The latter two are called deuterium and tritium, respectively. Even though different isotopes are the same chemical element, they can have vastly different properties. In this book, the particular example of helium-3 and helium-4 are discussed. (The numbers 3 and 4 are the masses of the isotopes. For example, tritium could be, but rarely is, called hydrogen-2.) Helium-4 is the most common isotope, being 700,000 times more plentiful than helium-3. Because helium-3 is 25 percent lighter than helium-4, however, it can move much faster. Helium has the interesting property of superfluidity in which in its liquid state it can flow without friction at very cold temperatures. Because of their different masses, helium-3 has two superfluid states, while helium-4 has only one.

Many isotopes are unstable, that is, they are radioactive. They release particles and through that release change, or decay, into other isotopes. Those isotopes in turn may decay into other isotopes. Eventually, a stable isotope is reached. For example, uranium-238 decays into isotopes of thorium, protactinium, radium, radon, polonium, and bismuth before ending at lead-206. The time it takes for half of a substance to decay into something else is called the half-life. In the aforementioned chain of uranium to lead, the first step, uranium-238 to thorium-234, has the longest half-life of 4.5 billion years, very nearly the same age as Earth. The shortest step, polonium-214 to lead-210, takes 0.00015 second.

The phenomenon of radioactivity has many practical uses. By measuring the amount of the radioactive isotope carbon-14 (which has a half-life of 5,730 years, roughly the span of recorded human history) that an artefact contains, archaeologists are able to accurately date that artefact and thus have revealed much about humanity's past. For example, in 1991 a mummified body was found encased in ice in the Italian Alps. Using carbon dating, it was determined that Otzi, as the mummy was later called, lived around 3300 BCE. Other successes of carbon dating have included Kennewick Man, a 9,400-year-old skeleton found in Washington state, the Dead Sea Scrolls, and the determination of the sequence of the construction of Stonehenge.

Another widespread use of radioactivity is in smoke detectors. Each household smoke detector contains a small amount of americium-241. Americium is an artificially produced chemical element. The americium-241 decays with a half-life of 432 years to become neptunium-237. In its decay, the americium-241 produces a steady stream of alpha particles, which are made up of two protons and two neutrons. These alpha particles collide with oxygen and nitrogen atoms in the air and ionize them. These ions are collected at electrodes in the smoke detector. However, smoke de-ionizes the oxygen and nitrogen and thus they are not collected at the electrode, which sets off the alarm.

Of course, for most people the most immediate association of radioactivity is nothing so benign as determining when a Neolithic man lived or preventing people from dying in fires. It is known as a deadly harmful force that should be avoided. Taboo subjects or people are sometimes metaphorically referred to as radioactive, in testimony to the belief that radioactivity is to be shunned and feared.

The particles, X-rays, and gamma rays given off in radioactivity can cause great injury, pain, and even death if experienced in sufficient doses. Radiation ionizes atoms within the human body, and those new ions and free radicals (molecules with an extra electron) can cause bonds within other molecules to break down in an attack on a person's biochemistry. It was not long after German physicist Wilhelm Roentgen's discovery of X-rays that the harmful effects of radiation became apparent.

The great energies found inside the atom are revealed in the processes of nuclear fission and nuclear fission. In the former an atom is split apart, and in the latter atoms are joined together. Nuclear fission can happen both naturally and artificially. Two prime examples of the latter are nuclear reactors and the atomic bomb. In both the reactor and the bomb, a fission process is started in which the neutrons released split apart other atoms. When those atoms split, neutrons are released that split apart other atoms and so on in what is called a chain reaction. In the atom bomb, the chain reaction is allowed to "run away" and release an enormous amount of energy that can destroy a city. Of course, such an explosion would be disastrous in a nuclear reactor, so rods made of a material such as cadmium that absorbs neutrons are inserted into the reactor core and thus control the reaction.

One sees the results of nuclear fusion every day in the sunlight that bathes Earth. In a process called the proton–proton cycle, four hydrogen nuclei are fused together to form a helium nucleus. The energy that is released comes from the difference in mass between the four hydrogen atoms and the helium nucleus. Although the energy is in the form of gamma rays, they lose energy over the hundreds of thousands of years it takes the gamma ray photons to emerge from the Sun.

The direct conversion of mass to energy in nuclear fusion means that it is much more efficient than any other form of energy production, such as coal, natural gas, or oil. Scientists have worked on trying to make fusion energy a reality for more than 60 years. Some critics have regarded nuclear fusion as six decades of wasted effort with the functioning fusion reactor always "ten years from now." However, scientists working on nuclear fusion have been able to claim steady, if slow, progress. Research is still ongoing, and the next great step in the quest for nuclear fusion energy source, the large tokamak ITER, is under construction in France and is scheduled to be complete in 2017.

Regardless of whether or not ITER is the longed-for breakthrough in nuclear fusion, the study of the atom will remain a vital area of physics. This book offers a fascinating and concise overview of nuclear physics for the science buff and the casual enthusiast alike.

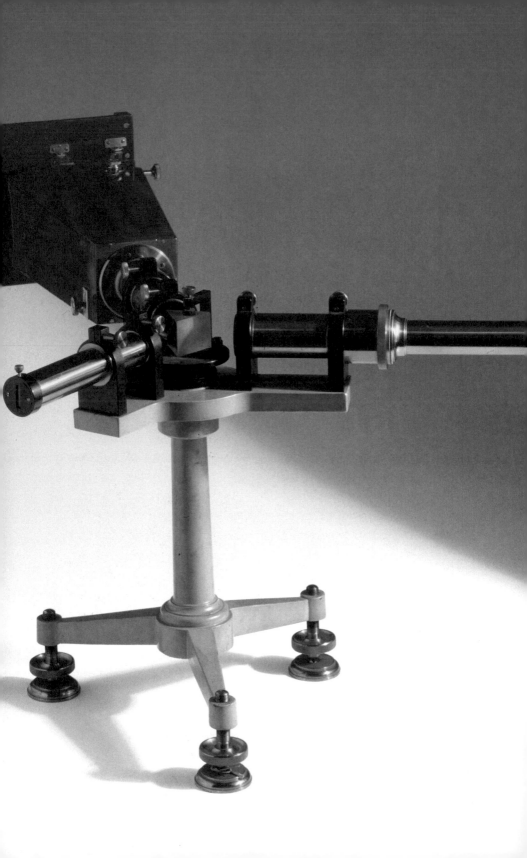

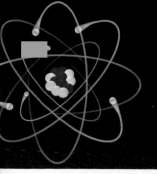
The concept of the atom that Western scientists accepted in broad outline from the 1600s until about 1900 originated with Greek philosophers in the 5th century BCE. Their speculation about a hard, indivisible fundamental particle of nature was replaced slowly by a scientific theory supported by experiment and mathematical deduction. It was 2,000 years before modern physicists realized that the atom is indeed divisible and that it is not hard, solid, or immutable.

WHAT IS AN ATOM?

The atom is the smallest unit into which matter can be divided without the release of electrically charged particles. It also is the smallest unit of matter that has the characteristic properties of a chemical element. As such, the atom is the basic building block of chemistry.

Most of the atom is empty space. The rest consists of a positively charged nucleus of protons and neutrons surrounded by a cloud of negatively charged electrons. The nucleus is small and dense compared with the electrons, which are the lightest charged particles in nature. Electrons are attracted to any positive charge by their electric force. In an atom, electric forces bind the electrons to the nucleus.

Because of the nature of quantum mechanics, no single image has been entirely satisfactory at visualizing the atom's various characteristics, which thus forces physicists to use complementary pictures of the atom to explain different properties. In some respects, the electrons in an atom behave like particles orbiting the nucleus. In others, the electrons behave like waves frozen in position around the nucleus. Such wave patterns, called orbitals, describe the distribution of individual electrons. The behaviour of an atom is strongly influenced by these orbital properties, and its chemical properties are determined by orbital groupings known as shells. What follows in this chapter is a historical survey of the most influential concepts about the atom that have been formulated through the centuries.

THE ATOMIC PHILOSOPHY OF THE EARLY GREEKS

Leucippus of Miletus (5th century BCE) is thought to have originated the atomic philosophy. His famous disciple, Democritus of Abdera, named the building blocks of matter *atomos*, meaning literally "indivisible," about 430 BCE. Democritus believed that atoms were uniform, solid, hard, incompressible, and indestructible and that they moved in infinite numbers through empty space until stopped. Differences in atomic shape and size determined the various properties of matter. In Democritus's philosophy, atoms existed not only for matter but also for such qualities as perception and the human soul. For example, sourness was caused by needle-shaped atoms, while the colour white was composed of smooth-surfaced atoms. The atoms of the soul were considered to be particularly fine. Democritus developed his atomic philosophy as a middle ground between two opposing Greek theories about reality and the illusion of change. He argued that matter was subdivided into indivisible and immutable particles that created the appearance of change when they joined and separated from others.

The philosopher Epicurus of Samos (341–270 BCE) used Democritus's ideas to try to quiet the fears of superstitious Greeks. According to Epicurus's materialistic philosophy, the entire universe was composed exclusively of atoms and void, and so even the gods were subject to natural laws.

Most of what is known about the atomic philosophy of the early Greeks comes from Aristotle's attacks on it and from a long poem, *De rerum natura* ("On the Nature of Things"), which the Latin poet and philosopher Titus Lucretius Carus (*c.* 95–55 BCE) wrote to popularize its ideas. The Greek atomic theory is significant historically and philosophically, but it has no scientific value. It was not based on observations of nature, measurements, tests, or experiments. Instead, the Greeks used mathematics and reason almost exclusively when they wrote about physics. Like the later theologians of the Middle Ages, they wanted an all-encompassing theory to explain the universe, not merely a detailed experimental view of a tiny portion of it. Science constituted only one aspect of their broad philosophical system. Thus, Plato and Aristotle attacked Democritus's atomic theory on philosophical grounds rather than on scientific ones. Plato valued abstract ideas more than the physical world and rejected the notion that attributes such as goodness and beauty were "mechanical manifestations of material atoms." Where Democritus believed that matter could not move through space without a vacuum and that light was the rapid movement of particles through a void, Aristotle rejected the existence of vacuums because he could not conceive of bodies falling equally fast through a void. Aristotle's conception prevailed in medieval Christian Europe where science was based on revelation and reason, whereas the Roman Catholic theologians rejected Democritus as materialistic and atheistic.

THE EMERGENCE OF
EXPERIMENTAL SCIENCE

De rerum natura, which was rediscovered in the 15th century, helped fuel a 17th-century debate between orthodox Aristotelian views and the new experimental science. The poem was printed in 1649 and popularized by Pierre Gassendi, a French priest who tried to separate Epicurus's atomism from its materialistic background by arguing that God created atoms.

Soon after the Italian scientist Galileo Galilei expressed his belief that vacuums can exist (1638), scientists began studying the properties of air and partial vacuums to test the relative merits of Aristotelian orthodoxy and the atomic theory. The experimental evidence about air was only gradually separated from this philosophical controversy.

The Anglo-Irish chemist Robert Boyle began his systematic study of air in 1658 after he learned that Otto von Guericke, a German physicist and engineer, had invented an improved air pump four years earlier. In 1662 Boyle published the first physical law expressed in the form of an equation that describes the functional dependence of two variable quantities. This formulation became known as Boyle's law. From the beginning, Boyle wanted to analyze the elasticity of air quantitatively, not just qualitatively, and to separate the particular experimental problem about air's "spring" from the surrounding philosophical issues. Pouring mercury into the open end of a closed J-shaped tube, Boyle forced the air in the short side of the tube to contract under the pressure of the mercury on top. By doubling the height of the mercury column, he roughly doubled the pressure and halved the volume of air. By tripling the pressure, he cut the volume of air to a third, and so on.

This behaviour can be formulated mathematically in the relation $PV = P'V'$, where P and V are the pressure and volume under one set of conditions and P' and V' represent them under different conditions. Boyle's law says that pressure and volume are inversely related for a given quantity of gas. Although it is only approximately true for real gases, Boyle's law is an extremely useful idealization that played an important role in the development of atomic theory.

Soon after his air-pressure experiments, Boyle wrote that all matter is composed of solid particles arranged into molecules to give material its different properties. He explained that all things are

> made of one Catholick Matter common to them all, and . . . differ but in the shape, size, motion or rest, and texture of the small parts they consist of.

In France Boyle's law is called Mariotte's law after the physicist Edme Mariotte, who independently discovered the empirical relationship in 1676. Mariotte realized that the law holds true only under constant temperatures; otherwise, the volume of gas expands when heated or contracts when cooled.

Forty years later Isaac Newton expressed a typical 18th-century view of the atom that was similar to that of Democritus, Gassendi, and Boyle. In the last query in his book *Opticks* (1704), Newton stated:

> All these things being considered, it seems probable to me that God in the Beginning form'd Matter in solid, massy, hard, impenetrable, moveable Particles, of such Sizes and Figures, and with such other Properties, and in such Proportion to Space, as most conduced to the End for which he form'd them; and that these primitive Particles

being Solids, are incomparably harder than any porous Bodies compounded of them; even so very hard, as never to wear or break in pieces; no ordinary Power being able to divide what God himself made one in the first Creation.

By the end of the 18th century, chemists were just beginning to learn how chemicals combine. In 1794 Joseph-Louis Proust of France published his law of definite proportions (also known as Proust's law). He stated that the components of chemical compounds always combine in the same proportions by weight. For example, Proust found that no matter where he got his samples of the compound copper carbonate, they were composed by weight of five parts copper, four parts oxygen, and one part carbon.

EXPERIMENTAL FOUNDATION OF ATOMIC CHEMISTRY

The English chemist and physicist John Dalton extended Proust's work and converted the atomic philosophy of the Greeks into a scientific theory between 1803 and 1808. His book *A New System of Chemical Philosophy* (*Part I*, 1808; *Part II*, 1810) was the first application of atomic theory to chemistry. It provided a physical picture of how elements combine to form compounds and a phenomenological reason for believing that atoms exist. His work, together with that of Joseph-Louis Gay-Lussac of France and Amedeo Avogadro of Italy, provided the experimental foundation of atomic chemistry.

On the basis of the law of definite proportions, Dalton deduced the law of multiple proportions, which stated that when two elements form more than one compound by combining in more than one proportion by weight, the weight of one element in one of the compounds is in simple, integer ratios to its weights in the other compounds. For example, Dalton knew that oxygen and carbon can combine to form two different compounds and that carbon dioxide (CO_2) contains twice as much oxygen by weight as carbon monoxide (CO). In this case the ratio of oxygen in one compound to the amount of oxygen in the other is the simple integer ratio 2:1. Although Dalton called his theory "modern" to differentiate it from Democritus's philosophy, he retained the Greek term *atom* to honour the ancients.

Dalton had begun his atomic studies by wondering why the different gases in the atmosphere do not separate, with the heaviest on the bottom and the lightest on the top. He decided that atoms are not infinite in variety as had been supposed and that they are limited to one of a kind for each element. Proposing that all the atoms of a given element have the same fixed mass, he concluded that elements react in definite proportions to form compounds because their constituent atoms react in definite proportion to produce compounds. He then tried to figure out the masses for well-known compounds. To do so, Dalton made a faulty but understandable assumption that the simplest hypothesis about atomic combinations was true. He maintained that the molecules of an element would always be single atoms. Thus, if two elements form only one compound, he believed that one atom of one element combined with one atom of another element. For example, describing the formation of water, he said that one atom of hydrogen and one of oxygen would combine to form HO instead of H_2O. Dalton's mistaken belief that atoms join together by attractive forces was accepted and formed the basis of most of 19th-century chemistry. As long as scientists worked with masses as ratios, a consistent chemistry could be developed because they did not need to know whether the atoms were separate or joined together as molecules.

Gay-Lussac soon took the relationship between chemical masses implied by Dalton's atomic theory and expanded it to volumetric relationships of gases. In 1809 he published two observations about gases that have come to be known as Gay-Lussac's law of combining gases. The first part of the law says that when gases combine chemically, they do so in numerically simple volume ratios. Gay-Lussac illustrated this part of his law with three oxides of nitrogen. The compound NO has equal parts of nitrogen and oxygen by volume. Similarly, in the compound N_2O the two parts by volume of nitrogen combine with one part of oxygen. He found corresponding volumes of nitrogen and oxygen in NO_2. Thus, Gay-Lussac's law relates volumes of the chemical constituents within a compound, unlike Dalton's law of multiple proportions, which relates only one constituent of a compound with the same constituent in other compounds.

The second part of Gay-Lussac's law states that if gases combine to form gases, the volumes of the products are also in simple numerical ratios to the volume of the original gases. This part of the law was illustrated by the combination of carbon monoxide and oxygen to form carbon dioxide. Gay-Lussac noted that the volume of the carbon dioxide is equal to the volume of carbon monoxide and is twice the volume of oxygen. He did not realize, however, that the reason that only half as much oxygen is needed is because the oxygen molecule splits in two to give a single atom to each molecule of carbon monoxide. In his "Mémoire sur la combinaison des substances gazeuses, les unes avec les autres" (1809; "Memoir on the Combination of Gaseous Substances with Each Other"), Gay-Lussac wrote:

Thus it appears evident to me that gases always combine in the simplest proportions when they act on one

another; and we have seen in reality in all the preceding
examples that the ratio of combination is 1 to 1, 1 to 2 or 1
to 3 ... Gases ... in whatever proportions they may com-
bine, always give rise to compounds whose elements by
volume are multiples of each other ... Not only, however,
do gases combine in very simple proportions, as we have
just seen, but the apparent contraction of volume which
they experience on combination has also a simple relation
to the volume of the gases, or at least to one of them.

Gay-Lussac's work raised the question of whether atoms differ from molecules and, if so, how many atoms and molecules are in a volume of gas. Amedeo Avogadro, building on Dalton's efforts, solved the puzzle, but his work was ignored for 50 years. In 1811 Avogadro proposed two hypotheses: (1) The atoms of elemental gases may be joined together in molecules rather than existing as separate atoms, as Dalton believed. (2) Equal volumes of gases contain equal numbers of molecules. These hypotheses explained why only half a volume of oxygen is necessary to combine with a volume of carbon monoxide to form carbon dioxide. Each oxygen molecule has two atoms, and each atom of oxygen joins one molecule of carbon monoxide.

Until the early 1860s, however, the allegiance of chemists to another concept espoused by the eminent Swedish chemist Jöns Jacob Berzelius blocked acceptance of Avogadro's ideas. (Berzelius was influential among chemists because he had determined the atomic weights of many elements extremely accurately.) Berzelius contended incorrectly that all atoms of a similar element repel each other because they have the same electric charge. He thought that only atoms with opposite charges could combine to form molecules.

Because early chemists did not know how many atoms were in a molecule, their chemical notation systems were in a state of chaos by the mid-19th century. Berzelius and his followers, for example, used the general formula MO for the chief metallic oxides, while others assigned the formula used today, M_2O. A single formula stood for different substances, depending on the chemist: H_2O_2 was water or hydrogen peroxide; C_2H_4 was methane or ethylene. Proponents of the system used today based their chemical notation on an empirical law formulated in 1819 by the French scientists Pierre-Louis Dulong and Alexis-Thérèse Petit concerning the specific heat of elements. According to the Dulong-Petit law, the specific heat of all elements is the same on a per atom basis. This law, however, was found to have many exceptions and was not fully understood until the development of quantum theory in the 20th century.

To resolve such problems of chemical notation, the Sicilian chemist Stanislao Cannizzaro revived Avogadro's ideas in 1858 and expounded them at the First International Chemical Congress, which met in Karlsruhe, Germany, in 1860. Lothar Meyer, a noted German chemistry professor, wrote later that when he heard Avogadro's theory at the congress, "It was as though scales fell from my eyes, doubt vanished, and was replaced by a feeling of peaceful certainty." Within a few years, Avogadro's hypotheses were widely accepted in the world of chemistry.

ATOMIC WEIGHTS AND THE PERIODIC TABLE

As more and more elements were discovered during the 19th century, scientists began to wonder how the physical properties of the elements were related to their atomic weights. During the 1860s several schemes were suggested. The Russian chemist Dmitry Ivanovich Mendeleyev based his system on the atomic weights of the elements as determined by Avogadro's theory of diatomic molecules. In his paper of 1869 introducing the periodic law, he credited Cannizzaro for using "unshakeable and indubitable" methods to determine atomic weights.

> *The elements, if arranged according to their atomic weights, show a distinct periodicity of their properties . . . Elements exhibiting similarities in their chemical behavior have atomic weights which are approximately equal (as in the case of Pt, Ir, Os) or they possess atomic weights which increase in a uniform manner (as in the case of K, Rb, Cs).*

Skipping hydrogen because it is anomalous, Mendeleyev arranged the 63 elements known to exist at the time into six groups according to valence. Valence, which is the combining power of an element, determines the proportions of the elements in a compound. For example, H_2O combines oxygen with a valence of 2 and hydrogen with a valence of 1. Recognizing that chemical qualities change gradually as atomic weight increases, Mendeleyev predicted that a new

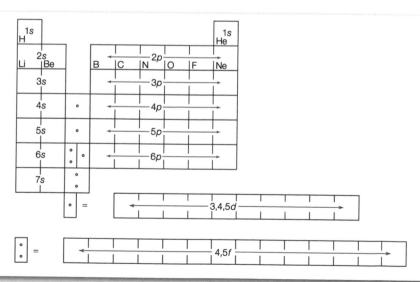

Periodic table of the elements showing the valence shells. Encyclopædia Britannica, Inc.

element must exist wherever there was a gap in atomic weights between adjacent elements. His system was thus a research tool and not merely a system of classification. Mendeleyev's periodic table raised an important question, however, for future atomic theory to answer: Where does the pattern of atomic weights come from?

KINETIC THEORY OF GASES

Whereas Avogadro's theory of diatomic molecules was ignored for 50 years, the kinetic theory of gases was rejected for more than a century. The kinetic theory relates the independent motion of molecules to the mechanical and thermal properties of gases—namely, their pressure, volume, temperature, viscosity, and heat conductivity. Three men—Daniel Bernoulli in 1738, John Herapath in 1820, and John James Waterston in 1845—independently developed the theory. The kinetic theory of gases, like the theory of diatomic molecules, was a simple physical idea that chemists ignored in favour of an elaborate explanation of the properties of gases.

Bernoulli, a Swiss mathematician and scientist, worked out the first quantitative mathematical treatment of the kinetic theory in 1738 by picturing gases as consisting of an enormous number of particles in very fast, chaotic motion. He derived Boyle's law by assuming that gas pressure is caused by the direct impact of particles on the walls of their container. He understood the difference between heat and temperature, realizing that heat makes gas particles move faster and that temperature merely measures the propensity of heat to flow from one body to another. In spite of its accuracy, Bernoulli's theory remained virtually unknown during the 18th century and early 19th century for several reasons. First, chemistry was more popular than physics among scientists of the day, and Bernoulli's

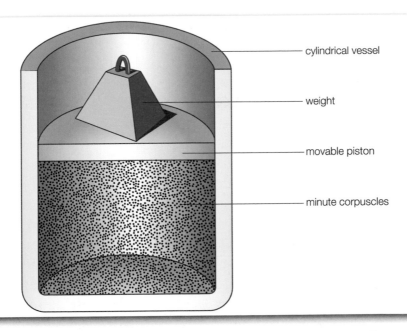

Bernoulli model of gas pressure. As conceived by Daniel Bernoulli in Hydrodynamica *(1738), gases consist of numerous particles in rapid, random motion. He assumed that the pressure of a gas is produced by the direct impact of the particles on the walls of the container.* Encyclopædia Britannica, Inc.; based on Daniel Bernoulli, Hydrodynamica (1738)

theory involved mathematics. Second, Newton's reputation ensured the success of his more comprehensible theory that gas atoms repel one another. Finally, Joseph Black, another noted British scientist, developed the caloric theory of heat, which proposed that heat was an invisible substance permeating matter. At the time, the fact that heat could be transmitted by light seemed a persuasive argument that heat and motion had nothing to do with each other.

Herapath, an English amateur physicist ignored by his contemporaries, published his version of the kinetic theory in 1821. He also derived an empirical relation akin to Boyle's law but did not understand correctly the role of heat and temperature in determining the pressure of a gas.

Waterston's efforts met with a similar fate. Waterston was a Scottish civil engineer and amateur physicist who could not even get his work published by the scientific community, which had become increasingly professional throughout the 19th century. Nevertheless, Waterston made the first statement of the law of equipartition of energy, according to which all kinds of particles have equal amounts of thermal energy. He derived practically all the consequences of the fact that pressure exerted by a gas is related to the number of molecules per cubic centimetre, their mass, and their mean squared velocity. He derived the basic equation of kinetic theory, which reads $P = NMV^2$. Here P is the pressure of a volume of gas, N is the number of molecules per unit volume, M is the mass of the molecule, and V^2 is the average velocity squared of the molecules. Recognizing that the kinetic energy of a molecule is proportional to MV^2 and that the heat energy of a gas is proportional to the temperature, Waterston expressed the law as $PV/T =$ a constant.

During the late 1850s, a decade after Waterston had formulated his law, the scientific community was finally ready to accept a kinetic theory of gases. The studies of heat undertaken by the English physicist James Prescott Joule during the 1840s had shown that heat is a form of energy. This work, together with the law of the conservation of energy that he helped establish, had persuaded scientists to discard the caloric theory by the mid-1850s. The caloric theory had required that a substance contain a definite amount of caloric (i.e., a hypothetical weightless fluid) to be turned into heat. Experiments showed that any amount of heat can be generated in a substance by putting enough energy into it, however, so there was no point to hypothesizing such a special fluid as caloric.

At first, after the collapse of the caloric theory, physicists had nothing with which to replace it. Joule, however, discovered Herapath's kinetic theory and used it in 1851 to calculate the velocity of hydrogen molecules. Then the German physicist Rudolf Clausius developed the kinetic theory mathematically in 1857, and the scientific world took note. Clausius and two other physicists, the Scot James Clerk Maxwell and the Austrian Ludwig Eduard Boltzmann (who developed the kinetic theory of gases in the 1860s), introduced sophisticated mathematics into physics for the first time since Newton. In his 1860 paper "Illustrations of the Dynamical Theory of Gases," Maxwell used probability theory to produce his famous distribution function for the velocities of gas molecules. Employing Newtonian laws of mechanics, he also provided a mathematical basis for Avogadro's theory. Maxwell, Clausius, and Boltzmann assumed that gas particles were in constant motion, that they were tiny compared with their space, and that their interactions were very brief. They then related the motion of the particles to pressure, volume, and temperature. Interestingly, none of the three committed himself on the nature of the particles.

STUDIES OF THE PROPERTIES OF ATOMS

In the 19th century, the small scales of the atomic became amenable to scientific study. The indivisible particles of Democritus now had sizes, as well as other properties such as electric charge. Atoms also contained even smaller particles, the electrons.

SIZE OF ATOMS

The first modern estimates of the size of atoms and the numbers of atoms in a given volume were made by the German chemist Joseph Loschmidt in 1865. Loschmidt used the results of kinetic theory and some rough estimates to do his calculation. The size of the atoms and the distance between them in the gaseous state are related both to the contraction of gas upon liquefaction and to the mean free path traveled by molecules in a gas. The mean free path, in turn, can be found from the thermal conductivity and diffusion rates in the gas. Loschmidt calculated the size of the atom and the spacing between atoms by finding a solution common to these relationships. His result for Avogadro's number is remarkably close to the present accepted value of about 6.022×10^{23}. The precise definition of Avogadro's number is the number of atoms in 12 grams of the carbon isotope C-12. Loschmidt's result for the diameter of an atom was approximately 10^{-8} cm.

Much later, in 1908, the French physicist Jean Perrin used Brownian motion to determine Avogadro's number. Brownian motion, first observed in 1827 by the Scottish botanist Robert Brown, is the continuous movement of tiny particles suspended in water. Their movement is caused by the thermal motion of water molecules bumping into the particles. Perrin's argument for determining Avogadro's number makes an analogy between particles in the liquid and molecules in the atmosphere. The thinning of air at high altitudes depends on the balance between the gravitational force pulling the molecules down and their thermal motion forcing them up. The relationship between the weight of the particles and the height of the atmosphere would be the same for Brownian particles suspended in water. Perrin counted particles of gum mastic at different heights in his water sample and inferred the mass of atoms from the rate of decrease. He then divided the result into the molar weight of atoms to determine Avogadro's number. After Perrin, few scientists could disbelieve the existence of atoms.

ELECTRIC PROPERTIES OF ATOMS

While atomic theory was set back by the failure of scientists to accept simple physical ideas like the diatomic molecule and the kinetic theory of gases, it was also delayed by the preoccupation of physicists with mechanics for almost 200 years, from Newton to the 20th century. Nevertheless, several 19th-century investigators, working in the relatively ignored fields of electricity, magnetism, and optics, provided important clues about the interior of the atom. The studies in electrodynamics made by the English physicist Michael Faraday and those of Maxwell indicated for the first time that something existed apart from palpable matter, and data obtained by Gustav Robert Kirchhoff of Germany about elemental spectral lines raised questions that would be answered only in the 20th century by quantum mechanics.

Until Faraday's electrolysis experiments, scientists had no conception of the nature of the forces binding atoms together in a molecule. Faraday concluded that electrical forces existed inside the molecule after he had produced an electric current and a chemical reaction in a solution with the electrodes of a voltaic cell. No matter what solution or electrode material he used, a fixed quantity of current sent through an electrolyte always caused a specific amount of material to form on an electrode of the electrolytic cell. Faraday concluded that each ion of a given chemical compound has exactly the same charge. Later he discovered that the ionic charges are integral multiples of a single unit of charge, never fractions.

On the practical level, Faraday did for charge what Dalton had done for the chemical combination of atomic masses. That is to say, Faraday demonstrated that it takes a definite amount of charge to convert an ion of an element into an atom of the element and that the amount of charge depends on the element used. The unit of charge that releases one gram-equivalent weight of a simple ion is called the faraday in his honour. For example, one faraday of charge passing through water releases one gram of hydrogen and eight grams of oxygen. In this manner, Faraday gave scientists a rather precise value for the ratios of the masses of atoms to the electric charges of ions. The ratio of the mass of the hydrogen atom to the charge of the electron was found to be 1.035×10^{-8} kilogram per coulomb. Faraday did not know the size of his electrolytic unit of charge in units such as coulombs any more than Dalton knew the magnitude of his unit of atomic weight in grams. Nevertheless, scientists could easily determine the ratio of these units.

More significantly, Faraday's work was the first to imply the electrical nature of matter and the existence of subatomic particles and a fundamental unit of charge. Faraday wrote:

> *The atoms of matter are in some way endowed or associated with electrical powers, to which they owe their most striking qualities, and amongst them their mutual chemical affinity.*

Faraday did not, however, conclude that atoms cause electricity.

Light and Spectral Lines

In 1865 Maxwell unified the laws of electricity and magnetism in his publication "A Dynamical Theory of the Electromagnetic Field." In this paper he concluded that light is an electromagnetic wave. His theory was confirmed by the German physicist Heinrich Hertz, who produced radio waves with sparks in 1887. With light understood

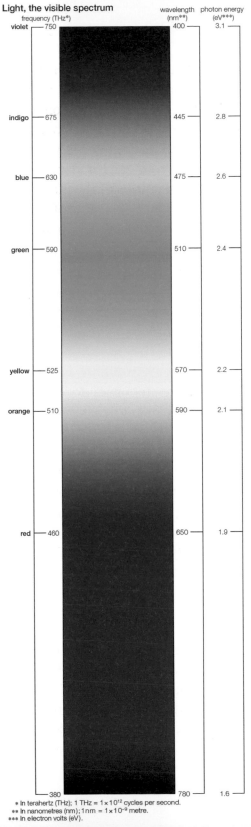

Light, the visible spectrum

frequency (THz*)		wavelength (nm**)	photon energy (eV***)
violet	750	400	3.1
indigo	675	445	2.8
blue	630	475	2.6
green	590	510	2.4
yellow	525	570	2.2
orange	510	590	2.1
red	460	650	1.9
	380	780	1.6

* In terahertz (THz); 1 THz = 1 × 10¹² cycles per second.
** In nanometres (nm); 1nm = 1 × 10⁻⁹ metre.
*** In electron volts (eV).

The visible solar spectrum, ranging from the shortest visible wavelengths (violet light, at 400 nm) to the longest (red light, at 700 nm). Encyclopædia Britannica, Inc.

as an electromagnetic wave, Maxwell's theory could be applied to the emission of light from atoms. The theory failed, however, to describe spectral lines and the fact that atoms do not lose all their energy when they radiate light. The problem was not with Maxwell's theory of light itself but rather with its description of the oscillating electron currents generating light. Only quantum mechanics could explain this behaviour.

By far the richest clues about the structure of the atom came from spectral line series. Mounting a particularly fine prism on a telescope, the German physicist and optician Joseph von Fraunhofer had discovered between 1814 and 1824 hundreds of dark lines in the spectrum of the Sun. He labeled the most prominent of these lines with the letters A through G. Together they are now called Fraunhofer lines. A generation later Kirchhoff heated different elements to incandescence in order to study the different coloured vapours emitted. Observing the vapours through a spectroscope, he discovered that each element has a unique and characteristic pattern of spectral lines. Each element produces the same set of identifying lines, even when it is combined chemically with other elements. In 1859 Kirchhoff and the German chemist Robert Wilhelm Bunsen discovered two new elements—cesium and rubidium—by first observing their spectral lines.

Johann Jakob Balmer, a Swiss secondary-school teacher with a penchant for numerology, studied hydrogen's spectral lines and found a constant relationship between the wavelengths of the element's four visible lines. In 1885 he published a generalized mathematical formula for all the lines of hydrogen. The Swedish physicist Johannes Rydberg extended Balmer's work in 1890 and found a general rule applicable to many elements. Soon more series were discovered elsewhere in the spectrum of hydrogen and in the spectra of other elements as well. Stated in terms of the frequency of the light rather than its wavelength, the formula may be expressed:

$$v = R(1/n^2 - 1/m^2).$$

Here v is the frequency of the light, n and m are integers, and R is the Rydberg constant. In the Balmer lines m is equal to 2 and n takes on the values 3, 4, 5, and 6.

DISCOVERY OF ELECTRONS

During the 1880s and '90s scientists searched cathode rays for the carrier of the electrical properties in matter. Their work culminated in the discovery by English physicist J.J. Thomson of the electron in 1897. The existence of the electron showed that the 2,000-year-old conception of the atom as a homogeneous particle was wrong and that in fact the atom has a complex structure.

Cathode-ray studies began in 1854 when Heinrich Geissler, a glassblower and technical assistant to the German physicist Julius Plücker, improved the vacuum tube. Plücker discovered cathode rays in 1858 by sealing two electrodes inside the tube, evacuating the air, and forcing electric current between the electrodes. He found a green glow on the wall of his glass tube and attributed it to rays emanating from the cathode. In 1869, with better vacuums, Plücker's pupil Johann W. Hittorf saw a shadow cast by an object placed in front of the cathode. The shadow proved that the cathode rays originated from the cathode. The English physicist and chemist William Crookes investigated cathode rays in 1879 and found that they were bent by a magnetic field. The direction of deflection suggested that they were negatively charged particles. As the luminescence did not depend on what gas had been in the vacuum or what metal the electrodes were made of, he surmised that the rays were a property of the electric current itself. As a result of Crookes's work, cathode rays were widely studied, and the tubes came to be called Crookes tubes.

Although Crookes believed that the particles were electrified charged particles, his work did not settle the issue of whether cathode rays were particles or radiation similar to light. By the late 1880s the controversy over the nature of cathode rays had divided the physics community into two camps. Most French and British physicists, influenced by Crookes, thought that cathode rays were electrically charged particles because they were affected by magnets. Most German physicists, however, believed that the rays were waves because they traveled in straight lines and were unaffected by gravity. A crucial test of the nature of the cathode rays was how they would be affected by electric fields. Heinrich Hertz, the aforementioned German physicist, reported that the cathode rays were not deflected when they passed between two oppositely charged plates in an 1892 experiment. In England J.J. Thomson thought Hertz's vacuum might have been faulty and that residual gas might have reduced the effect of the electric field on the cathode rays.

Thomson repeated Hertz's experiment with a better vacuum in 1897. He directed the cathode rays between two parallel aluminum plates to the end of a tube where they were observed as luminescence on the glass. When the top aluminum plate was negative, the rays moved down; when the upper plate was positive, the rays moved up. The deflection was proportional to the difference in potential between the plates. With both magnetic and electric deflections observed, it was clear that cathode rays were negatively charged particles. Thomson's discovery established the particulate nature of electricity. Accordingly, he called his particles electrons.

From the magnitude of the electrical and magnetic deflections, Thomson could calculate the ratio of mass to charge for the electrons. This ratio was known for atoms from electrochemical studies. Measuring and comparing it with the number for an atom, he discovered that the mass of the electron was minuscule, merely 1/1,836 that of a hydrogen ion. When scientists realized that an electron was virtually 1,000 times lighter than the smallest atom, they understood how cathode rays could penetrate metal sheets and how electric current could flow through copper wires. In deriving the mass-to-charge ratio, Thomson had calculated the electron's velocity. It was 1/10 the speed of light, thus amounting to roughly 30,000 km (18,000 miles) per second. Thomson emphasized that

> *we have in the cathode rays matter in a new state, a state in which the subdivision of matter is carried very much further than in the ordinary gaseous state; a state in which all matter, that is, matter derived from different sources such as hydrogen, oxygen, etc., is of one and the same kind; this matter being the substance from which all the chemical elements are built up.*

Thus, the electron was the first subatomic particle identified, the smallest and the fastest bit of matter known at the time.

MILLIKAN OIL-DROP EXPERIMENT

In 1909 the American physicist Robert Andrews Millikan greatly improved a method employed by Thomson for directly measuring the electron charge. He began by measuring the course of charged water droplets in an electrical field. The results suggested that the charge on the droplets is a multiple of the elementary electric charge, but the experiment was not accurate enough to be convincing.

In Millikan's subsequent experiment, he produced the first direct and compelling measurement of the electric charge of a single electron by measuring the minute electric charge that is present on many of the droplets in an oil mist. The force on any electric charge in an electric field is equal to the product of the charge and the electric field. Millikan was able to measure both the amount of electric force and magnitude of electric field on the tiny charge of an isolated oil droplet and from the data determine the magnitude of the charge itself.

Millikan's original experiment or any modified version, such as the following, is called the oil-drop experiment. A closed chamber with transparent sides is fitted with two parallel metal plates, which acquire a positive or negative charge when an electric current is applied. At the start of the experiment, an atomizer sprays a fine mist of oil droplets into the upper portion of the chamber. Under the influence of gravity and air resistance, some of the oil droplets fall through a small hole cut in the top metal plate. When the space between the metal plates is ionized by radiation (e.g., X-rays), electrons from the air attach themselves to the falling oil droplets, causing them to acquire a negative charge. A light source, set at right angles to a viewing microscope, illuminates the oil droplets and makes them appear as bright stars while they fall. The mass of a single charged droplet can be calculated by observing how fast it falls. By adjusting the potential difference, or voltage, between the metal plates, the speed of the droplet's motion can be increased or decreased. When the amount of upward electric force equals the known downward gravitational force, the charged droplet remains stationary. The amount of voltage needed to suspend a droplet is used along with its mass to determine the overall electric charge on the droplet. Through repeated application of this method, the values of the electric charge on individual oil drops are always whole-number multiples of a lowest value—that value being the elementary electric charge itself (about 1.602×10^{-19} coulomb). From the time of Millikan's original experiment, this method offered convincing proof that electric charge exists in basic natural units. All subsequent distinct methods of measuring the basic unit of electric charge point to its having the same fundamental value.

Millikan's electron-charge experiment was the first to detect and measure the effect of an individual subatomic particle. Besides confirming the particulate nature of electricity, his experiment also supported previous determinations of Avogadro's number. Avogadro's number times the unit of charge gives Faraday's constant, the amount of charge required to electrolyze one mole of a chemical ion.

IDENTIFICATION OF POSITIVE IONS

In addition to electrons, positively charged particles also emanate from the anode in an energized Crookes tube. The German physicist Wilhelm Wien analyzed these positive rays in 1898 and found that the particles have a mass-to-charge ratio more than 1,000 times larger than that of the electron. Because the ratio of the particles is also comparable to the mass-to-charge ratio of the residual atoms in the discharge tubes, scientists suspected that the rays were actually ions from the gases in the tube.

In 1913 Thomson refined Wien's apparatus to separate different ions and measure their mass-to-charge ratio on photographic plates. He sorted out the many ions in various charge states produced in a discharge tube. When he conducted his atomic mass experiments with neon gas, he found that a beam of neon atoms subjected to electric and magnetic forces split into two parabolas instead of one on a photographic plate. Chemists had assumed the atomic weight of neon was 20.2, but the traces on Thomson's photographic plate suggested atomic weights of 20.0 and 22.0, with the former parabola much stronger than the latter. He concluded that neon consisted of two stable isotopes: primarily neon-20, with a small percentage of neon-22. Eventually a third isotope, neon-21, was discovered in minute quantities. It is now known that 1,000 neon atoms will contain an average of 909 atoms of neon-20, 88 of neon-22, and 3 of neon-21. Dalton's assumptions that all atoms of an element have an identical mass and that the atomic weight of an element is its mass were thus disproved. Today the atomic weight of an element is recognized as the weighted average of the masses of its isotopes.

Francis William Aston, an English physicist, improved Thomson's technique when he developed the mass spectrograph in 1919. This device spread out the beam of positive ions into a "mass spectrum" of lines similar to the way light is separated into a spectrum. Aston analyzed about 50 elements over the next six years and discovered that most have isotopes.

Discovery of Radioactivity

Like Thomson's discovery of the electron, the discovery of radioactivity in uranium by the French physicist Henri Becquerel in 1896 forced scientists to radically change their ideas about atomic structure. Radioactivity demonstrated that the atom was neither indivisible nor immutable. Instead of serving merely as an inert matrix for electrons, the atom could change form and emit an enormous amount of energy. Furthermore, radioactivity itself became an important tool for revealing the interior of the atom.

The German physicist Wilhelm Conrad Röntgen had discovered X-rays in 1895, and Becquerel thought they might be related to fluorescence and phosphorescence, processes in which substances absorb and emit energy as light. In the course of his investigations, Becquerel stored some photographic plates and uranium salts in a desk drawer. Expecting to find the plates only lightly fogged, he developed them and was surprised to find sharp images of the salts. He then began experiments that showed that uranium salts emit a penetrating radiation independent of external influences. Becquerel also demonstrated that the radiation could discharge electrified bodies. In this case discharge means the removal of electric charge, and it is now understood that the radiation, by ionizing molecules of air, allows the air to conduct an electric current. Early studies of radioactivity relied on measuring ionization power or on observing the effects of radiation on photographic plates.

In 1898 the French physicists Pierre and Marie Curie discovered the strongly radioactive elements polonium

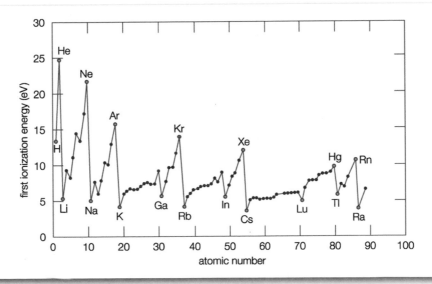

First ionization energies of the elements. Encyclopædia Britannica, Inc.

and radium, which occur naturally in uranium minerals. Marie coined the term *radioactivity* for the spontaneous emission of ionizing, penetrating rays by certain atoms.

Experiments conducted by the British physicist Ernest Rutherford in 1899 showed that radioactive substances emit more than one kind of radiation. It was determined that part of the radiation is 100 times more penetrating than the rest and can pass through aluminum foil one-fiftieth of a millimetre thick. Rutherford named the less penetrating emanations alpha rays and the more powerful ones beta rays, after the first two letters of the Greek alphabet. Investigators who in 1899 found that beta rays were deflected by a magnetic field concluded that they are negatively charged particles similar to cathode rays. In 1903 Rutherford found that alpha rays were deflected slightly in the opposite direction, showing that they are massive, positively charged particles. Much later Rutherford proved that alpha rays are nuclei of helium atoms by collecting the rays in an evacuated tube and detecting the buildup of helium gas over several days.

A third kind of radiation was identified by the French chemist Paul Villard in 1900. Designated as the gamma ray, it is not deflected by magnets and is much more penetrating than alpha particles. Gamma rays were later shown to be a form of electromagnetic radiation, like light or X-rays, but with much shorter wavelengths. Because of these shorter wavelengths, gamma rays have higher frequencies and are even more penetrating than X-rays.

In 1902, while studying the radioactivity of thorium, Rutherford and the English chemist Frederick Soddy discovered that radioactivity was associated with changes inside the atom that transformed thorium into a different element. They found that thorium continually generates a chemically different substance that is intensely radioactive. The radioactivity eventually makes the new element disappear. Watching the process, Rutherford and Soddy formulated the exponential decay law, which states that a fixed fraction of the element will decay in each unit of time. For example, half of the thorium product decays in four days, half the remaining sample in the next four days, and so on.

Until the 20th century, physicists had studied subjects, such as mechanics, heat, and electromagnetism, that they could understand by applying common sense or by extrapolating from everyday experiences. The discoveries of the electron and radioactivity, however, showed that classical Newtonian mechanics could not explain phenomena at atomic and subatomic levels. As the primacy of classical mechanics crumbled during the early 20th century, quantum mechanics was developed to replace it. Since then experiments and theories have led physicists into a world that is often extremely abstract and seemingly contradictory.

MODELS OF ATOMIC STRUCTURE

J.J. Thomson's discovery of the negatively charged electron had raised theoretical problems for physicists as early as 1897, because atoms as a whole are electrically neutral. Where was the neutralizing positive charge and what held it in place? Between 1903 and 1907 Thomson tried to solve the mystery by adapting an atomic model that had been first proposed by the Scottish scientist William Thomson (Lord Kelvin) in 1902. According to the Thomson atomic model, often referred to as the "plum-pudding" model, the atom is a sphere of uniformly distributed positive charge about one angstrom in diameter. Electrons are embedded in a regular pattern, like raisins in a plum pudding, to neutralize the positive charge. The advantage of the Thomson atom was that it was inherently stable: if the

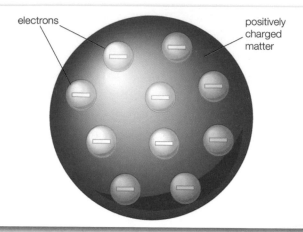

Thomson atomic model. William Thomson (also known as Lord Kelvin) envisioned the atom as a sphere with a uniformly distributed positive charge and embedded within it enough electrons to neutralize the positive charge. Encyclopædia Britannica, Inc.

electrons were displaced, they would attempt to return to their original positions. In another contemporary model, the atom resembled the solar system or the planet Saturn, with rings of electrons surrounding a concentrated positive charge. The Japanese physicist Nagaoka Hantaro in particular developed the "Saturnian" system in 1904. The atom, as postulated in this model, was inherently unstable because, by radiating continuously, the electron would gradually lose energy and spiral into the nucleus. No electron could thus remain in any particular orbit indefinitely.

Rutherford's Nuclear Model

Rutherford overturned Thomson's model in 1911 with his famous gold-foil experiment, in which he demonstrated that the atom has a tiny, massive nucleus. Five years earlier Rutherford had noticed that alpha particles beamed through a hole onto a photographic plate would make a sharp-edged picture, while alpha particles beamed through a sheet of mica only 0.002 cm thick would make an impression with blurry edges. For some particles the blurring corresponded to a two-degree deflection. Remembering those results, Rutherford had his postdoctoral fellow, Hans Geiger, and an undergraduate student, Ernest Marsden, refine the experiment. The young physicists beamed alpha particles through gold foil and detected them as flashes of light or scintillations on a screen. The gold foil was only 0.00004 cm thick. Most of the alpha particles went straight through the foil, but some were deflected by the foil and hit a spot on a screen placed off to one side. Geiger and Marsden found that about one in 20,000 alpha particles had been deflected 45° or more.

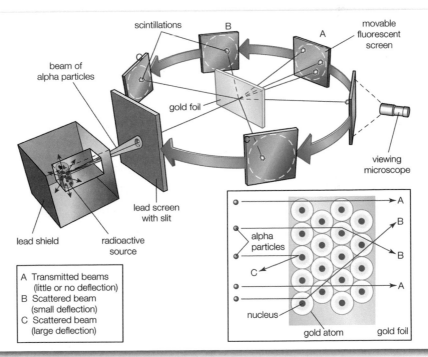

The Rutherford gold-foil experiment. In 1911 physicist Ernest Rutherford disproved William Thomson's model of the atom as a uniformly distributed substance. Because a few of the alpha particles in his beam were scattered by large angles after striking the gold foil, Rutherford knew that the gold atom's mass must be concentrated in a tiny, dense nucleus. Encyclopædia Britannica, Inc.

Rutherford asked why so many alpha particles passed through the gold foil while a few were deflected so greatly. "It was almost as incredible as if you fired a 15-inch shell at a piece of tissue paper, and it came back to hit you," Rutherford said later.

On consideration, I realized that this scattering backwards must be the result of a single collision, and when I made calculations I saw that it was impossible to get anything of that order of magnitude unless you took a system in which the greater part of the mass of the atom was concentrated in a minute nucleus. It was then that I had the idea of an atom with a minute massive centre carrying a charge.

Many physicists distrusted the Rutherford atomic model because it was difficult to reconcile with the chemical behaviour of atoms. The model suggested that the charge on the nucleus was the most important

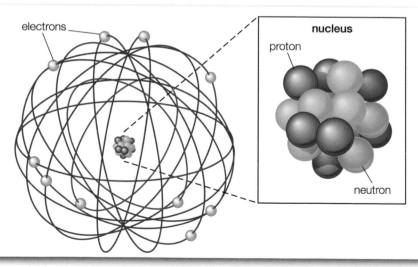

The Rutherford atomic model. Physicist Ernest Rutherford envisioned the atom as like a miniature solar system, with electrons orbiting around a massive nucleus. Encyclopædia Britannica, Inc.

characteristic of the atom, determining its structure. On the other hand, Mendeleyev's periodic table of the elements had been organized according to the atomic masses of the elements, implying that the mass was responsible for the structure and chemical behaviour of atoms.

MOSELEY'S X-RAY STUDIES

Henry Gwyn Jeffreys Moseley, a young English physicist killed in World War I, confirmed that the positive charge on the nucleus revealed more about the fundamental structure of the atom than Mendeleyev's atomic mass. Moseley studied the spectral lines emitted by heavy elements in the X-ray region of the electromagnetic spectrum. He built on the work done by several other British physicists — Charles Glover Barkla, who had studied X-rays produced by the impact of electrons on metal plates, and William Bragg and his son Lawrence, who had developed a precise method of using crystals to reflect X-rays and measure their wavelength by diffraction. Moseley applied their method systematically to measure the spectra of X-rays produced by many elements.

Moseley found that each element radiates X-rays of a different and characteristic wavelength. The wavelength and frequency vary in a regular pattern according to the charge on the nucleus. He called this charge the atomic number. In his first experiments, conducted in 1913, Moseley used what was called the *K* series of X-rays to study the elements up to zinc. The following year he extended this work using another series of X-rays, the *L* series. Moseley was conducting his research at the same time that the Danish theoretical physicist Niels Bohr was developing his quantum shell model of the atom. The two conferred and shared data as their work progressed, and Moseley framed his equation in terms of Bohr's theory by identifying the K series of X-rays with the most-bound shell in Bohr's theory, the $N = 1$ shell, and identifying the L series of X-rays with the next shell, $N = 2$.

Moseley presented formulas for the X-ray frequencies that were closely related to Bohr's formulas for the spectral lines in a hydrogen atom. Moseley showed that the frequency of a line in the X-ray spectrum is proportional to the square of the charge on the nucleus. The constant of proportionality depends on whether the X-ray is in the K or L series. This is the same relationship that Bohr used in his formula applied to the Lyman and Balmer series of spectral lines. The regularity of the differences in X-ray frequencies allowed Moseley to order the elements by atomic number from aluminum to gold. He observed that, in some cases, the order by atomic weights was incorrect. For example, cobalt has a larger atomic mass than nickel, but Moseley found that it has atomic number 27 while nickel has 28. When Mendeleyev constructed the periodic table, he based his system on the atomic masses of the elements and had to put cobalt and nickel out of order to make the chemical properties fit better. In a few places where Moseley found more than one integer between elements, he predicted correctly that a new element would be discovered. Because there is just one element for each atomic number, scientists could be confident for the first time of the completeness of the periodic table. No unexpected new elements would be discovered.

BOHR'S SHELL MODEL

In 1913 Bohr proposed his quantized shell model of the atom to explain how electrons can have stable orbits around the nucleus. The motion of the electrons in the Rutherford model was unstable because, according to classical mechanics and electromagnetic theory, any charged particle moving on a curved path emits electromagnetic radiation. Thus, the electrons would lose energy and spiral into the nucleus. To remedy the stability problem, Bohr modified the Rutherford model by requiring that the electrons move in orbits of fixed size and energy. The energy of an electron depends on the size of the orbit and is lower for smaller orbits. Radiation can occur only when the electron jumps from one orbit to another. The atom will be completely stable in the state with the smallest orbit,

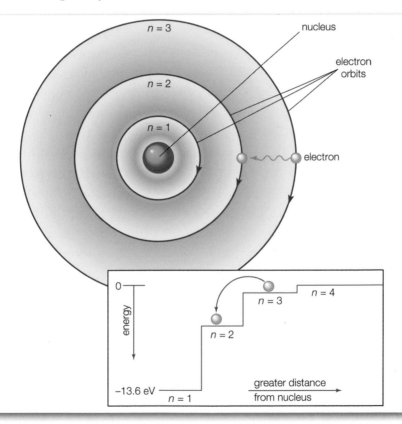

The Bohr atom. The electron travels in circular orbits around the nucleus. The orbits have quantized sizes and energies. Energy is emitted from the atom when the electron jumps from one orbit to another closer to the nucleus. Shown here is the first Balmer transition, in which an electron jumps from orbit n = 3 to orbit n = 2, producing a photon of red light with an energy of 1.89 eV and a wavelength of 656 nanometres. Encyclopædia Britannica, Inc.

since there is no orbit of lower energy into which the electron can jump.

Bohr's starting point was to realize that classical mechanics alone could never explain the atom's stability. A stable atom has a certain size so that any equation describing it must contain some fundamental constant or combination of constants with a dimension of length. The classical fundamental constants—namely, the charges and the masses of the electron and the nucleus—cannot be combined to make a length. Bohr noticed, however, that the quantum constant formulated by the German physicist Max Planck has dimensions which, when combined with the mass and charge of the electron, produce a measure of length. Numerically, the measure is close to the known size of atoms. This encouraged Bohr to use Planck's constant in searching for a theory of the atom.

Planck had introduced his constant in 1900 in a formula explaining the light radiation emitted from heated bodies. According to classical theory, comparable amounts of light energy should be produced at all frequencies. This is not only contrary to observation but also implies the absurd result that the total energy radiated by a heated body should be infinite. Planck postulated that energy can only be emitted or absorbed in discrete amounts, which he called *quanta* (Latin for "how much"). The energy quantum is related to the frequency of the light by a new fundamental constant, *h*. When a body is heated, its radiant energy in a particular frequency range is, according to classical theory, proportional to the temperature of the body. With Planck's hypothesis, however, the radiation can be emitted only in quantum amounts of energy. If the radiant energy is less than the quantum of energy, the amount of light in that frequency range will be reduced. Planck's formula correctly describes radiation from heated bodies. Planck's constant has the dimensions of action, which may be expressed as units of energy multiplied by time, units of momentum multiplied by length, or units of angular momentum. For example, Planck's constant can be written as $h = 6.6 \times 10^{-34}$ joule·seconds.

In 1905 Albert Einstein extended Planck's hypothesis by proposing that the radiation itself can carry energy only in quanta. According to Einstein, the energy (E) of the quantum is related to the frequency (v) of the light by Planck's constant in the formula $E = hv$. Using Planck's constant, Bohr obtained an accurate formula for the energy levels of the hydrogen atom. He postulated that the angular momentum of the electron is quantized (i.e., it can have only discrete values). He assumed that otherwise electrons obey the laws of classical mechanics by traveling around the nucleus in circular orbits. Because of the quantization, the electron orbits have fixed sizes and energies. The orbits are labeled by an integer, the quantum number n. In Bohr's model, radius a_n of the orbit n is given by the formula $a_n = h^2 n^2 \varepsilon_0 / \pi^2$, where ε_0 is the electric constant. As Bohr had noticed, the radius of the $n = 1$ orbit is approximately the same size as an atom.

With his model, Bohr explained how electrons could jump from one orbit to another only by emitting or absorbing energy in fixed quanta. For example, if an electron jumps one orbit closer to the nucleus, it must emit energy equal to the difference of the energies of the two orbits. Conversely, when the electron jumps to a larger orbit, it must absorb a quantum of light equal in energy to the difference in orbits.

Bohr's model accounts for the stability of atoms because the electron cannot lose more energy than it has in the smallest orbit, the one with $n = 1$. The model also explains the Balmer formula for the spectral lines of hydrogen. The light energy is the difference in energies between the two orbits in the Bohr formula. Using

Einstein's formula to deduce the frequency of the light, Bohr not only explained the form of the Balmer formula but also explained accurately the value of the constant of proportionality R.

The usefulness of Bohr's theory extends beyond the hydrogen atom. Bohr himself noted that the formula also applies to the singly ionized helium atom, which, like hydrogen, has a single electron. The nucleus of the helium atom has twice the charge of the hydrogen nucleus, however. In Bohr's formula the charge of the electron is raised to the fourth power. Two of those powers stem from the charge on the nucleus, and the other two come from the charge on the electron itself. Bohr modified his formula for the hydrogen atom to fit the helium atom by doubling the charge on the nucleus. Moseley applied Bohr's formula with an arbitrary atomic charge Z to explain the K- and L-series X-ray spectra of heavier atoms. The German physicists James Franck and Gustav Hertz confirmed the existence of quantum states in atoms in experiments reported in 1914. They made atoms absorb energy by bombarding them with electrons. The atoms would only absorb discrete amounts of energy from the electron beam. When the energy of an electron was below the threshold for producing an excited state, the atom would not absorb any energy.

Bohr's theory had major drawbacks, however. Except for the spectra of X-rays in the K and L series, it could not explain properties of atoms having more than one electron. The binding energy of the helium atom, which has two electrons, was not understood until the development of quantum mechanics. Several features of the spectrum were inexplicable even in the hydrogen atom. High-resolution spectroscopy shows that the individual spectral lines of hydrogen are divided into several closely spaced fine lines. In a magnetic field the lines split even farther apart. The German physicist Arnold Sommerfeld

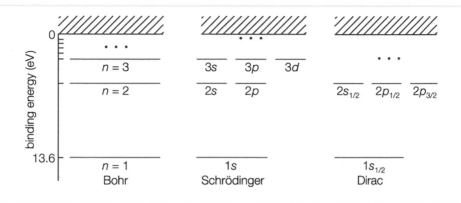

Energy levels of the hydrogen atom, according to Bohr's model and quantum mechanics using the Schrödinger equation and the Dirac equation. Encyclopædia Britannica, Inc.

modified Bohr's theory by quantizing the shapes and orientations of orbits to introduce additional energy levels corresponding to the fine spectral lines.

The quantization of the orientation of the angular momentum vector was confirmed in an experiment in 1922 by other German physicists, Otto Stern and Walther Gerlach. Their experiment took advantage of the magnetism associated with angular momentum. An atom with angular momentum has a magnetic moment like a compass needle that is aligned along the same axis. The researchers passed a beam of silver atoms through a magnetic field, one that would deflect the atoms to one side or another according to the orientation of their magnetic moments. In their experiment Stern and Gerlach found only two deflections, not the continuous distribution of deflections that would have been seen if the magnetic moment had been oriented in any direction. Thus, it was determined that the magnetic moment and the angular momentum of an atom can have only two orientations. The discrete orientations of the orbits explain some of the magnetic field effects—namely, the so-called normal

Zeeman effect, which is the splitting of a spectral line into three separate subsidiary lines. These lines correspond to quantum jumps in which the angular momentum along the magnetic field is increased by one unit, decreased by one unit, or left unchanged.

Spectra in magnetic fields displayed additional splittings that showed that the description of the electrons in atoms was still incomplete. In 1925 Samuel Abraham Goudsmit and George Eugene Uhlenbeck, two graduate students in physics at the University of Leiden in the Netherlands, added a quantum number to account for the division of some spectral lines into more subsidiary lines than can be explained with the original quantum numbers. Goudsmit and Uhlenbeck postulated that an electron has an internal spinning motion and that the corresponding angular momentum is one-half of the orbital angular momentum quantum. Independently, the Austrian-born physicist Wolfgang Pauli also suggested adding a two-valued quantum number for electrons, but for different reasons. He needed this additional quantum number to formulate his exclusion principle, which serves as the atomic basis of the periodic table and the chemical behaviour of the elements. According to the Pauli exclusion principle, one electron at most can occupy an orbit, taking into account all the quantum numbers. Pauli was led to this principle by the observation that an alkali metal atom in a magnetic field has a number of orbits in the shell equal to the number of electrons that must be added to make the next noble gas. These numbers are twice the number of orbits available if the angular momentum and its orientation are considered alone.

In spite of these modifications, by the early 1920s Bohr's model seemed to be a dead end. It could not explain the number of fine spectral lines and many of the frequency shifts associated with the Zeeman effect. Most daunting, however, was its inability to explain the rich spectra of multielectron atoms. In fact, efforts to generalize the model to multielectron atoms had proved futile, and physicists despaired of ever understanding them.

THE LAWS OF QUANTUM MECHANICS

Within a few short years, scientists developed a consistent theory of the atom that explained its fundamental structure and its interactions. Crucial to the development of the theory was new evidence indicating that light and matter have both wave and particle characteristics at the atomic and subatomic levels. Theoreticians had objected to the fact that Bohr had used an ad hoc hybrid of classical Newtonian dynamics for the orbits and some quantum postulates to arrive at the energy levels of atomic electrons. The new theory ignored the fact that electrons are particles and treated them as waves. By 1926 physicists had developed the laws of quantum mechanics, also called wave mechanics, to explain atomic and subatomic phenomena.

The duality between the wave and particle nature of light was highlighted by the American physicist Arthur Holly Compton in an X-ray scattering experiment conducted in 1922. Compton sent a beam of X-rays through a target material and observed that a small part of the beam was deflected off to the sides at various angles. He found that the scattered X-rays had longer wavelengths than the original beam, and the change could be explained only by assuming that the X-rays scattered from the electrons in the target as if the X-rays were particles with discrete amounts of energy and momentum. When X-rays are scattered, their momentum is partially transferred to the electrons. The recoil electron takes some energy from an X-ray, and as a result the X-ray frequency is shifted. Both the discrete amount of momentum and the frequency

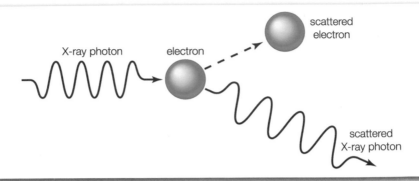

X-ray photon   electron   scattered electron   scattered X-ray photon

The Compton effect. When a beam of X-rays is aimed at a target material, some of the beam is deflected, and the scattered X-rays have a greater wavelength than the original beam. The physicist Arthur Holly Compton concluded that this phenomenon could only be explained if the X-rays were understood to be made up of discrete bundles or particles, now called photons, that lost some of their energy in the collisions with electrons in the target material and then scattered at lower energy. Encyclopædia Britannica, Inc.

shift of the light scattering are completely at variance with classical electromagnetic theory, but they are explained by Einstein's quantum formula.

Louis-Victor de Broglie, a French physicist, proposed in his 1923 doctoral thesis that all matter and radiations have both particle- and wavelike characteristics. Until the emergence of the quantum theory, physicists had assumed that matter was strictly particulate. In his quantum theory of light, Einstein proposed that radiation has characteristics of both waves and particles. Believing in the symmetry of nature, Broglie postulated that ordinary particles such as electrons may also have wave characteristics. Using the old-fashioned word *corpuscles* for particles, Broglie wrote,

> *For both matter and radiations, light in particular, it is necessary to introduce the corpuscle concept and the wave concept at the same time. In other words, the existence of corpuscles accompanied by waves has to be assumed in all cases.*

Broglie's conception was an inspired one, but at the time it had no empirical or theoretical foundation. The Austrian physicist Erwin Schrödinger had to supply the theory.

Schrödinger's Wave Equation

In 1926 the Schrödinger equation, essentially a mathematical wave equation, established quantum mechanics in widely applicable form. To understand how a wave equation is used, it is helpful to think of an analogy with the vibrations of a bell, violin string, or drumhead. These vibrations are governed by a wave equation, since the motion can propagate as a wave from one side of the object to the other. Certain vibrations in these objects are simple modes that are easily excited and have definite frequencies. For example, the motion of the lowest vibrational mode in a drumhead is in phase all over the drumhead with a pattern that is uniform around it, and the highest amplitude of the vibratory motion occurs in the middle of the drumhead. In more complicated, higher frequency modes, the motion on different parts of the vibrating drumhead are out of phase, with inward motion on one part at the same time that there is outward motion on another.

Schrödinger postulated that the electrons in an atom should be treated like the waves on the drumhead. The different energy levels of atoms are identified with the simple vibrational modes of the wave equation. The equation is solved to find these modes, and then the energy of an electron is obtained from the frequency of the mode and from Einstein's quantum formula, $E = h\nu$. Schrödinger's wave equation gives the same energies as Bohr's original formula but with a much more precise description of an electron in an atom. The lowest energy level of the hydrogen atom, called the ground state, is analogous to the motion in the lowest vibrational mode of the drumhead. In the atom

43

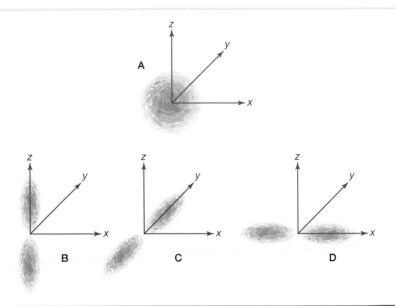

Electron densities in wave functions of the Schrödinger equation. (A) The lowest s orbital, recognizable by its spherical symmetry and the absence of any nodes. (B, C, D) The three p orbitals. Encyclopædia Britannica, Inc.

the electron wave is uniform in all directions from the nucleus, is peaked at the centre of the atom, and has the same phase everywhere. Higher energy levels in the atom have waves that are peaked at greater distances from the nucleus. Like the vibrations in the drumhead, the waves have peaks and nodes that may form a complex shape. The different shapes of the wave pattern are related to the quantum numbers of the energy levels, including the quantum numbers for angular momentum and its orientation.

The year before Schrödinger produced his wave theory, the German physicist Werner Heisenberg published a mathematically equivalent system to describe energy levels and their transitions. In Heisenberg's method, properties of atoms are described by arrays of numbers called matrices, which are combined with special rules of multiplication. Today physicists use both wave functions and matrices, depending on the application. Schrödinger's picture is more useful for describing continuous electron distributions because the wave function can be more easily visualized. Matrix methods are more useful for numerical analysis calculations with computers and for systems that can be described in terms of a finite number of states, such as the spin states of the electron.

In 1929 the Norwegian physicist Egil Hylleraas applied the Schrödinger equation to the helium atom with its two electrons. He obtained only an approximate solution, but his energy calculation was quite accurate. With Hylleraas's explanation of the two-electron atom, physicists realized that the Schrödinger equation could be a powerful mathematical tool for describing nature on the atomic level, even if exact solutions could not be obtained.

ANTIPARTICLES AND THE ELECTRON'S SPIN

The English physicist Paul Dirac introduced a new equation for the electron in 1928. Because the Schrödinger equation does not satisfy the principles of relativity, it can be used to describe only those phenomena in which the particles move much more slowly than the velocity of light. To satisfy the conditions of relativity, Dirac was forced to postulate that the electron would have a particular form of wave function with four independent components, some of which describe the electron's spin. Thus, from the very beginning, the Dirac theory incorporated the electron's spin properties. The remaining components allowed additional states of the electron that had not yet been observed. Dirac interpreted them as antiparticles, with a charge opposite to that of electrons. The discovery of the positron in 1932 by the American physicist Carl David Anderson proved the existence of antiparticles and was a triumph for Dirac's theory.

After Anderson's discovery, subatomic particles could no longer be considered immutable. Electrons and positrons can be created out of the vacuum, given a source of energy such as a high-energy X-ray or a collision. They also can annihilate each other and disappear into some other form of energy. From this point, much of the history of subatomic physics has been the story of finding new kinds of particles, many of which exist for only fractions of a second after they have been created.

ADVANCES IN NUCLEAR AND SUBATOMIC PHYSICS

The 1920s witnessed further advances in nuclear physics with Rutherford's discovery of induced radioactivity. Bombardment of light nuclei by alpha particles produced new radioactive nuclei. In 1928 the Russian-born American physicist George Gamow explained the lifetimes in alpha radioactivity using the Schrödinger equation. His explanation used a property of quantum mechanics that allows particles to "tunnel" through regions where classical physics would forbid them to be.

STRUCTURE OF THE NUCLEUS

The constitution of the nucleus was poorly understood at the time because the only known particles were the electron and the proton. It had been established that nuclei are typically about twice as heavy as can be accounted for by protons alone. A consistent theory was impossible until the English physicist James Chadwick discovered the neutron in 1932. He found that alpha particles reacted with beryllium nuclei to eject neutral particles with nearly the same mass as protons. Almost all nuclear phenomena can be understood in terms of a nucleus composed of neutrons and protons. Surprisingly, the neutrons and protons in the nucleus move to a large extent in orbitals as though their wave functions were independent of one another. Each neutron or proton orbital is described by a stationary wave pattern with peaks and nodes and angular momentum quantum numbers. The theory of the nucleus based on these orbitals is called the shell nuclear model. It was introduced independently in 1948 by Maria Goeppert Mayer of the United States and Johannes Hans Daniel Jensen of West Germany, and it developed in succeeding decades into a comprehensive theory of the nucleus.

The interactions of neutrons with nuclei had been studied during the mid-1930s by the Italian-born American physicist Enrico Fermi and others. Nuclei readily capture neutrons, which, unlike protons or alpha particles, are not repelled from the nucleus by a positive charge. When a neutron is captured, the new nucleus has one higher unit of atomic mass. If a nearby isotope of that atomic mass is more stable, the new nucleus will be radioactive, convert the neutron to a proton, and assume the more stable form.

Nuclear fission was discovered by the German chemists Otto Hahn and Fritz Strassmann in 1938 during the course of experiments initiated and explained by Austrian physicist Lise Meitner. In fission a uranium nucleus captures a neutron and gains enough energy to trigger the inherent instability of the nucleus, which splits into two lighter nuclei of roughly equal size. The fission process releases more neutrons, which can be used to produce further fissions. The first nuclear reactor, a device designed to permit controlled fission chain reactions, was constructed at the University of Chicago under Fermi's direction, and the first self-sustaining chain reaction was achieved in this reactor in 1942. In 1945 American scientists produced the first fission bomb, also called an atomic bomb, which used uncontrolled fission reactions in either uranium or the artificial element plutonium. In 1952 American scientists used a fission explosion to ignite a fusion reaction in which isotopes of hydrogen combined thermally into heavier helium nuclei. This was the first thermonuclear bomb, also called an H-bomb, a weapon that can release hundreds or thousands of times more energy than a fission bomb.

QUANTUM FIELD THEORY AND THE STANDARD MODEL

Dirac not only proposed the relativistic equation for the electron but also initiated the relativistic treatment of interactions between particles known as quantum field theory. The theory allows particles to be created and destroyed and requires only the presence of suitable interactions carrying sufficient energy. Quantum field theory also stipulates that the interactions can extend over a distance only if there is a particle, or field quantum, to carry the force. The electromagnetic force, which can operate over long distances, is carried by the photon, the quantum of light. Because the theory allows particles to interact with their own field quanta, mathematical difficulties arose in applying the theory.

The theoretical impasse was broken as a result of a measurement carried out in 1946 and 1947 by the American physicist Willis Eugene Lamb, Jr. Using microwave techniques developed during World War II, he showed that the hydrogen spectrum is actually about one-tenth of one percent different from Dirac's theoretical picture. Later the German-born American physicist Polykarp Kusch found a similar anomaly in the size of the magnetic moment of the electron. Lamb's results were announced at a famous Shelter Island Conference held in the United States in 1947. The German-born American physicist Hans Bethe and others realized that the so-called Lamb shift was probably caused by electrons and field quanta that may be created from the vacuum. The previous mathematical difficulties were overcome by Richard Feynman, Julian Schwinger, and Tomonaga Shin'ichirō, who shared the 1965 Nobel Prize for Physics, and Freeman Dyson, who showed that their various approaches were mathematically identical. The new theory, called quantum electrodynamics, was found to explain all the measurements to very high precision. Apparently, quantum electrodynamics provides a complete theory of how electrons behave under electromagnetism.

Beginning in the 1960s, similarities were found between the weak force and electromagnetism. Sheldon Glashow, Abdus Salam, and Steven Weinberg combined the two forces in the electroweak theory, for which they shared the Nobel Prize for Physics in 1979. In addition to the photon, three field quanta were predicted as additional carriers of the force—the W particle, the Z particle, and the Higgs particle. The discoveries of the W and Z particles in 1983, with correctly predicted masses, established the validity of the electroweak theory. Physicists are still searching for the much heavier Higgs particle, whose exact mass is not specified by the theory.

In all, hundreds of subatomic particles have been discovered since the first unstable particle, the muon, was identified in cosmic rays in the 1930s. By the 1960s patterns emerged in the properties and relationships among subatomic particles that led to the quark theory. Combining the electroweak theory and the quark theory, a theoretical framework called the Standard Model was constructed, which includes all known particles and field quanta. In the Standard Model there are two broad categories of particles, the leptons and the quarks. Leptons include electrons, muons, and neutrinos, and, aside from gravity, they interact only with the electroweak force.

The quarks are subject to the strong force, and they combine in various ways to make bound states. The bound quark states, called hadrons, include the neutron and the proton. Three quarks combine to form a proton, a neutron, or any of the massive hadrons known as baryons. A quark combines with an antiquark to form mesons such as the pion. Quarks have never been observed, and physicists do not expect to find one. The strength of the strong force is so great that quarks cannot be separated from each other outside hadrons. The existence of quarks has been confirmed indirectly in several ways, however. In experiments conducted with high-energy electron accelerators starting in 1967, physicists observed that some of the electrons bombarded onto proton targets were deflected at large angles. As in Rutherford's gold-foil experiment, the large-angle deflection implies that hadrons have an internal structure containing very small charged objects. The small objects are presumed to be quarks. To accommodate quarks and their peculiar properties, physicists developed a new quantum field theory, known as quantum chromodynamics, during the mid-1970s. This theory explains qualitatively the confinement of quarks to hadrons. Physicists believe that the theory should explain all aspects of hadrons. However, mathematical difficulties in dealing with the strong interactions in quantum chromodynamics are more severe than those of quantum electrodynamics, and rigorous calculations of hadron properties have not been possible. Nevertheless, numerical calculations using the largest computers seem to confirm the validity of the theory.

CHAPTER 2
THE ATOM:
COMPONENTS AND PROPERTIES

Most matter consists of an agglomeration of molecules, which can be separated relatively easily. Molecules, in turn, are composed of atoms joined by chemical bonds that are more difficult to break. Each individual atom consists of smaller particles—namely, electrons and nuclei. These particles are electrically charged, and the electric forces on the charge are responsible for holding the atom together. Attempts to separate these smaller constituent particles require ever-increasing amounts of energy and result in the creation of new subatomic particles, many of which are charged.

An atom consists largely of empty space. The nucleus is the positively charged centre of an atom and contains most of its mass. It is composed of protons, which have a positive charge, and neutrons, which have no charge. Protons, neutrons, and the electrons surrounding them are long-lived particles present in all ordinary, naturally occurring atoms. Other subatomic particles may be found in association with these three types of particles. They can be created only with the addition of enormous amounts of energy, however, and are very short-lived.

All atoms are roughly the same size, whether they have 3 or 90 electrons. Approximately 50 million atoms of solid matter lined up in a row would measure 1 cm (0.4 inch). A convenient unit of length for measuring atomic sizes is the angstrom (Å), defined as 10^{-10} metre. The radius of an atom measures 1–2 Å. Compared with the overall size of the atom, the nucleus is even more minute. It is in the same proportion to the atom as a marble is to a football field. In volume the nucleus takes up only 10^{-14} metres of the space in the atom (i.e., 1 part in 100,000). A convenient unit of length for measuring nuclear sizes is the femtometre (fm), which equals 10^{-15} metre. The diameter of a nucleus depends on the number of particles it contains and ranges from about 4 fm for a light nucleus such as carbon to 15 fm for a heavy nucleus such as lead. In spite of the small size of the nucleus, virtually all the mass of the atom is concentrated there. The protons are massive, positively charged particles, whereas the neutrons have no charge and are slightly more massive than the protons. The fact that nuclei can have anywhere from 1 to about 250 protons and neutrons accounts for their wide variation in mass. The lightest nucleus, that of hydrogen, is 1,836 times more massive than an electron, while heavy nuclei are nearly 500,000 times more massive.

ATOMIC NUMBER

The single most important characteristic of an atom is its atomic number (usually denoted by the letter Z), which is defined as the number of units of positive charge (protons) in the nucleus. For example, if an atom has a Z of 6, it is carbon, while a Z of 92 corresponds to uranium. A neutral atom has an equal number of protons and electrons so that the positive and negative charges exactly balance. Because it is the electrons that determine how one atom interacts with another, in the end it is the number of protons in the nucleus that determines the chemical properties of an atom.

ATOMIC MASS AND ISOTOPES

The number of neutrons in a nucleus affects the mass of the atom but not its chemical properties. Thus, a nucleus with six protons and six neutrons will have the same chemical properties as a nucleus with six protons and eight neutrons, although the two masses will be different. Nuclei with the same number of protons but different numbers of neutrons are said to be isotopes of each other. All chemical elements have many isotopes.

It is usual to characterize different isotopes by giving the sum of the number of protons and neutrons in the nucleus—a quantity called the atomic mass number. In the above example, the first atom would be called carbon-12 or ^{12}C (because it has six protons and six neutrons), while the second would be carbon-14 or ^{14}C.

The mass of atoms is measured in terms of the atomic mass unit, which is defined to be $\frac{1}{12}$ of the mass of an atom of carbon-12, or $1.6605402 \times 10^{-24}$ gram. The mass of an atom consists of the mass of the nucleus plus that of the electrons, so the atomic mass unit is not exactly the same as the mass of the proton or neutron.

THE ELECTRON

The smallest particle that makes up the atom is the electron. The number of electrons and their placement in the atoms of an element determine the properties of that element.

CHARGE, MASS, AND SPIN

Scientists have known since the late 19th century that the electron has a negative electric charge. The value of this charge was first measured by the American physicist Robert Millikan between 1909 and 1910. In Millikan's oil-drop experiment, he suspended tiny oil drops in a chamber containing an oil mist. By measuring the rate of fall of the oil drops, he was able to determine their weight. Oil drops that had an electric charge (acquired, for example, by friction when moving through the air) could then be slowed down or stopped by applying an electric force. By comparing applied electric force with changes in motion, Millikan was able to determine the electric charge on each drop. After he had measured many drops, he found that the charges on all of them were simple multiples of a single number. This basic unit of charge was the charge on the electron, and the different charges on the oil drops corresponded to those having 2, 3, 4, . . . extra electrons on them. The charge on the electron is now accepted to be $1.60217733 \times 10^{-19}$ coulomb. For this work Millikan was awarded the Nobel Prize for Physics in 1923.

The charge on the proton is equal in magnitude to that on the electron but opposite in sign—that is, the proton has a positive charge. Because opposite electric charges attract each other, there is an attractive force between electrons and protons. This force is what keeps electrons in orbit around the nucleus, something like the way that gravity keeps Earth in orbit around the Sun.

The electron has a mass of about $9.1093897 \times 10^{-28}$ gram. The mass of a proton or neutron is about 1,836 times larger. This explains why the mass of an atom is primarily determined by the mass of the protons and neutrons in the nucleus.

The electron has other intrinsic properties. One of these is called spin. The electron can be pictured as being something like Earth, spinning around an axis of rotation. In fact, most elementary particles have this property. Unlike Earth, however, they exist in the subatomic world and are governed by the laws of quantum mechanics. Therefore, these particles cannot spin in any arbitrary way, but only at certain specific rates. These rates can be $\frac{1}{2}$, 1, $\frac{3}{2}$, 2, . . . times a basic unit of rotation. Like protons and neutrons, electrons have spin $\frac{1}{2}$.

Particles with half-integer spin are called fermions, for the Italian American physicist Enrico Fermi, who investigated their properties in the first half of the 20th century. Fermions have one important property that will help explain both the way that electrons are arranged in their orbits and the way that protons and neutrons are arranged inside the nucleus. They are subject to the Pauli exclusion principle (named for the Austrian physicist Wolfgang Pauli), which states that no two fermions can occupy the same state. For example, the two electrons in a helium atom must have different spin directions if they occupy the same orbit.

Because a spinning electron can be thought of as a moving electric charge, electrons can be thought of as tiny electromagnets. This means that, like any other magnet, an electron will respond to the presence of a magnetic field by twisting. (Think of a compass needle pointing north under the influence of Earth's magnetic field.) This fact is usually expressed by saying that electrons have a magnetic moment. In physics, magnetic moment relates the strength of a magnetic field to the torque experienced by a magnetic object. Because of their intrinsic spin, electrons have a magnetic moment given by 9.27×10^{-24} joule per tesla.

Orbits and Energy Levels

Unlike planets orbiting the Sun, electrons cannot be at any arbitrary distance from the nucleus. They can exist only in certain specific locations called allowed orbits. First explained by the Danish physicist Niels Bohr in 1913, this property is another result of quantum mechanics — specifically, the requirement that the angular momentum of an electron in orbit, like everything else in the quantum world, come in discrete bundles called quanta.

In the Bohr atom electrons can be found only in allowed orbits, and these allowed orbits are at different energies. The orbits are analogous to a set of stairs in which the gravitational potential energy is different for each step and in which a ball can be found on any step but never in between.

The laws of quantum mechanics describe the process by which electrons can move from one allowed orbit, or energy level, to another. As with many processes in the quantum world, this process is impossible to visualize. An electron disappears from the orbit in which it is located and reappears in its new location without ever appearing any place in between. This process is called a quantum leap or quantum jump, and it has no analog in the macroscopic world.

Because different orbits have different energies, whenever a quantum leap occurs, the energy possessed by the electron will be different after the jump. For example, if an electron jumps from a higher to a lower energy level, the lost energy will have to go somewhere and in fact will be emitted by the atom in a bundle of electromagnetic radiation. This bundle is known as a photon, and this emission of photons with a change of energy levels is the process by which atoms emit light.

In the same way, if energy is added to an atom, an electron can use that energy to make a quantum leap from a lower to a higher orbit. This energy can be supplied in many ways. One common way is for the atom to absorb a photon of just the right frequency. For example, when white light is shone on an atom, it selectively absorbs those frequencies corresponding to the energy differences between allowed orbits.

Each element has a unique set of energy levels, and so the frequencies at which it absorbs and emits light act as a kind of fingerprint, identifying the particular element. This property of atoms has given rise to spectroscopy, a science devoted to identifying atoms and molecules by the kind of radiation they emit or absorb.

This picture of the atom, with electrons moving up and down between allowed orbits, accompanied by the absorption or emission of energy, contains the essential features of the Bohr atomic model, for which Bohr received the Nobel Prize for Physics in 1922. His basic model does not work well in explaining the details of the structure of atoms more complicated than hydrogen, however. This requires the introduction of quantum mechanics. In quantum mechanics each orbiting electron is represented by a mathematical expression known as a wave function—something like a vibrating guitar string laid out along the path of the electron's orbit. These waveforms are called orbitals.

Electron Shells

In the quantum mechanical version of the Bohr atomic model, each allowed electron orbit is assigned a quantum number n that runs from 1 (for the orbit closest to the nucleus) to infinity (for orbits very far from the nucleus). All the orbitals that have the same value of n make up a shell. Inside each shell there may be subshells corresponding to different rates of rotation and orientation of orbitals and the spin directions of the electrons. In general, the farther away from the nucleus a shell is, the more subshells it will have.

This arrangement of possible orbitals explains a great deal about the chemical properties of different atoms. The easiest way to see this is to imagine building up complex atoms by starting with hydrogen and adding one proton and one electron (along with the appropriate number of neutrons) at a time. In hydrogen the lowest-energy orbit— called the ground state—corresponds to the electron

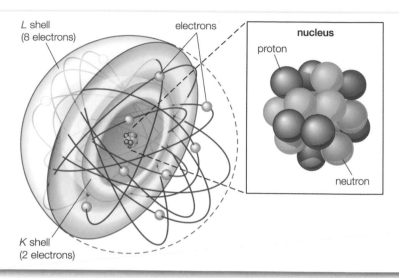

Shell atomic model. In the shell atomic model, electrons occupy different energy levels, or shells. The K and L shells are shown for a neon atom. Encyclopædia Britannica, Inc.

located in the shell closest to the nucleus. There are two possible states for an electron in this shell, corresponding to a clockwise spin and a counterclockwise spin (or, in the jargon of physicists, spin up and spin down).

The next most complex atom is helium, which has two protons in its nucleus and two orbiting electrons. These electrons fill the two available states in the lowest shell, producing what is called a filled shell. The next atom is lithium, with three electrons. Because the closest shell is filled, the third electron goes into the next higher shell. This shell has spaces for eight electrons, so that it takes an atom with 10 electrons (neon) to fill the first two levels. The next atom after neon, sodium, has 11 electrons, so that one electron goes into the next highest shell.

In the progression thus far, three atoms—hydrogen, lithium, and sodium—have one electron in the outermost shell. It is these outermost electrons that determine the chemical properties of an atom. Therefore, these three

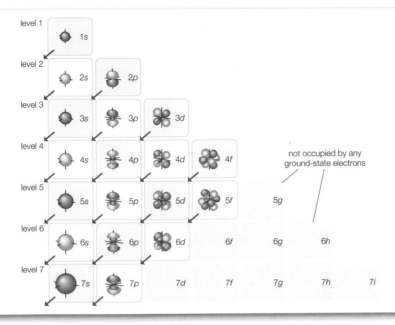

Atomic orbitals. Electrons fill in shell and subshell levels in a semiregular process, as indicated by the arrows above. After filling the first shell level (with just an s subshell), electrons move into the second level s subshell and then into the p subshell, before starting on another shell level. Because of its lower energy state, the 4s orbital fills before the 3d, and similarly for later s orbitals (for example, 6s fills before 4f). Encyclopædia Britannica, Inc.

elements should have similar properties, as indeed they do. For this reason, they appear in the same column of the periodic table of the elements, and the same principle determines the position of every element in that table. The outermost shell of electrons—called the valence shell—determines the chemical behaviour of an atom, and the number of electrons in this shell depends on how many are left over after all the interior shells are filled.

ATOMIC BONDS

Once the way atoms are put together is understood, the question of how they interact with each other can be addressed—in particular, how they form bonds to create molecules and macroscopic materials. There are three basic ways that the outer electrons of atoms can form bonds:

1. Electrons can be transferred from one atom to another.
2. Electrons can be shared between neighbouring atoms.
3. Electrons can be shared with all atoms in a material.

The first way gives rise to what is called an ionic bond. Consider as an example an atom of sodium, which has one electron in its outermost orbit, coming near an atom of chlorine, which has seven. Because it takes eight electrons to fill the outermost shell of these atoms, the chlorine

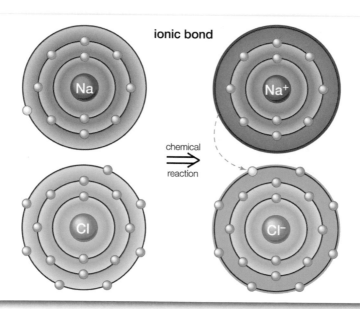

Ionic bond. An atom of sodium (Na) donates one of its electrons to an atom of chlorine (Cl) in a chemical reaction. The resulting positive ion (Na+) and negative ion (Cl-) form a stable molecule (sodium chloride, or common table salt) based on this ionic bond. Encyclopædia Britannica, Inc.

atom can be thought of as missing one electron. The sodium atom donates its single valence electron to fill the hole in the chlorine shell, forming a sodium chloride system at a lower total energy level.

An atom that has more or fewer electrons in orbit than protons in its nucleus is called an ion. Once the electron from its valence shell has been transferred, the sodium atom will be missing an electron. It therefore will have a positive charge and become a sodium ion. Simultaneously, the chlorine atom, having gained an extra electron, will take on a negative charge and become a chlorine ion. The electrical force between these two oppositely charged ions is attractive and locks them together. The resulting sodium chloride compound is a cubic crystal, commonly known as ordinary table salt.

The second bonding strategy is described by quantum mechanics. When two atoms come near each other, they can share a pair of outermost electrons (think of the atoms as tossing the electrons back and forth between them) to form a covalent bond. Covalent bonds are particularly common in organic materials, where molecules often contain long chains of carbon atoms (which have four electrons in their valence shells).

Finally, in some materials each atom gives up an outer electron that then floats freely—in essence, the electron is shared by all of the atoms within the material. The electrons form a kind of sea in which the positive ions float like marbles in molasses. This is called the metallic bond and, as the name implies, it is what holds metals together.

There are also ways for atoms and molecules to bond without actually exchanging or sharing electrons. In many molecules the internal forces are such that the electrons tend to cluster at one end of the molecule, leaving the other end with a positive charge. Overall, the molecule has no net electric charge—it is just that the positive

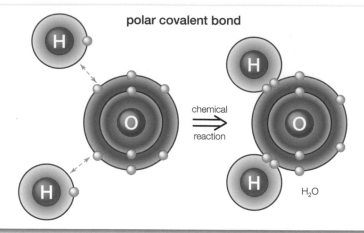

polar covalent bond

chemical
reaction

H_2O

Polar covalent bond. In polar covalent bonds, such as that between hydrogen and oxygen atoms, the electrons are not transferred from one atom to the other, because they are in an ionic bond. Instead, some outer electrons merely spend more time in the vicinity of the other atom. The effect of this orbital distortion is to induce regional net charges that hold the atoms together, such as in water molecules. Encyclopædia Britannica, Inc.

and negative charges are found at different places. For example, in water (H_2O) the electrons tend to spend most of their time near the oxygen atom, leaving the region of the hydrogen atoms with a positive charge. Molecules whose charges are arranged in this way are called polar molecules. An atom or ion approaching a polar molecule from its negative side, for example, will experience a stronger negative electric force than the more distant positive electric force. This is why so many substances dissolve in water: the polar water molecule can pull ions out of materials by exerting electric forces. A special case of polar forces occurs in what is called the hydrogen bond. In many situations, when hydrogen forms a covalent bond with another atom, electrons move toward that atom, and the hydrogen acquires a slight positive charge. The hydrogen, in turn, attracts another atom, thereby forming a kind of bridge between the two. Many important molecules, including DNA, depend on hydrogen bonds for their structure.

Finally, there is a way for a weak bond to form between two electrically neutral atoms. The Dutch physicist Johannes van der Waals first theorized a mechanism for such a bond in 1873, and it is now known as van der Waals forces. When two atoms approach each other, their electron clouds exert repulsive forces on each other, so that the atoms become polarized. In such situations, it is possible that the electrical attraction between the nucleus of one atom and the electrons of the other will overcome the repulsive forces between the electrons, and a weak bond will form. One example of this force can be seen in ordinary graphite pencil lead. In this material, carbon atoms are held together in sheets by strong covalent bonds, but the sheets are held together only by van der Waals forces. When a pencil is drawn across paper, the van der Waals forces break, and sheets of carbon slough off. This is what creates the dark pencil streak.

CONDUCTORS AND INSULATORS

The way that atoms bond together affects the electrical properties of the materials they form. For example, in materials held together by the metallic bond, electrons float loosely between the metal ions. These electrons will be free to move if an electrical force is applied. For example, if a copper wire is attached across the poles of a battery, the electrons will flow inside the wire. Thus, an electric current flows, and the copper is said to be a conductor.

The flow of electrons inside a conductor is not quite so simple, though. A free electron will be accelerated for a while but will then collide with an ion. In the collision process, some of the energy acquired by the electron will be transferred to the ion. As a result, the ion will move faster, and an observer will notice the wire's temperature rise. This conversion of electrical energy from the motion of the electrons to heat energy is called electrical resistance. In a material of high resistance, the wire heats up quickly as electric current flows. In a material of low resistance, such as copper wire, most of the energy remains with the moving electrons, so the material is good at moving electrical energy from one point to another. Its excellent conducting property, together with its relatively low cost, is why copper is commonly used in electrical wiring.

The exact opposite situation obtains in materials, such as plastics and ceramics, in which the electrons are all locked into ionic or covalent bonds. When these kinds of materials are placed between the poles of a battery, no current flows—there are simply no electrons free to move. Such materials are called insulators.

MAGNETIC PROPERTIES

The magnetic properties of materials are also related to the behaviour of electrons in atoms. An electron in orbit can be thought of as a miniature loop of electric current. According to the laws of electromagnetism, such a loop will create a magnetic field. Each electron in orbit around a nucleus produces its own magnetic field, and the sum of these fields, together with the intrinsic fields of the electrons and the nucleus, determines the magnetic field of the atom. Unless all of these fields cancel out, the atom can be thought of as a tiny magnet.

In most materials these atomic magnets point in random directions, so that the material itself is not magnetic. In some cases—for instance, when randomly oriented atomic magnets are placed in a strong external magnetic field—they line up, strengthening the external field in the process. This phenomenon is known as paramagnetism.

In a few metals, such as iron, the interatomic forces are such that the atomic magnets line up over regions a few thousand atoms across. These regions are called domains. In normal iron the domains are oriented randomly, so the material is not magnetic. If iron is put in a strong magnetic field, however, the domains will line up, and they will stay lined up even after the external field is removed. As a result, the piece of iron will acquire a strong magnetic field. This phenomenon is known as ferromagnetism. Permanent magnets are made in this way.

THE NUCLEUS

The primary constituents of the nucleus are the proton and the neutron, which have approximately equal mass and are much more massive than the electron. For reference, the accepted mass of the proton is $1.6726231 \times 10^{-24}$ gram, while that of the neutron is $1.6749286 \times 10^{-24}$ gram. The charge on the proton is equal in magnitude to that on the electron but is opposite in sign, while the neutron has no electrical charge. Both particles have spin $\frac{1}{2}$ and are therefore fermions and subject to the Pauli exclusion principle. Both also have intrinsic magnetic fields. The magnetic moment of the proton is $1.410606633 \times 10^{-26}$ joule per tesla, while that of the neutron is $0.9662364 \times 10^{-26}$ joule per tesla.

It would be wrong to picture the nucleus as just a collection of protons and neutrons, analogous to a bag of marbles. In fact, much of the effort in physics research during the second half of the 20th century was devoted to studying the various kinds of particles that live out their fleeting lives inside the nucleus. A more accurate picture of the nucleus would be of a seething cauldron where hundreds of different kinds of particles swarm around the protons and neutrons. It is now believed that these so-called elementary particles are made of still more-elementary objects, which have been given the name of quarks. Modern theories suggest that even the quarks may be made of still more fundamental entities called strings.

NUCLEAR FORCES

The forces that operate inside the nucleus are a mixture of those familiar from everyday life and those that operate only inside the atom. Two protons, for example, will repel each other because of their identical electrical force but will be attracted to each other by gravitation. Especially at the scale of elementary particles, the gravitational force is many orders of magnitude weaker than other fundamental forces, so it is customarily ignored when talking about the nucleus. Nevertheless, because the nucleus stays together in spite of the repulsive electrical force between protons, there must exist a counterforce— which physicists have named the strong force—operating at short range within the nucleus. The strong force has been a major concern in physics research since its existence was first postulated in the 1930s.

One more force—the weak force—operates inside the nucleus. The weak force is responsible for some of the radioactive decays of nuclei. The four fundamental forces— strong, electromagnetic, weak, and gravitational—are responsible for every process in the universe. One of the important strains in modern theoretical physics is the belief that, although they seem very different, they are different aspects of a single underlying force.

NUCLEAR SHELL MODEL

Many models describe the way protons and neutrons are arranged inside a nucleus. One of the most successful and simple to understand is the shell model. In this model the protons and neutrons occupy separate systems of shells, analogous to the shells in which electrons are found outside the nucleus. From light to heavy nuclei, the proton and neutron shells are filled (separately) in much the same way as electron shells are filled in an atom.

Like the Bohr atomic model, the nucleus has energy levels that correspond to processes in which protons and neutrons make quantum leaps up and down between their allowed orbits. Because energies in the nucleus are so much greater than those associated with electrons, however, the photons emitted or absorbed in these reactions tend to be in the X-ray or gamma ray portions of the electromagnetic spectrum, rather than the visible light portion.

When a nucleus forms from protons and neutrons, an interesting regularity can be seen: the mass of the nucleus is slightly less than the sum of the masses of the constituent protons and neutrons. This consistent discrepancy

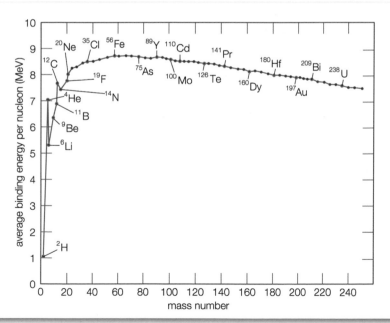

Nuclear binding energies, shown as a function of atomic mass number. Encyclopædia Britannica, Inc.

is not large—typically only a fraction of a percent—but it is significant. By Albert Einstein's principles of relativity, this small mass deficit can be converted into energy via the equation $E = mc^2$. Thus, in order to break a nucleus into its constituent protons and neutrons, energy must be supplied to make up this mass deficit. The energy corresponding to the mass deficit is called the binding energy of the nucleus, and, as the name suggests, it represents the energy required to tie the nucleus together. The binding energy varies across the periodic table and is at a maximum for iron, which is thus the most stable element.

RADIOACTIVE DECAY

The nuclei of most everyday atoms are stable—that is, they do not change over time. This statement is somewhat misleading, however, because nuclei that are not stable generally do not last long and hence tend not to be part of everyday experience. In fact, most of the known isotopes of nuclei are not stable. Instead, they go through a process called radioactive decay, a process that often changes the identity of the original atom.

In radioactive decay a nucleus will remain unchanged for some unpredictable period and then emit a high-speed particle or photon, after which a different nucleus will have replaced the original. Each unstable isotope decays at a different rate. That is, each has a different probability of decaying within a given period of time. A collection of identical unstable nuclei do not all decay at once. Instead, like popcorn popping in a pan, they will decay individually over a period of time. The time that it takes for half of the original sample to decay is called the half-life of the isotope. Half-lives of known isotopes range from microseconds to billions of years. Uranium-238 (^{238}U) has a half-life of about 4.5 billion years, which is approximately the time that has elapsed since the formation of the solar system. Thus, Earth has about half of the ^{238}U that it had when it was formed.

There are three different types of radioactive decay. In the late 19th century, when radiation was still mysterious, these forms of decay were denoted alpha, beta, and gamma. In alpha decay a nucleus ejects two protons and two neutrons, all locked together in what is called an alpha particle (later discovered to be identical to the nucleus of a normal helium atom). The daughter, or decayed, nucleus will have two fewer protons and two fewer neutrons than the original and hence will be the nucleus of a different chemical element. Once the electrons have rearranged themselves (and the two excess electrons have wandered off), the atom will, in fact, have changed identity.

In beta decay one of the neutrons in the nucleus turns into a proton, a fast-moving electron, and a particle called a neutrino. This emission of fast electrons is called beta radiation. The daughter nucleus has one fewer neutron and one more proton than the original and hence, again, is a different chemical element.

In gamma decay a proton or neutron makes a quantum leap from a higher to a lower orbit, emitting a high-energy photon in the process. In this case the chemical identity of the daughter nucleus is the same as the original.

When a radioactive nucleus decays, it often happens that the daughter nucleus is radioactive as well. This daughter will decay in turn, and the daughter nucleus of that decay may be radioactive as well. Thus, a collection of identical atoms may, over time, be turned into a mixture of many kinds of atoms because of successive decays. Such decays will continue until stable daughter nuclei are produced. This process, called a decay chain, operates everywhere in nature. For example, uranium-238 decays with a half-life of 4.5 billion years into thorium-234, which decays in 24 days into protactinium-234, which also decays. This process continues until it gets to lead-206, which is stable. Dangerous elements such as radium and radon are continually produced in Earth's crust as intermediary steps in decay chains.

NUCLEAR ENERGY

It is almost impossible to have lived at any time since the mid-20th century and not be aware that energy can be derived from the atomic nucleus. The basic physical principle behind this fact is that the total mass present after a nuclear reaction is less than before the reaction. This difference in mass, via the equation $E = mc^2$, is converted into what is called nuclear energy.

There are two types of nuclear processes that can produce energy—nuclear fission and nuclear fusion. In fission a heavy nucleus (such as uranium) is split into a collection of lighter nuclei and fast-moving particles. The energy at the end typically appears in the kinetic energy of the final particles. Nuclear fission is used in nuclear reactors to produce commercial electricity. It depends on the fact that a particular isotope of uranium (^{235}U) behaves in a particular way when it is hit by a neutron. The nucleus breaks apart and emits several particles. Included in the debris of the fission are two or three more free neutrons that can produce fission in other nuclei in a chain reaction. This chain reaction can be controlled and used to heat water into steam, which can then be used to turn turbines in an electrical generator.

Fusion refers to a process in which two or more light nuclei come together to form a heavier nucleus. The most

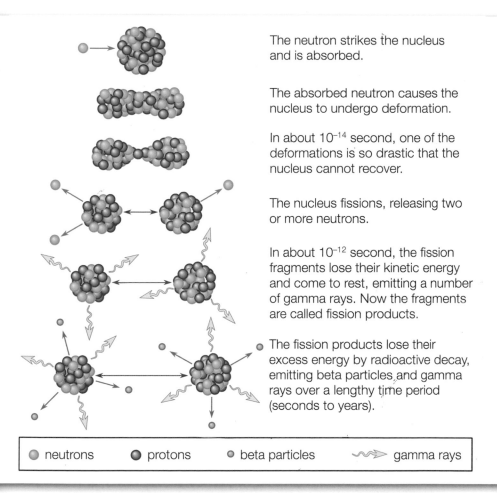

The neutron strikes the nucleus and is absorbed.

The absorbed neutron causes the nucleus to undergo deformation.

In about 10^{-14} second, one of the deformations is so drastic that the nucleus cannot recover.

The nucleus fissions, releasing two or more neutrons.

In about 10^{-12} second, the fission fragments lose their kinetic energy and come to rest, emitting a number of gamma rays. Now the fragments are called fission products.

The fission products lose their excess energy by radioactive decay, emitting beta particles and gamma rays over a lengthy time period (seconds to years).

● neutrons	● protons	● beta particles	〜〜▷ gamma rays

Sequence of events in the fission of a uranium nucleus by a neutron. Encyclopædia Britannica, Inc.

common fusion process in nature is one in which four protons come together to form a helium nucleus (two protons and two neutrons) and some other particles. This is the process by which energy is generated in stars. Scientists have not yet learned to produce a controllable, commercially useful nuclear fusion on Earth, which remains a goal for the future.

CHAPTER 3
ISOTOPES

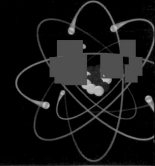

An isotope is a species of atoms of a chemical element with the same atomic number and position in the periodic table and nearly identical chemical behaviour but with different atomic masses and physical properties. Every chemical element has one or more isotopes.

An atom is first identified and labeled according to the number of protons in its nucleus. This atomic number is ordinarily given the symbol Z. The great importance of the atomic number derives from the observation that all atoms with the same atomic number have nearly, if not precisely, identical chemical properties. A large collection of atoms with the same atomic number constitutes a sample of an element. A bar of pure uranium, for instance, would consist entirely of atoms with atomic number 92. The periodic table of the elements assigns one place to every atomic number, and each of these places is labeled with the common name of the element, as, for example, calcium, radon, or uranium.

Not all the atoms of an element need have the same number of neutrons in their nuclei. In fact, it is precisely the variation in the number of neutrons in the nuclei of atoms that gives rise to isotopes. Hydrogen is a case in point. It has the atomic number 1. Three nuclei with one proton are known that contain 0, 1, and 2 neutrons, respectively. The three share the place in the periodic table assigned to atomic number 1 and hence are called isotopes (from the Greek *isos*, meaning "same," and *topos*, signifying "place") of hydrogen.

Many important properties of an isotope depend on its mass. The total number of neutrons and protons (symbol A), or mass number, of the nucleus gives approximately the mass measured on the so-called atomic-mass-unit (amu) scale. The numerical difference between the actual measured mass of an isotope and A is called either the mass excess or the mass defect (symbol Δ).

The specification of Z, A, and the chemical symbol (a one- or two-letter abbreviation of the element's name, say, Sy) in the form ^A_ZSy identifies an isotope adequately for most purposes. Thus, in the standard notation, $^1_1$H refers to the simplest isotope of hydrogen and $^{235}_{92}$U to an isotope of uranium widely used for nuclear power generation and nuclear weapons fabrication. (Authors who do not wish to use symbols sometimes write out the element name and mass number—hydrogen-1 and uranium-235 in the preceding examples.)

The term *nuclide* is used to describe particular isotopes, notably in cases where the nuclear rather than the chemical properties of an atom are to be emphasized. The lexicon of isotopes includes three other frequently used terms: *isotones* for isotopes of different elements with the same number of neutrons, *isobars* for isotopes of different elements with the same mass number, and *isomers* for isotopes identical in all respects except for the total energy content of the nuclei.

THE DISCOVERY OF ISOTOPES

Evidence for the existence of isotopes emerged from two independent lines of research, the first being the study of radioactivity. By 1910 it had become clear that certain processes associated with radioactivity, discovered some years before by French physicist Henri Becquerel, could

Henri Becquerel determined that some radioactive-associated processes could convert one element into another. Boyer/Roger Viollet/Getty Images

transform one element into another. In particular, ores of the radioactive elements uranium and thorium had been found to contain small quantities of several radioactive substances never before observed. These substances were thought to be elements and accordingly received special names. Uranium ores, for example, yielded ionium, and thorium ores gave mesothorium. Painstaking work completed soon afterward revealed, however, that ionium, once mixed with ordinary thorium, could no longer be retrieved by chemical means alone. Similarly, mesothorium was shown to be chemically indistinguishable from radium. As chemists used the criterion of chemical indistinguishability as part of the definition of an element, they were forced to conclude that ionium and mesothorium were not new elements after all, but rather new forms of old ones. Generalizing from these and other data, English chemist Frederick Soddy in 1910 observed that "elements of different atomic weights [now called atomic masses] may possess identical (chemical) properties" and so belong in the same place in the periodic table. With considerable prescience, he extended the scope of his conclusion to include not only radioactive species but stable elements as well. A few years later, Soddy published a comparison of the atomic masses of the stable element lead as measured in ores rich in uranium and thorium, respectively. He expected a difference because uranium and thorium decay into different isotopes of lead. The lead from the uranium-rich ore had an average atomic mass of 206.08 compared to 207.69 for the lead from the thorium-rich ore, thus verifying Soddy's conclusion.

The unambiguous confirmation of isotopes in stable elements not associated directly with either uranium or thorium followed a few years later with the development of the mass spectrograph by Francis William Aston. His work grew out of the study of positive rays (sometimes called canal rays), discovered in 1886 by Eugen Goldstein and soon thereafter recognized as beams of positive ions. As a student in the laboratory of J.J. Thomson, Aston had learned that the gaseous element neon produced two positive rays. The ions in the heavier ray had masses about two units, or 10 percent, greater than the ions in the lighter ray. To prove that the lighter neon had a mass very close to 20 and that the heavier ray was indeed neon and not a spurious signal of some kind, Aston had to construct an instrument that was considerably more precise than any other of the time. By 1919 he had done so and convincingly argued for the existence of neon-20 and neon-22. Information from his and other laboratories accumulated rapidly in the ensuing years, and by 1935 the principal isotopes and their relative proportions were known for all but a handful of elements.

NUCLEAR STABILITY

Isotopes are said to be stable if, when left alone, they show no perceptible tendency to change spontaneously. Under the proper conditions, however, say in a nuclear reactor or particle accelerator or in the interior of a star, even stable isotopes may be transformed, one into another. The ease or difficulty with which these nuclear transformations occur varies considerably and reflects differing degrees of stability in the isotopes. Accordingly, it is important and useful to measure stability in more quantitative terms.

A uniform scale of nuclear stability, one that applies to stable and unstable isotopes alike, is based on a comparison of measured isotope masses with the masses of their constituent electrons, protons, and neutrons. For this purpose, electrons and protons are paired together as hydrogen atoms. The actual masses of all the stable isotopes differ appreciably from the sums of their individual particle masses. For example, the isotope $^{12}_{6}C$, which has a particularly stable nucleus, has an atomic mass defined to be exactly 12 amu. The total separate masses of 6 electrons and 6 protons (treated as 6 hydrogen atoms) and of 6 neutrons add up to 12.09894 amu. The difference, Δm, between the actual mass of the assembled isotope and the masses of the particles gives a measure of the stability of the isotope: the larger and more negative the value of Δm, the greater the stability of the isotope. The difference in mass is often expressed as energy by using Albert Einstein's relativity equation in the form $E = (\Delta m)c^2$. Here, c is the speed of light. The quantity of energy calculated in this way is called the nuclear binding energy (E_B).

A single mathematical equation accurately reproduces the nuclear binding energies of more than 1,000 nuclides. It can be written in the form

$$E_B(\text{MeV}) = c_1 A \left[1 - k\left\{\frac{N-Z}{A}\right\}^2\right] - c_2 A^{2/3} \left[1 - k\left\{\frac{N-Z}{A}\right\}^2\right]$$
$$- c_3 Z^2 A^{-1/3} + c_4 Z^2 A^{-1} + \delta.$$

In this equation N is the number of neutrons in the nucleus. The terms $c_1 = 15.8$, $c_2 = 18.3$, $c_3 = 0.714$, $c_4 = 1.211$, and $k = 1.79$, while δ may take any of several values. The numerical values of these terms do not come from theory but from a selection process that ensures the best possible agreement with experimental data. However, theory helps justify, at least qualitatively, the mathematical form of each term. Modeled on an analogy to a liquid drop, the first term represents the favourable contribution to the binding of the nucleus made by short-range, attractive nuclear forces between neutrons and protons. The second term corrects the first by allowing for the expectation that nucleons at the surface of the nucleus, unlike those in the interior, do not experience forces of nuclear attraction equally from all sides. Both the first and second terms have a second empirical component of the form $k[(N - Z)/A]^2$, which is referred to as the symmetry energy. It vanishes (neither helps nor hinders binding) when N is equal to Z (when the nucleus is "symmetric"), but then works increasingly to destabilize the nucleus as N and Z grow apart. The third term symbolizes the coulombic, or electrostatic, energy of repulsion of the protons. Its derivation assumes a uniform distribution of charge within the nucleus. The fourth term makes a small correction to the third. This correction is necessitated by the observation that the nuclear charge distribution becomes somewhat more spread out near the surface of the nucleus. The last term, the so-called pairing energy, takes on any one of three values depending on whether N and Z are both even ($\delta = 11/\sqrt{A}$), their sum is odd ($\delta = 0$), or both are odd ($\delta = -11/\sqrt{A}$). More detailed treatments sometimes give other values for δ as well.

The largest observed deviations from the equation occur at certain favoured numbers (magic numbers) of neutrons or protons (2, 8, 20, 28, 50, 82, and 126). Magic nuclei are more stable than the binding energy equation would predict. The isotope of helium with 2 neutrons and 2 protons is said to be doubly magic. The shell nuclear model helps to explain its stability.

Division of the binding energy E_B by A, the mass number, yields the binding energy per nucleon. This important quantity reaches a maximum value for nuclei in the vicinity of iron. When two deuterium atoms fuse to form helium, the binding energy per nucleon increases and energy is released. Similarly, when the nucleus of an atom of ^{235}U fissions into two smaller nuclei, the binding energy per nucleon again increases with a concomitant release of energy.

RADIOACTIVE ISOTOPES

Only a small fraction of the isotopes are known to be stable indefinitely. All the others disintegrate spontaneously with the release of energy by processes broadly designated as radioactive decay. Each "parent" radioactive isotope eventually decays into one or at most a few stable isotope "daughters" specific to that parent. The radioactive parent tritium (^{3}H, or hydrogen-3), for example, always turns into the daughter helium-3 (^{3}He) by emitting an electron.

Under ordinary conditions, the disintegration of each radioactive isotope proceeds at a well-defined and characteristic rate. Thus, without replenishment, any radioactive isotope will ultimately vanish. Some isotopes, however, decay so slowly that they persist on Earth today even after the passage of more than 4.5 billion years since the last significant injection of freshly synthesized atoms from some nearby star. Examples of such long-lived radioisotopes include potassium-40, rubidium-87, neodymium-144, uranium-235, uranium-238, and thorium-232.

In this context, the widespread occurrence of radioisotopes that decay more rapidly, such as radon-222 and carbon-14, may at first seem puzzling. The explanation of the apparent paradox is that nuclides in this category are continually replenished by specialized nuclear processes: by the slow decay of uranium in Earth in the case of radon and by the interactions of cosmic rays with the atmosphere in the case of carbon-14. Nuclear testing and the release of material from nuclear reactors also introduce radioactive isotopes into the environment.

Nuclear physicists have expended great effort to create isotopes not detected in nature, partly as a way to test theories of nuclear stability. In 2006 a team of researchers at the Joint Institute for Nuclear Research in Dubna, near Moscow, and at the Lawrence Livermore National Laboratory, in Livermore, Calif., U.S., announced the creation of element 118, with 118 protons and 176 neutrons. Like most isotopes of elements heavier than uranium, it is radioactive, decaying in fractions of a second into more common elements.

ELEMENTAL AND ISOTOPIC ABUNDANCES

The composition of any object can be given as a set of elemental and isotopic abundances. One may speak, for example, of the composition of the ocean, the solar system, or indeed the Galaxy in terms of its respective elemental and isotopic abundances. Formally, the phrase *elemental abundances* usually connotes the amounts of the elements in an object expressed relative to one particular element (or isotope of it) selected as the standard for comparison. Isotopic abundances refer to the relative proportions of the stable isotopes of each element. They are most often quoted as atom percentages.

Since the late 1930s, geochemists, astrophysicists, and nuclear physicists have joined together to try to explain the observed pattern of elemental and isotopic abundances. A more or less consistent picture has emerged. Hydrogen, much helium, and some lithium isotopes are thought to have formed at the time of the big bang—the primordial explosion from which the universe is believed to have originated. The rest of the elements come, directly or indirectly, from stars. Cosmic rays produce a sizable proportion of the elements with mass numbers between 5 and 10, which are relatively rare. A substantial body of evidence shows that stars synthesize the heavier elements by nuclear processes collectively termed nucleosynthesis.

In the first instance, then, nucleosynthesis determines the pattern of elemental abundances everywhere. The pattern is not immutable, for not all stars are alike and once matter escapes from stars it may undergo various processes of physical and chemical separation. A newly formed small planet, for example, may not exert enough gravitational attraction to capture the light gases hydrogen and helium. Conversely, the processes that change elemental abundances normally alter isotopic abundances to a much lesser degree. Thus, virtually all terrestrial and meteoritic iron analyzed to date consists of 5.8 percent ^{54}Fe, 91.72 percent ^{56}Fe, 2.2 percent ^{57}Fe, and 0.28 percent ^{58}Fe. The relative constancy of the isotopic abundances makes it possible to tabulate meaningful average atomic masses for the elements. The availability of atomic masses is crucial to chemists.

Although there is general agreement on how the elements formed, the interpretation of elemental and isotopic abundances in specific bodies continues to occupy the attention of scientists. They obtain their raw data from several sources. Most knowledge concerning abundances comes from the study of Earth, meteorites, and the Sun.

Currently accepted estimates of solar system (as opposed to terrestrial) abundances are pieced together mainly from two sources. Chemical analyses of Type I carbonaceous chondrites, a special kind of meteorite, provide information about all but the most volatile elements (i.e., those that existed as gases that the parent body of the meteorite could not trap in representative amounts). Spectroscopic analysis of light from the Sun furnishes information about the volatile elements deficient in meteorites.

To the extent that the Sun resembles other stars, the elemental and isotopic abundances of the solar system have universal significance. The solar system pattern has several notable features. First, the lighter isotopes, those of hydrogen and helium, constitute more than 98 percent of the mass. Heavier isotopes make up scarcely 2 percent. Second, apart from the exceptions discussed in the following text, as A or Z increases through the periodic table of the elements, abundances generally decrease. For

Study of the composition of meteorites, as well as Earth and the Sun, can reveal a great deal of information about abundances. Peter Kneffel/AFP/ Getty Images

example, the solar system as a whole contains about one million times more carbon, nitrogen, and oxygen than the much heavier elements platinum and gold, though the proportions of the latter may vary widely from object to object. The decrease in abundance with increasing mass reflects in part the successive nature of nucleosynthesis. In nucleosynthesis a nuclide of lower mass often serves as the seed or target for the production of a nuclide of higher mass. As the conversion of the lower mass target to the higher mass product is usually far from complete, abundances tend to decrease as mass increases. A third feature of interest is that stable isotopes with even numbers of protons and neutrons occur more often than do isotopes with odd ones (the so-called odd-even effect). Out of the almost 300 stable nuclides known, only five have odd numbers of both protons and neutrons; more than half have even values of Z and N. Fourth, among the isotopes with even Z and N certain species stand out by virtue of their considerable nuclear stability and comparatively high abundances. Nuclides that have equal and even numbers of neutrons and protons, the "alpha-particle" nuclides, fall into this category, which includes carbon-12, magnesium-24, and argon-36. Finally, peaks in the abundance distribution occur near the special values of Z and N defined above as magic numbers. The high abundances manifest the extra nuclear stability that the magic numbers confer. Elements with enhanced abundances include nickel ($Z = 28$), tin ($Z = 50$), and lead ($Z = 82$).

The study of cosmic rays and of the light emitted by stars yields information about elemental and isotopic abundances outside the solar system. Cosmic rays are ions with high energy that are given off by stars. The Sun produces cosmic rays, too, but of much lower average energy than those reaching the solar system from outside. The abundance pattern in cosmic rays resembles that of the solar system in many ways, suggesting that solar and over-all galactic abundances may be similar. Two explanations have been advanced to account for why solar and cosmic-ray abundances do not agree in all respects. The first is that cosmic rays undergo nuclear reactions (i.e., collisions that transform their nuclei) as they pass through interstellar matter. The second is that material from unusual stars with exotic compositions may be more prominent in cosmic rays.

The determination of elemental and isotopic abundances in stars of the Milky Way Galaxy and of more distant galaxies poses formidable experimental difficulties. Research in the field is active and reveals trends in composition among stars that are consistent with nucleosynthetic theory. The "metallicity"—or proportion of heavy elements—in stars, for instance, seems to increase with stellar age. In addition, many stars with compositions far different from that of the solar system are known. Their existence has led some investigators to doubt whether the concept of cosmic, as opposed to solar-system, abundances is meaningful. For the present it is perhaps enough to quote the American astrophysicist James W. Truran:

> *The local pattern of abundances is generally representative. The gross abundance features throughout our galaxy, in other galaxies, and even apparently in quasars are generally similar to those of solar system matter, testifying to the fact that the underlying stellar systems share the same nucleosynthetic processes.*

VARIATIONS IN ISOTOPIC ABUNDANCES

Although isotopic abundances are fairly constant throughout the solar system, variations do occur. Variations in stable isotopic abundances are usually less than 1 percent, but they can be larger. Whatever their size, they provide geologists and astronomers with valuable clues to the histories of the objects under study. Several different processes can cause abundances to vary, among them radioactive decay and mass fractionation.

RADIOACTIVE DECAY

This process transmutes an isotope of one element into an isotope of another, such as potassium-40 (^{40}K) to argon-40 (^{40}Ar) or uranium-235 (^{235}U) to lead-207 (^{207}Pb). As a consequence, the isotopic composition of the daughter element produced by the radioactive decay—argon or lead in the cases cited—may vary significantly from sample to sample. The variations become especially pronounced when the material under study forms with only a small amount of the daughter element present initially. The isotopic composition of argon in Earth's atmosphere is a case in point.

Compared to stellar or solar-system abundances, atmospheric argon contains a much higher proportion of ^{40}Ar and much less ^{36}Ar and ^{38}Ar. The excess ^{40}Ar in the atmosphere evidently leaked out of crustal rocks and other potassium-bearing materials where it was produced by the decay of ^{40}K. Because Earth trapped a relatively small amount of cosmically normal argon during its accretion, the ^{40}Ar generated since then by radioactive decay dominates the isotopic pattern in the atmosphere.

MASS FRACTIONATION

Physical and/or chemical processes affect differently the isotopes of an element. When the effect is systematic, increasing or decreasing steadily as mass number increases, the new pattern of isotopic abundances is said to be mass fractionated with respect to some standard pattern. For small fractionations—a few percent or less—the normal isotopic ratio M_h/M_l changes by an amount proportional to $\Delta m = M_h - M_l$, where M_l is the mass of the lighter isotope. For oxygen subjected to mass fractionation the percentage change of the ratio $^{18}O/^{16}O$ should be twice that in the ratio $^{17}O/^{16}O$. Sometimes a set of samples will form from a single reservoir but with each one having experienced a different degree of mass fractionation. A graph of one isotopic ratio, M_h/M_l, against a second, $M_{h'}/M_l$, will then yield a straight line of slope $(M_h - M_l)/(M_{h'} - M_l)$. Such plots find important use in deciding whether groups of objects originated from a common source and how those groups evolved. When the oxygen isotope abundances of samples from Earth and the Moon are considered in this way, the results suggest that both the planet and its satellite are members of a family of objects distinct from the families to which most meteorites belong.

Other Causes of Isotopic Abundance Variations

Several other causes may contribute to observed variations in isotopic abundances. First, in rare instances, materials can preserve the isotopic signatures of unusual material from other stars. In particular, certain meteorites contain microscopic diamonds and silicon carbide grains thought to predate the formation of the solar system. These grains escaped thorough blending with average solar system matter by virtue of their resistance to thermal processing and to chemical reactions. Second, planetary atmospheres and the surface of airless bodies in the solar system undergo intense irradiation by high-energy particles, which affects their isotopic composition. Finally, certain kinds of chemical reactions induced by light can lead to changes in isotopic composition.

PHYSICAL PROPERTIES ASSOCIATED WITH ISOTOPES

Broadly speaking, differences in the properties of isotopes can be attributed to either of two causes: differences in mass or differences in nuclear structure. Scientists usually refer to the former as isotope effects and to the latter by a variety of more specialized names. The isotopes of helium afford examples of both kinds. Mass effects are considered first.

Helium has two stable isotopes, ^{3}He and ^{4}He, and exists in the gaseous state under normal conditions. At a given temperature and pressure, any volume of ^{4}He will weigh one-third more than the same volume of ^{3}He. More generally, for the same spatial distribution of atoms, the substance with the heavier isotope is expected to have the larger density. When deuterium, $^2_1$H, is substituted for hydrogen, $^1_1$H, to form heavy water, $^2_1$H$_2$O, its density is about 10 percent greater than that of normal H$_2$O.

A second difference related directly to mass concerns atomic velocities. Lighter species travel at higher average

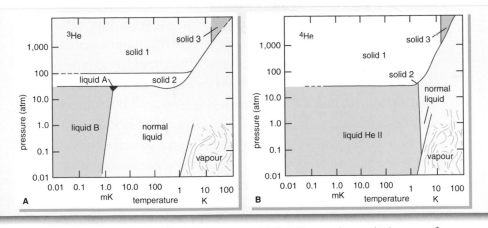

The phase diagrams of (A) helium-3 and (B) helium-4 show which states of these isotopes are stable. Copyright Encyclopædia Britannica; rendering for this edition by Rosen Educational Services

speeds. Atoms of ^{3}He, on the average, move 15 percent faster than those of gaseous ^{4}He at the same temperature. Many other properties that depend on atomic motion, such as the thermal conductivity and viscosity of gases, manifest predictable isotope effects.

Contrasts in the behaviour of the helium isotopes extend to the liquid and solid states and are attributable to the effects of both mass and nuclear structure. It will be noted that ^{3}He forms three distinguishable liquid phases of which two are superfluids, while ^{4}He may exist only as two distinct liquids of which one is a superfluid. Unlike all other isotopes of the elements in the periodic table, neither ^{3}He nor ^{4}He solidifies under low pressures at a temperature near absolute zero, 0 Kelvin (K) (-273 °C, or -459 °F).

Several other differences between isotopes depend on nuclear structure rather than on nuclear mass. First, radioactivity results from the interplay, distinctive for each nucleus, of nuclear and electrostatic forces between neutrons, protons, and electrons. Helium-6, for example, is radioactive, whereas helium-4 is stable. Second, the spatial distribution of the protons in the nucleus affects in measurable ways the behaviour of the surrounding electrons. The addition of one neutron to the nucleus of an isotope allows the protons to spread out and to occupy a larger region of space. An added neutron may also cause the nucleus to assume a nonspherical shape. Any electron that spends time close to the nucleus will be sensitive to these changes. In particular, the new distribution of nuclear charge changes the way that the electron (or, more strictly, the atom as a whole) emits or absorbs light. Finally, nuclei may have angular momentum or spin. The term *spin* derives from a simple picture of the nucleus as a lumpy ball of protons and neutrons rotating about an axis. The number and the arrangement of neutrons and protons in a

nucleus determine its spin, with higher spins corresponding roughly to faster rotation. About half of all stable
nuclei have nonzero spin, so they act as tiny magnets, a
fact that has far-reaching consequences. Scientists often
describe the magnetic character of a nucleus in terms of
a quantity closely related to spin called the nuclear magnetic moment. The larger the nuclear magnetic moment
of a nucleus, the more that nucleus will "feel" the force
exerted by any nearby magnet. For example, a hydrogen
nucleus, ^1H, and a tritium nucleus, ^3H, have about the
same nuclear magnetic moment and react about equally
when placed between the poles of a horseshoe magnet. In
contrast, the same horseshoe magnet will affect a deuterium nucleus (^2H) about twice as much and the nucleus of
a ^{12}C atom, which has no spin, not at all.

EFFECT OF ISOTOPES ON ATOMIC AND MOLECULAR SPECTRA

The study of how atoms and molecules interact with
electromagnetic radiation, of which visible light is one
form, is called spectroscopy. Spectroscopy has contributed much to the understanding of isotopes, and vice
versa. To the extent that the characteristic spectrum of an
atom or a molecule (i.e., the light emitted or absorbed by
it) is regarded as a physical property, the special relation
between spectroscopy and isotopy warrants individual
treatment here.

Atoms typically absorb or emit light exclusively at
certain frequencies. Quantum mechanics explains this
observation in a general way by associating with each atom
(or molecule) well-defined states of energy. The atom may
pass from one state to another only when energy is supplied (or removed) in the amount separating one state
from another.

Precise measurements of the light emitted by isotopes of an element show small but significant differences termed shifts by spectroscopists. On the whole, these shifts are quite small. They originate in both mass and nuclear structure effects. The effects due to mass are largest for light isotopes. As nuclear mass increases, they decrease by an amount roughly proportional to $1/A^2$ and become insignificant in the heavier elements.

The effects due to nuclear structure relate primarily to the angular momentum, the magnetic moment, and the so-called electric quadrupole moment of the nucleus. The latter measures deviations from sphericity in the charge distribution. The magnetic moment and its attendant effects form the foundation of nuclear magnetic resonance (NMR), a field that has become very important in many branches of science.

Once of interest mainly to academic physicists and chemists, the methods of NMR now find widespread application in medical imaging facilities. In a simple experiment for NMR, a tubeful of liquid methane, $^{12}C^1H_4$, at low temperature, might be set between the poles of a very strong external magnet. According to the laws of quantum mechanics, the axes of the ^1H nuclei may orient themselves in one of only two possible directions. The "poles" of the ^1H nucleus may either line up (approximately) with those of the external magnet, north to north and south to south; or the two sets of poles may oppose each other, as when a compass needle aligns itself with Earth's magnetic field. The former orientation (N to N and S to S) has the higher energy. A ^1H nucleus in the lower-energy state can move to the higher-energy state by absorbing light. With the magnets used today, light in the radiowave portion of the electromagnetic spectrum carries the right amount of energy to cause the transitions, i.e., to flip the nucleus on its axis. The task of the NMR spectroscopist is to determine precisely which frequencies make nuclear spin changes occur and with what likelihood. Results may be reported as "NMR spectra," graphs that show the probability that any given frequency of light will induce a transition. The great power of NMR derives from the observation that the spectra reflect the structure of the molecule studied, that is, the linkage of atoms within the molecule. For example, in the molecule methanol, CH_3OH, three atoms of hydrogen bind to carbon, C, and one atom of hydrogen binds to oxygen, O. Broad (low resolution) peaks at two different frequencies in the proton NMR spectrum of methanol show the existence of the two distinct chemical environments for hydrogen. The mathematical difference between frequencies, adjusted to take into account the strength of the external magnetic field, is an example of what spectroscopists call a chemical shift. Chemists refer to published libraries of chemical shifts both to identify the substances present in samples of unknown composition and to infer the structures of newly synthesized molecules. Nuclei popular for NMR studies include ^1H, ^{13}C, ^{15}N, ^{17}O, and ^{31}P.

Molecular Vibrations

When atoms join together in molecules, they can enter into characteristic vibrations and rotations. Just as an atom has a set of energy states associated primarily with the possible configurations of its electrons, so molecules have sets of energy states associated with their vibrations and rotations, as well as a set of electronic states. Light of the correct energy will induce changes from one vibrational (and/or rotational) state to another. Two ways in which isotopy relates to molecular vibrations, in particular, can be illustrated with the simplest of all molecules—diatomic molecules, which consist of only two atoms. Vibrational spectroscopy shows that isotopically heavier diatomic molecules have higher bond energies. (Bond energy is the amount of energy needed to separate the two atoms.) Quantum mechanical theory makes it possible to calculate from vibrational spectra just how much stronger the bond to the heavier isotope is. The differences between the chemical bond energies of isotopes help to explain why the isotopes do not behave identically in chemical reactions. The second relation concerns the spacing between vibrational energy levels: the vibrational energy levels of an isotopically heavier molecule lie closer together. Consequently, it takes less energy to excite $^{18}O-^{18}O$ from one vibrational level to the next than it does $^{16}O-^{16}O$. Spectroscopists made good use of this fact when they inferred from the spectra of isotopically mixed diatoms the existence of previously unknown isotopes. Oxygen-18 was discovered in this way.

IMPORTANCE IN THE STUDY OF POLYATOMIC MOLECULES

This second point, the distinguishability of the vibrational spectra of isotopically different molecules, is of great importance in the study of polyatomic molecules (molecules that contain three or more atoms). One key issue for chemists is the nature of the vibrations in polyatomic molecules: How do the nuclei of the atoms oscillate in relation to each other? The answer to this question bears strongly on what transient shapes the molecule may assume, how it will react with other molecules, and the rate at which it will do so. It is usually impossible to obtain this information from a study of the vibrational spectra of molecules made from atoms at natural abundance levels. Fortunately, the systematic substitution of heavier isotopes at known points in polyatomic molecules gives rise to new sets of vibrational spectra that clarify the nature of the atomic motions.

There is a second, fundamental reason for investigating the vibrational spectra of isotopically substituted, or "labeled," molecules. In interpreting spectra, spectroscopists rely on the mathematical results of quantum theory. Often, a close analysis of vibrational spectra of labeled molecules offers the best means for testing the soundness of the prevailing theoretical understanding of molecules.

CHEMICAL EFFECTS OF ISOTOPIC SUBSTITUTION

As isotopic abundances remain almost constant during most chemical processes, chemists do not normally distinguish the behaviour of one isotope from that of another. Indeed, in the limit of high temperatures, isotopes distribute themselves at random without preference for any particular chemical form. Nonetheless, under certain circumstances, nonrandom isotopic effects can become appreciable. Specifically, the lower the temperature and the lighter the isotope, the more noticeable the effects are likely to be. The reason is that the heavier isotopes tend to displace the lighter ones in those molecules where the heavy isotopes form the strongest chemical bond.

The exchange reaction $H_2 + D_2 \rightarrow 2HD$ provides an example of random behaviour at high temperature and isotope-specific behaviour at lower ones. If two volumes of gas consisting, respectively, of H_2 and D_2 only, are mixed, the hydrogen–hydrogen and deuterium–deuterium bonds will gradually break and new molecules will form until the vessel contains an appreciable quantity of HD as well as of H_2 and D_2. At high temperatures the amount of HD observed at equilibrium approaches that predicted on the basis of probability (entropy) considerations alone (i.e., a random distribution). How much would that be? A mathematical analysis shows that the concentrations of H_2, D_2, and HD should be equal to $(fH)^2$, $(fD)^2$, and $2(fH)(fD)$, respectively, to a very good approximation. Here fX represents the fractional concentration of atom X.

Experiment shows that as temperature increases, the concentrations of H_2, D_2, and HD approach the values expected. Although gratifying, the corroboration provides little information of chemical interest because the same results apply equally to the nitrogen isotopes ^{14}N and ^{15}N, to the chlorine isotopes ^{35}Cl and ^{37}Cl, and to many other pairs that differ greatly from hydrogen in their chemical behaviour. The variations from the random statistical distribution that occur at lower temperatures are more interesting to a chemist because of what they reveal about the particular element.

At low temperatures the formation of D_2 (and H_2) is favoured at the expense of HD. A detailed theoretical treatment traces the cause of this favouritism to the comparative strength of the deuterium–deuterium bond. The result can be generalized: at equilibrium, the heavier isotope tends to concentrate wherever it forms the strongest chemical bond. For example, in the exchange reaction

$$R-H + R'-D \longrightarrow R-D + R'-H,$$

the hydrogen and deuterium switch partners. One may think of the hydrogen and deuterium as competing for the more attractive partner, supposed here to be R rather than R'. In accordance with the aforementioned generalization, the deuterium will tend to monopolize R, with which, by hypothesis, it forms a stronger bond than it does with R'. Deuterium has a slight edge in the competition for R in spite of the fact that the hydrogen must also form a stronger bond with R than with R'.

Special quantities called chemical equilibrium constants express in quantitative terms the extent to which a chemical reaction favours products (the substances written to the right of the arrow) or reactants (the substances written to the left of the arrow). For reactions of the type cited, which chemists call exchange reactions, equilibrium constants are typically within a few percent of the values expected for a random distribution. The largest variations are observed for the low-Z elements, such as hydrogen. The variations are quite small for elements with higher atomic numbers, seldom exceeding 1 percent.

As previously implied, the equilibrium constants for exchange reactions change slightly with temperature. The American chemist Harold C. Urey put this fact to use when he devised a method for inferring the temperature at which carbonates formed in the sea. He noted that, given a choice between water (H_2O) and carbonate (CO_3^{2-}, a principal constituent of seashells), the isotope ^{18}O shows a slight preference for the carbonate. The preference increases as temperature decreases. By measuring the $^{18}O/^{16}O$ ratio in a sample of carbonate and comparing it with the ratio in local seawater, it is possible to calculate a temperature at which the carbonate and the water equilibrated.

Although isotopic substitutions usually change chemical equilibrium constants by small amounts, they can increase the rates of chemical reactions by a factor of 10 or more in the most extreme cases.

EFFECT OF ISOTOPIC SUBSTITUTION ON REACTION RATES

Chemical reactions take place when chemical bonds between atoms break or form. In the laboratory, chemical reactions proceed at well-defined rates. By introducing a heavy isotope into a reacting molecule, one may change the rate at which the molecule reacts. Two factors determine the size of the change.

The first factor is where the isotopic substitution is made in the reacting molecule. The largest effects, primary isotope effects, occur when one introduces a new isotope in the reaction "centre" (i.e., the place in the molecule where chemical bonds are broken and/or formed during the reaction). If the isotope is placed some distance from the reaction centre, however, it produces a much smaller, secondary isotope effect.

The second factor determining the size of the change in reaction rate is the relative, or percentage, difference in the masses of the original and substituted isotopes. The 300 percent difference in mass between ^3H (tritium) and ^1H can lead to more than 15-fold changes in reaction rates.

Both primary and secondary isotope effects decrease rapidly with increasing atomic number because the percentage difference in mass between isotopes tends to decrease. The substitution of deuterium for hydrogen, for example, may slow a reaction down by a factor of six. In contrast, the substitution of ^{18}O for ^{16}O would typically change a reaction rate by only a few percent. There is a much larger relative mass difference between hydrogen and deuterium than there is between ^{18}O and ^{16}O.

Primary isotope effects are often interpreted in terms of what is known as transition-state theory. The theory postulates that to react, molecules must first reorganize themselves into a special, energy-rich configuration called a transition state. Other things being equal, the more energy required to form the transition state, the slower the reaction will be. A reaction in which a hydrogen atom shifts from one large molecule, symbolized as R–H, to another, symbolized as R′–H, furnishes an example:

$$R-H + R' \longrightarrow R \cdots H \cdots R' \longrightarrow R + H-R'.$$

The middle structure with the dotted lines represents a transition state. The energy needed to form the transition state and hence the rate of reaction depends on the strength of the R–H bond among other factors. As deuterium would form a stronger bond to R than hydrogen, it follows that the substitution of deuterium for hydrogen would slow the reaction down. The amount by which the reaction slows down would depend heavily on just how much stronger the R–D bond is than the R–H bond.

ISOTOPE SEPARATION AND ENRICHMENT

Most elements are found as mixtures of several isotopes. For certain applications in industry, medicine, and science, samples enriched in one particular isotope are needed. Many methods have therefore been developed to separate the isotopes of an element from one another. Each method is based on some difference—sometimes a very slight one—between the physical or chemical properties of the isotopes of an element.

MASS SPECTROMETRY

Although the instrumentation normally serves analytical purposes, when suitably modified a mass spectrometer can also be used on a larger scale to prepare a purified sample of virtually any isotope. Uranium-235 for the first atomic bomb was separated with specially built mass

The mass spectrometer can be used to prepare a sample of many different isotopes. SSPL via Getty Images

spectrometers. Because of its high operational costs, this method is ordinarily restricted to the production of a few milligrams to a few grams of various stable isotopes for scientific investigation.

DISTILLATION

The same factors that lead to the enrichment of alcohol in the vapour above a solution of water and alcohol permit the enrichment of isotopes. At temperatures below 220 °C (428 °F), for example, light water ($_1^1H_2O$) vaporizes to a slightly greater extent than heavy water ($_1^2H_2O$, or D_2O). The distillation of normal water, which contains both molecules, produces a vapour slightly enriched in $_1^1H_2O$. The residual liquid retains a correspondingly enhanced concentration of heavy water. It is usually, though not always, true that the molecule with the lighter isotope will be more volatile. Similarly, distillation of liquefied carbon monoxide through several kilometres of piping yields a residue enriched in the heavier of carbon's two stable isotopes, ^{13}C. Compounds made from the ^{13}C-enriched material are needed for certain medical tests, such as one that detects the ulcer-causing bacterium *Helicobacter pylori*.

Chemical Exchange Reactions

Slight differences between the preferences of isotopes for one chemical form over another can serve as the basis for separation. The preparation of nitrogen enriched in ^{15}N by ion-exchange techniques illustrates this principle. Ammonia in water $NH_3(aq)$ will bind to a so-called ion-exchange resin (R–H). When poured over a vertical column of resin, a solution of ammonia reacts to form a well-defined horizontal band at the top of the column. The addition of a solution of lye (sodium hydroxide) will force the band of ammonia to move down the column. As the resin holds $^{15}NH_3$ slightly more tenaciously than $^{14}NH_3$, the $^{14}NH_3$ tends to concentrate at the leading, or bottom, edge of the band and the $^{15}NH_3$ at the trailing, or topmost, edge. Solutions depleted or enriched in ^{15}N are collected as they wash off the column.

Gaseous Diffusion

Gases can diffuse through the small pores present in many materials. The diffusion proceeds in a random manner as gas molecules bounce off the walls of the porous medium. The average time a molecule of gas takes to traverse such a barrier depends on its velocity and certain other factors. According to the kinetic theory of gases, at a given temperature a lighter molecule will have a larger average velocity than a heavier one. This result provides the basis for a separation method that was once widely used to produce uranium enriched in the readily fissionable isotope ^{235}U, which is needed for nuclear reactors and nuclear weapons. (Natural uranium contains only about 0.7 percent ^{235}U, with the remainder of the isotopic mixture consisting almost entirely of ^{238}U.) In the separation process, natural uranium in the form of uranium hexafluoride (UF_6) gas is diffused from one compartment of a chamber to another through a porous barrier. Since the molecules of $^{235}UF_6$ travel at a higher velocity than those of $^{238}UF_6$, they pass into the second compartment more rapidly than the latter. Because the percentage of ^{235}U increases only slightly after traversal of the barrier, the process must be repeated hundreds of thousands of times to obtain the desired concentration of the isotope.

Gas Centrifugation

When a mixture of gaseous molecules spins at high speed in a specially designed closed container, the heaviest species will concentrate near the outer walls and the lightest near the axis. The American physicist Jesse W. Beams used a gas centrifuge to separate isotopes, specifically the isotopes of chlorine, for the first time in 1936. Much subsequent work focused on the separation of $^{235}UF_6$ from $^{238}UF_6$, for which the gas centrifuge promised considerable savings in energy costs. Today, more than two-thirds of the world's enriched uranium is produced by this method, which is expected by 2020 to supplant completely the gas diffusion method. Gas centrifuge facilities also produce and sell gram-to-kilogram quantities of the isotopes of numerous other elements for scientific and medical purposes.

Photochemical Enrichment Methods

As discussed earlier, the frequencies of light absorbed by isotopes differ slightly. Once an atom has absorbed radiation and reached an excited state, its chemical properties may become quite different from what they were in the initial, or ground, state. Certain chemical and physical processes—the loss of an electron, for example—may proceed from an excited state that would not occur at all in the ground state. This observation is the nub of photochemical methods for isotope separation in which light is used to excite one and only one isotope of an element. In atomic vapour laser isotope separation (AVLIS), the starting material is the element itself. In molecular laser isotope separation (MLIS), the starting material is a chemical compound containing the element. Ordinary light sources are not suitable for isotope separation because they emit a broad range of frequencies that excites all the isotopes of an element. For this reason, the large-scale implementation of AVLIS and MLIS had to await improvements in lasers—devices that produce intense light within exquisitely narrow bands of frequencies.

The use of laser-based methods to separate the isotopes of uranium attracted great attention in the closing decades of the 20th century. Proponents foresaw that these methods would consume less energy and waste less starting material than, for example, gaseous diffusion plants. In several countries, government-sponsored research concentrated on processes that begin with ordinary metallic uranium. Upon heating in an oven, the uranium vaporizes and escapes as a beam of atoms through a small hole. Several large, high-powered lasers tuned to the correct frequencies shine on the beam and cause the ^{235}U atoms (but not the ^{238}U atoms) to lose electrons. In this (ionized) form the ^{235}U particles are attracted to and collect on a charged plate. Ironically, just as this technology came to maturity, various geopolitical factors—relatively abundant fossil fuels, a surfeit of weapons-grade uranium from Russia, progress toward nuclear disarmament, and concerns about the safety of nuclear reactors and about preserving jobs in the nuclear industry—idled the first large-scale laser-enrichment facility in the United States. Even so, it seems safe to predict that laser separation will have a role to play in producing nuclear fuels.

Both government and private laboratories have been active in developing laser separation methods for rare stable isotopes of other elements. Such isotopes have applications in medicine and in the life sciences. They may serve, for example, as the starting material from which to make the radioactive isotopes needed for nuclear medicine or as tags put on drugs to monitor their action inside patients.

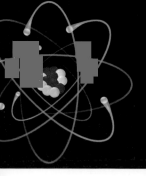

CHAPTER 4

RADIOACTIVITY

R adioactivity is a property exhibited by certain types of matter of emitting energy and subatomic particles spontaneously. It is, in essence, an attribute of individual atomic nuclei.

An unstable nucleus will decompose spontaneously, or decay, into a more stable configuration but will do so only in a few specific ways by emitting certain particles or certain forms of electromagnetic energy. Radioactive decay is a property of several naturally occurring elements as well as of artificially produced isotopes of the elements. The rate at which a radioactive element decays is expressed in terms of its half-life (i.e., the time required for one-half of any given quantity of the isotope to decay). Half-lives range from more than 1,000,000,000 years for some nuclei to less than 10^{-9} second. The product of a radioactive decay process—called the daughter of the parent isotope—may itself be unstable, in which case it, too, will decay. The process continues until a stable nuclide has been formed.

THE NATURE OF RADIOACTIVE EMISSIONS

The emissions of the most common forms of spontaneous radioactive decay are the alpha (α) particle, the beta (β) particle, the gamma (γ) ray, and the neutrino. The alpha particle is actually the nucleus of a helium-4 atom, with two positive charges ^4_2He. Such charged atoms are called ions. The neutral helium atom has two electrons outside its nucleus balancing these two charges. Beta particles may be negatively charged (beta minus, symbol e^-), or positively charged (beta plus, symbol e^+). The beta minus [β⁻] particle is actually an electron created in the nucleus during beta decay without any relationship to the orbital electron cloud of the atom. The beta plus particle, also called the positron, is the antiparticle of the electron; and when brought together, two such particles will mutually annihilate each other. Gamma rays are electromagnetic radiations such as radio waves, light, and X-rays. Beta radioactivity also produces the neutrino and antineutrino, particles that have no charge and scant mass, symbolized by v and $\bar{v}$, respectively.

In the less common forms of radioactivity, fission fragments, neutrons, or protons may be emitted. Fission fragments are themselves complex nuclei with usually between one-third and two-thirds the charge Z and mass A of the parent nucleus. Neutrons and protons are, of course, the basic building blocks of complex nuclei, having approximately unit mass on the atomic scale and having zero charge or unit positive charge, respectively. The neutron cannot long exist in the free state. It is rapidly captured by nuclei in matter. Otherwise, in free space it will undergo beta-minus decay to a proton, an electron, and an antineutrino with a half-life of 12.8 minutes. The proton is the nucleus of ordinary hydrogen and is stable.

TYPES OF RADIOACTIVITY

The early work on natural radioactivity associated with uranium and thorium ores identified two distinct types of radioactivity: alpha and beta decay.

ALPHA DECAY

In alpha decay, an energetic helium ion (alpha particle) is ejected, leaving a daughter nucleus of atomic number two less than the parent and of atomic mass number four less than the parent. An example is the decay (symbolized by an arrow) of the abundant isotope of uranium, ^{238}U, to a thorium daughter plus an alpha particle:

$$^{238}_{92}\text{U} \longrightarrow \,^{234}_{90}\text{Th} + \,^{4}_{2}\text{He}$$

$$Q_\alpha = 4.268 \text{ MeV}$$

$$t_{1/2} = 4.51 \times 10^9 \text{ years}$$

Given for this and subsequent reactions are the energy released (Q) in millions of electron volts (MeV) and the half-life ($t_{1/2}$). It should be noted that in alpha decays the charges, or number of protons, shown in subscript are in balance on both sides of the arrow, as are the atomic masses, shown in superscript.

BETA-MINUS DECAY

In beta-minus decay, an energetic negative electron is emitted, producing a daughter nucleus of one higher atomic number and the same mass number. An example is the decay of the uranium daughter product thorium-234 into protactinium-234:

$$^{234}_{90}\text{Th} \longrightarrow \,^{234}_{91}\text{Pa} + e^- + \bar{\nu}$$

$$Q_{\beta+} = .263 \text{ MeV}$$

$$t_{1/2} = 24.1 \text{ days}$$

In the reaction for beta decay, $\bar{\nu}$ represents the anti-neutrino. Here, the number of protons is increased by one in the reaction, but the total charge remains the same, because an electron, with negative charge, is also created.

Gamma Decay

A third type of radiation, gamma radiation, usually accompanies alpha or beta decay. Gamma rays are photons and are without rest mass or charge. Alpha or beta decay may simply proceed directly to the ground (lowest energy) state of the daughter nucleus without gamma emission, but the decay may also proceed wholly or partly to higher energy states (excited states) of the daughter. In the latter case, gamma emission may occur as the excited states transform to lower energy states of the same nucleus. (Alternatively to gamma emission, an excited nucleus may transform to a lower energy state by ejecting an electron from the cloud surrounding the nucleus. This orbital electron ejection is known as internal conversion and gives rise to an energetic electron and often an X-ray as the atomic cloud fills in the empty orbital of the ejected electron. The ratio of internal conversion to the alternative gamma emission is called the internal-conversion coefficient.)

Isomeric Transitions

There is a wide range of rates of half-lives for the gamma-emission process. Usually dipole transitions, in which the gamma ray carries off one ℏ unit of angular momentum, are fast, less than nanoseconds (one nanosecond equals 10^{-9} second). The law of conservation of angular momentum requires that the sum of angular momenta of the radiation and daughter nucleus is equal to the angular momentum (spin) of the parent. If the spins of initial and final states differ by more than one, dipole radiation is forbidden, and gamma emission must proceed more slowly by a higher multipole (quadrupole, octupole, etc.) gamma transition. If the gamma-emission half-life exceeds about one nanosecond, the excited nucleus is said to be in a metastable, or isomeric, state (the names for a long-lived excited state), and it is customary to classify the decay as another type of radioactivity, an isomeric transition. An example of isomerism is found in the protactinium-234 nucleus of the uranium-238 decay chain:

$$^{234m}_{91}\text{Pa} \longrightarrow ^{234}_{91}\text{Pa} + \gamma$$

$$Q_\gamma = 0.0698 \text{ MeV}$$

$$t_{1/2} = 1.17 \text{ min}$$

The letter *m* following the mass number stands for metastable and indicates a nuclear isomer.

Beta-Plus Decay

During the 1930s new types of radioactivity were found among the artificial products of nuclear reactions: beta-plus decay, or positron emission, and electron capture. In beta-plus decay an energetic positron is created and emitted, along with a neutrino, and the nucleus transforms to a daughter, lower by one in atomic number and the same in mass number. For instance, carbon-11 ($Z = 6$) decays to boron-11 ($Z = 5$), plus one positron and one neutrino:

$$^{11}_{6}\text{C} \longrightarrow ^{11}_{5}\text{B} + e^+ + \nu$$

$$Q_{\beta^+} = 0.97 \text{ MeV}$$

$$t_{1/2} = 20.4 \text{ min}$$

Electron Capture

Electron capture (EC) is a process in which decay follows the capture by the nucleus of an orbital electron. It is similar to positron decay in that the nucleus transforms to a daughter of one lower atomic number. It differs in that an orbital electron from the cloud is captured by the nucleus with subsequent emission of an atomic X-ray as the orbital vacancy is filled by an electron from the cloud about the nucleus. An example is the nucleus of beryllium-7 capturing one of its inner electrons to give lithium-7:

$$Q_{EC} = 0.8616 \text{ MeV}$$

$$^{7}_{4}\text{Be} + e^{-} \longrightarrow {}^{7}_{3}\text{Li} + \nu$$

$$t_{1/2} = 53 \text{ days}$$

The overall energy release, Q_{EC}, is necessarily a calculated value because there is no general practical means of measuring the neutrino energies accompanying EC decay. With a few electron-capturing nuclides, it has been possible to measure directly the decay energy by measurement of a rare process called inner bremsstrahlung (braking radiation). In this process the energy release is shared between the neutrino and a gamma ray. The measured distribution of gamma-ray energies indicates the total energy

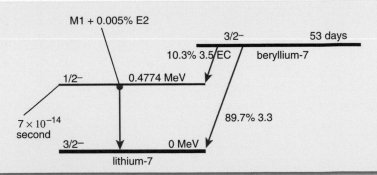

Radioactive decay of beryllium-7 to lithium-7 by electron capture (EC). Copyright Encyclopædia Britannica; rendering for this edition by Rosen Educational Services

release. Usually there is so much ordinary gamma radiation with radioactive decay that the inner bremsstrahlung is unobservable.

SPONTANEOUS FISSION

Yet another type of radioactivity is spontaneous fission. In this process the nucleus splits into two fragment nuclei of roughly half the mass of the parent. This process is only barely detectable in competition with the more prevalent alpha decay for uranium, but for some of the heaviest artificial nuclei, such as fermium-256, spontaneous fission becomes the predominant mode of radioactive decay. Kinetic-energy releases from 150 to 200 MeV may occur as the fragments are accelerated apart by the large electrical repulsion between their nuclear charges. The reaction is as follows:

$$^{111}_{52}\text{Te} \longrightarrow {}^{111}_{51}\overset{*}{\text{Sb}} + e^+ + \nu \qquad Q_{\beta^+} \text{ uncertain}$$
$$\quad \longrightarrow {}^{110}_{50}\text{Sn} + p \qquad E_{max\,p} = 3.7 \text{ MeV}$$
$$t_{1/2} = 19.5 \text{ sec}$$

Only one of several product sets is shown. A few neutrons are always emitted in fission of this isotope, a feature essential to chain reactions. Spontaneous fission is not to be confused with induced fission, the process involved in nuclear reactors. Induced fission is a property of uranium-235, plutonium-239, and other isotopes to undergo fission after absorption of a slow neutron. Other than the requirement of a neutron capture to initiate it, induced fission is quite similar to spontaneous fission regarding total energy release, numbers of secondary neutrons, and so on.

PROTON RADIOACTIVITY

Proton radioactivity was discovered in 1970 in an excited isomeric state of cobalt-53, ^{53m}Co, 1.5 percent of which emits protons:

$$^{53m}_{27}\text{Co} \begin{cases} \xrightarrow{1.5\%} {}^{52}_{26}\text{Fe} + p & Q_p = 1.57 \text{ MeV} \\ \xrightarrow{98.5\%} {}^{53}_{26}\text{Fe} + e^+ + v & t_{1/2} = 0.243 \text{ sec} \end{cases}$$

SPECIAL BETA-DECAY PROCESSES

In addition to the above types of radioactivity, there is a special class of rare beta-decay processes that gives rise to heavy-particle emission. In these processes the beta decay partly goes to a high excited state of the daughter nucleus, and this state rapidly emits a heavy particle.

One such process is beta-delayed neutron emission, which is exemplified by the following reaction:

$$^{17}_{7}\text{N} \longrightarrow {}^{17*}_{8}\text{O} + e^- + \bar{v} \qquad Q_{\beta-} = 8.68 \text{ MeV}$$
$$\downarrow \; ^{16}_{8}\text{O} + n \qquad E_{max\,n} = 1.81 \text{ MeV}$$
$$t_{1/2} = 4.16 \text{ sec}$$

(The asterisk denotes the short-lived intermediate excited states of oxygen-17, and $E_{max\,n}$ denotes the maximum energy observed for emitted neutrons.) There is a small production of delayed neutron emitters following nuclear fission, and these radioactivities are especially important in providing a reasonable response time to allow control of nuclear fission reactors by mechanically moved control rods.

Among the positron emitters in the light-element region, a number beta decay partly to excited states that are unstable with respect to emission of an alpha particle. Thus, these species exhibit alpha radiation with the half-life of the beta emission. Both the positron decay from boron-8 and electron decay from lithium-8 are beta-delayed alpha emission, because ground as well as excited states of beryllium-8 are unstable with respect to breakup into two alpha particles. Another example, sodium-20 (^{20}Na) decays successively neon-20 (^{20}Ne; the asterisk again indicating the short-lived intermediate state) and finally oxygen-16:

$$^{20}_{11}\text{Na} \longrightarrow \overset{*}{^{20}_{10}\text{Ne}} + e^+ + \nu \qquad Q_{\beta^+} = 13.0 \text{ MeV}$$

$$\longrightarrow {^{16}_{8}\text{O}} + \alpha \qquad E_{max\,\alpha} = 4.44 \text{ MeV}$$

$$t_{1/2} = 0.39 \text{ sec}$$

In a few cases, positron decay leads to an excited nuclear state unable to bind a proton. In these cases, proton radiation appears with the half-life of the beta transition. The combination of high positron-decay energy and low proton-binding energy in the daughter ground state is required. In the following example, tellurium-111 (^{111}Te) yields antimony-111 (^{111}Sb) and then tin-110 (^{110}Sn) successively:

$$^{111}_{52}\text{Te} \longrightarrow \overset{*}{^{111}_{51}\text{Sb}} + e^+ + \nu \qquad Q_{\beta^+} \text{ uncertain}$$

$$\longrightarrow {^{110}_{50}\text{Sn}} + p \qquad E_{max\,p} = 3.7 \text{ MeV}$$

$$t_{1/2} = 19.5 \text{ sec}$$

HEAVY-ION RADIOACTIVITY

In 1980 A. Sandulescu, D.N. Poenaru, and W. Greiner described calculations indicating the possibility of a new type of decay of heavy nuclei intermediate between alpha decay and spontaneous fission. The first observation of heavy-ion radioactivity was that of a 30-MeV, carbon-14 emission from radium-223 by H.J. Rose and G.A. Jones in 1984. The ratio of carbon-14 decay to alpha decay is about 5×10^{-10}. Observations also have been made of carbon-14 from radium-222, radium-224, and radium-226, as well as neon-24 from thorium-230, protactinium-231, and uranium-232. Such heavy-ion radioactivity, like alpha decay and spontaneous fission, involves quantum-mechanical tunneling through the potential-energy barrier. Shell effects play a major role in this phenomenon, and in all cases observed to date the heavy partner of carbon-14 or neon-24 is close to doubly magic lead-208.

OCCURRENCE OF RADIOACTIVITY

Some species of radioactivity occur naturally on Earth. A few species have half-lives comparable to the age of the elements (about 6×10^9 years), so that they have not decayed away after their formation in stars. Notable among these are uranium-238, uranium-235, and thorium-232. Also, there is potassium-40, the chief source of irradiation of the body through its presence in potassium of tissue. Of lesser significance are the beta emitters vanadium-50, rubidium-87, indium-115, tellurium-123, lanthanum-138, lutetium-176, and rhenium-187, and the alpha emitters cerium-142, neodymium-144, samarium-147, gadolinium-152, dysprosium-156, hafnium-174, platinum-190, and lead-204. Besides these approximately 10^9-year species, there are the shorter-lived daughter activities fed by one or another of the aforementioned species, for example, by various nuclei of the elements between lead ($Z = 82$) and thorium ($Z = 90$).

Another category of natural radioactivity includes species produced in the upper atmosphere by cosmic ray bombardment. Notable are 5,720-year carbon-14 and 12.3-year tritium (hydrogen-3), 53-day beryllium-7, and 2,700,000-year beryllium-10. Meteorites are found to contain additional small amounts of radioactivity, the result of cosmic ray bombardments during their history outside Earth's atmospheric shield. Activities as short-lived as 35-day argon-37 have been measured in fresh falls of meteorites. Nuclear explosions since 1945 have injected additional radioactivities into the environment, consisting of both nuclear fission products and secondary products formed by the action of neutrons from nuclear weapons on surrounding matter.

The fission products encompass most of the known beta emitters in the mass region 75–160. They are formed in varying yields, rising to maxima of about 7 percent per fission in the mass region 92–102 (light peak of the fission yield versus atomic mass curve) and 134–144 (heavy peak). Two kinds of delayed hazards caused by radioactivity are recognized. First, the general radiation level is raised by fallout settling to Earth. Protection can be provided by concrete or earth shielding until the activity has decayed to a sufficiently low level. Second, ingestion or inhalation of even low levels of certain radioactive species can pose a special hazard, depending on the half-life, nature of radiations, and chemical behaviour within the body.

Nuclear reactors also produce fission products but under conditions in which the activities may be contained. Containment and waste-disposal practices should keep the activities confined and eliminate the possibility of leaching into groundwaters for times that are long compared to the half-lives. A great advantage of thermonuclear fusion power over fission power, if it can be practically realized, is not only that its fuel reserves, heavy hydrogen and lithium, are vastly greater than uranium, but also that the generation of radioactive fission product wastes can be largely avoided. In this connection, it may be noted that a major source of heat in the interior of both Earth and the Moon is provided by radioactive decay. Theories about the formation and evolution of Earth, the Moon, and other planets must take into account these large heat production sources.

Desired radioactivities other than natural activities and fission products may be produced either by irradiation of certain selected target materials by reactor neutrons or by charged particle beams or gamma ray beams of accelerators.

Radioactive decay provides a major source of heat within the Moon. NASA/ JPL/USGS

ENERGETICS AND KINETICS OF RADIOACTIVITY

In radioactive processes, a particle is released. How much energy do these particles contain? How is this amount of energy measured?

ENERGY RELEASE IN RADIOACTIVE TRANSITIONS

Consideration of the energy release of various radioactive transitions leads to the fundamental question of nuclear binding energies and stabilities. A much-used method of displaying nuclear-stability relationships is an isotope chart, with those positions on the same horizontal row corresponding to a given proton number (Z) and those on the same vertical column to a given neutron number (N). An irregular bold line surrounds the region of presently known nuclei. The area encompassed by this is often referred to as the valley of stability because the chart may be considered a map of a binding energy surface, the lowest areas of which are the most stable. The most tightly bound nuclei of all are the abundant iron and nickel isotopes. Near the region of the valley containing the heaviest nuclei (largest mass number A; i.e., largest number of nucleons, $N + Z$), the processes of alpha decay and spontaneous fission are most prevalent; both these processes relieve the energetically unfavourable concentration of positive charge in the heavy nuclei.

Along the region that borders on the valley of stability on the upper left-hand side (toward higher Z) are the positron-emitting and electron-capturing radioactive nuclei, with the energy release and decay rates increasing the farther away the nucleus is from the stability line. Along the lower right-hand border region (toward lower Z), beta-minus decay is the predominant process, with energy release and decay rates increasing the farther the nucleus is from the stability line.

Some areas of the chart are "deformed regions" in which nuclei should exhibit cigar shapes; elsewhere the nuclei are spherical. Far from the valley of stability, nuclei would be unbound with respect to neutron or proton loss and would be exceedingly short-lived (less than 10^{-19} second).

CALCULATION AND MEASUREMENT OF ENERGY

By the method of closed energy cycles, it is possible to use measured radioactive-energy-release (Q) values for alpha and beta decay to calculate the energy release for unmeasured transitions. An illustration is provided by the cycle of four nuclei:

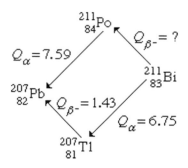

In this cycle, energies from two of the alpha decays and one beta decay are measurable. The unmeasured beta-decay energy for bismuth-211, $Q_{\beta^-}(\text{Bi})$, is readily calculated because conservation of energy requires the sum of Q values around the cycle to be zero. Thus, $Q_{\beta^-}(\text{Bi}) + 7.59 - 1.43 - 6.75 = 0$. Solving this equation gives $Q_{\beta^-}(\text{Bi}) = 0.59$ MeV. This calculation by closed energy cycles can be extended from stable lead-207 back up the chain of alpha and beta decays to its natural precursor uranium-235 and beyond. In this manner the nuclear binding energies of a series of nuclei can be linked together. Because alpha decay decreases the mass number A by 4, and beta decay does not change A, closed α-β-cycle calculations based on lead-207 can link up only those nuclei with mass numbers of the general type $A = 4n + 3$, in which n is an integer. Another, the $4n$ series, has as its natural precursor thorium-232 and its stable end product lead-208. Another, the $4n + 2$ series, has uranium-238 as its natural precursor and lead-206 as its end product.

In early research on natural radioactivity, the classification of isotopes into the series cited earlier was of great significance because they were identified and studied as families. Newly discovered radioactivities were given symbols relating them to the family and order of occurrence therein. Thus, thorium-234 was known as UX_1, the isomers of protactinium-234 as UX_2 and UZ, uranium-234 as U_{II}, and so forth. These original symbols and names are occasionally encountered in more recent literature but are mainly of historical interest. The remaining $4n + 1$ series is not naturally occurring but comprises well-known artificial activities decaying down to stable thallium-205.

To extend the knowledge of nuclear binding energies, it is clearly necessary to make measurements to supplement the radioactive-decay energy cycles. In part, this extension can be made by measurement of Q values of artificial nuclear reactions. For example, the neutron-binding energies of the lead isotopes needed to link the energies of the four radioactive families together can be measured by determining the threshold gamma-ray energy to remove a neutron (photonuclear reaction), or the energies of incoming deuteron and outgoing proton in the reaction can be measured to provide this information.

Further extensions of nuclear-binding-energy measurements rely on precision mass spectroscopy. By ionizing, accelerating, and magnetically deflecting various nuclides, their masses can be measured with great precision. A precise measurement of the masses of atoms involved in radioactive decay is equivalent to direct measurement of the energy release in the decay process. The atomic mass of naturally occurring but radioactive potassium-40 is measured to be 39.964008 amu. Potassium-40 decays predominantly by β-emission to calcium-40, having a measured mass 39.962589. Through Einstein's equation, energy is equal to mass (m) times velocity of light (c) squared, or $E = mc^2$, the energy release (Q) and the mass difference, Δm, are related, the conversion factor being one amu, equal to 931.478 MeV. Thus, the excess mass of potassium-40 over calcium-40 appears as the total energy release Q_β in the radioactive decay $Q_{\beta-} = (39.964008 - 39.962589) \times 931.478$ MeV = 1.31 M eV. The other neighbouring isobar (same mass number, different atomic number) to argon-40 is also of lower mass, 39.962384, than potassium-40. This mass difference converted to energy units gives an energy release of 1.5 MeV, this being the energy release for EC decay to argon-40. The maximum energy release for positron emission is always less than that for electron capture by twice the rest mass energy of an electron ($2m_oc^2 = 1.022$ MeV). Thus, the maximum positron energy for this reaction is 1.5 - 1.02, or 0.48 MeV.

To connect alpha-decay energies and nuclear mass differences requires a precise knowledge of the alpha-particle (helium-4) atomic mass. The mass of the parent minus the sum of the masses of the decay products gives the energy release. Thus, for alpha decay of plutonium-239 to uranium-235 and helium-4 the calculation goes as follows:

$$
\begin{array}{ll}
M(^{239}\text{Pu}) & 239.05216 \\
-M(^{235}\text{U}) & -235.04393 \\
-M(^{4}\text{He}) & \underline{-\ \ \ 4.00260} \\
& 0.00563 \times 931.478 \\
\multicolumn{2}{c}{Q_\alpha = 5.24 \text{ MeV}}
\end{array}
$$

By combining radioactive-decay-energy information with nuclear-reaction Q values and precision mass spectroscopy, extensive tables of nuclear masses have been prepared. From them the Q values of unmeasured reactions or decay may be calculated.

Alternative to the full mass, the atomic masses may be expressed as mass defect, symbolized by the Greek letter delta, Δ (the difference between the exact mass M and the integer A, the mass number), either in energy units or atomic mass units.

ABSOLUTE NUCLEAR BINDING ENERGY

The absolute nuclear binding energy is the hypothetical energy release if a given nuclide were synthesized from Z separate hydrogen atoms and N (equal to $A - Z$) separate neutrons. An example is the calculation giving the absolute binding energy of the stablest of all nuclei, iron-56:

$$
\begin{array}{ll}
26 \times M(^1\text{H}) & 26 \times 1.007825 = 26.20345 \\
30 \times M(n) & 30 \times 1.008665 = 30.25995 \\
M(^{56}\text{Fe}) & -\,55.93493 \\
& \text{binding energy} = 0.52847 \times 931.478 = \\
& \phantom{\text{binding energy} = 0.5284} 492.58 \text{ MeV}
\end{array}
$$

$$
\text{average binding energy}
$$
$$
\text{per nucleon of } ^{56}\text{Fe} = 492.58/56 = 8.796 \text{ MeV}
$$

A general survey of the average binding energy per nucleon (for nuclei of all elements grouped according to ascending mass) shows a maximum at iron-56 falling off gradually on both sides to about 7 MeV at helium-4 and to about 7.4 MeV for the most massive nuclei known. Most of the naturally occurring nuclei are thus not stable in an absolute nuclear sense. Nuclei heavier than iron would gain energy by degrading into nuclear products closer to iron, but it is only for the elements of greatest mass that the rates of degradation processes such as alpha decay and spontaneous fission attain observable rates. In a similar manner, nuclear energy is to be gained by fusion of most elements lighter than iron. The coulombic repulsion between nuclei, however, keeps the rates of fusion reactions unobservably low unless the nuclei are subjected to temperatures of greater than 10^7 K. Only in the hot cores of the Sun and other stars or in thermonuclear bombs or controlled fusion plasmas are these temperatures attained and nuclear-fusion energy released.

NUCLEAR MODELS

There are various models of the atomic nucleus that can be used to explain radioactivity. The three models described here apply to different types of atoms.

THE LIQUID-DROP MODEL

The average behaviour of the nuclear binding energy can be understood with the model of a charged liquid drop. In this model, the aggregate of nucleons has the same properties of a liquid drop, such as surface tension, cohesion, and deformation. There is a dominant attractive-binding-energy term proportional to the number of nucleons A. From this must be subtracted a surface-energy term proportional to surface area and a coulombic repulsion energy proportional to the square of the number of protons and inversely proportional to the nuclear radius. Furthermore, there is a symmetry-energy term of quantum-mechanical origin favouring equal numbers of protons and neutrons. Finally, there is a pairing term that gives slight extra binding to nuclei with even numbers of neutrons or protons.

The pairing-energy term accounts for the great rarity of odd–odd nuclei (the terms odd–odd, even–even,

even–odd, and odd–even refer to the evenness or oddness of proton number, Z, and neutron number, N, respectively) that are stable against beta decay. The sole examples are deuterium, lithium-6, boron-10, and nitrogen-14. A few other odd–odd nuclei, such as potassium-40, occur in nature, but they are unstable with respect to beta decay. Furthermore, the pairing-energy term makes for the larger number of stable isotopes of even-Z elements, compared to odd-Z, and for the lack of stable isotopes altogether in element 43, technetium, and element 61, promethium.

The beta-decay energies of so-called mirror nuclei afford one means of estimating nuclear sizes. For example, the neon and fluorine nuclei, $^{19}_{10}Ne_9$ and $^{19}_9F_{10}$, are mirror nuclei because the proton and neutron numbers of one of them equal the respective neutron and proton numbers of the other. Thus, all binding-energy terms are the same in each except for the coulombic term, which is inversely proportional to the nuclear radius. Such calculations along with more direct determinations by high-energy electron scattering and energy measurements of X-rays from muonic atoms (hydrogen atoms in which the electrons are replaced by negative muons) establish the nuclear charge as roughly uniformly distributed in a sphere of radius 1.2 $A^{1/3} \times 10^{-13}$ centimetre. That the radius is proportional to the cube root of the mass number has the great significance that the average density of all nuclei is nearly constant.

Careful examination of nuclear-binding energies reveals periodic deviations from the smooth average behaviour of the charged-liquid-drop model. An extra binding energy arises in the neighbourhood of certain numbers of neutrons or protons, the so-called magic numbers (2, 8, 20, 28, 50, 82, and 126). Nuclei such as $^4_2He_2$, $^{16}_8O_8$, $^{40}_{20}Ca_{20}$, $^{48}_{20}Ca_{28}$, and $^{208}_{82}Pb_{126}$ are especially stable species, doubly magic, in view of their having both proton and neutron numbers magic.

THE SHELL MODEL

In the preceding section, the overall trends of nuclear binding energies were described in terms of a charged-liquid-drop model. Yet there were noted periodic binding-energy irregularities at the magic numbers. The periodic occurrence of magic numbers of extra stability is strongly analogous to the extra electronic stabilities occurring at the atomic numbers of the noble-gas atoms. The explanations of these stabilities are quite analogous in atomic and nuclear cases as arising from filling of particles into quantized orbitals of motion. The completion of filling of a shell of orbitals is accompanied by an extra stability. The nuclear model accounting for the magic numbers is, as previously noted, the shell model. In its simplest form, this model can account for the occurrence of spin zero for all even–even nuclear ground states. The nucleons fill pairwise into orbitals with angular momenta canceling. The shell model also readily accounts for the observed nuclear spins of the odd-mass nuclei adjacent to doubly magic nuclei, such as $^{208}_{82}Pb$. Here, the spins of 1/2 for neighbouring $^{207}_{81}Tl$ and $^{207}_{82}Pb$ are accounted for by having all nucleons fill pairwise into the lowest energy orbits and putting the odd nucleon into the last available orbital before reaching the doubly magic configuration (the Pauli exclusion principle dictates that no more than two nucleons may occupy a given orbital, and their spins must be oppositely directed). Calculations show the last available orbitals below lead-208 to have angular momentum 1/2. Likewise, the spins of 9/2 for $^{209}_{82}Pb$ and $^{209}_{83}Bi$ are understandable because spin-9/2 orbitals are the next available orbitals beyond doubly magic lead-208. Even the associated magnetization, as expressed by the magnetic dipole moment, is rather well explained by the simple spherical-shell model.

The orbitals of the spherical-shell model are labeled in a notation close to that for electronic orbitals in atoms. The orbital configuration of calcium-40 has protons and neutrons filling the following orbitals: $1s_{1/2}$, $1p_{3/2}$, $1p_{1/2}$, $1d_{5/2}$, and $1d_{3/2}$. The letter denotes the orbital angular momentum in usual spectroscopic notation, in which the letters s, p, d, f, g, h, i, etc., represent integer values of l running from zero for s (not to be confused with spins) through six for i. The fractional subscript gives the total angular momentum j with values of $l + 1/2$ and $l - 1/2$ allowed, as the intrinsic spin of a nucleon is $1/2$. The first integer is a radial quantum number taking successive values 1, 2, 3, etc., for successively higher energy values of an orbital of given l and j. Each orbital can accommodate a maximum of $2j + 1$ nucleons. The parity associated with an orbital is even (+) if l is even (s, d, g, i) and odd (-) if l is odd (p, f, h).

An example of a spherical-shell-model interpretation is provided by the beta-decay scheme of 2.2-minute thallium-209 shown below, in which spin and parity are given for each state. The ground and lowest excited states of lead-209 are to be associated with occupation by the 127th neutron of the lowest available orbitals above the closed shell of 126.

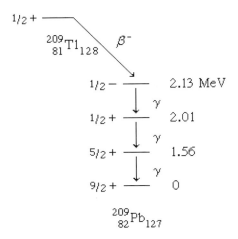

Note that there are available $g_{9/2}$, $d_{5/2}$, and $s_{1/2}$ orbitals with which to explain the ground and first two excited states. Low-lying states associated with the $i_{11/2}$ and $j_{15/2}$ orbitals are known from nuclear-reaction studies, but they are not populated in the beta decay.

The 2.13-MeV state that receives the primary beta decay is not so simply interpreted as the other states. It is to be associated with the promotion of a neutron from the $3p_{1/2}$ orbital below the 126 shell closure. The density (number per MeV) of states increases rapidly above this excitation, and the interpretations become more complex and less certain.

By suitable refinements, the spherical-shell model can be extended further from the doubly magic region. Primarily, it is necessary to drop the approximation that nucleons move independently in orbitals and to invoke a residual force, mainly short-range and attractive, between the nucleons. The spherical-shell model augmented by residual interactions can explain and correlate around the magic regions a large amount of data on binding energies, spins, magnetic moments, and the spectra of excited states.

THE COLLECTIVE MODEL

For nuclei more removed from the doubly magic regions, the spherical-shell model encounters difficulty in explaining the large observed electric quadrupole moments indicating cigar-shaped nuclei. For these nuclei a hybrid of liquid-drop and shell models, the collective model, has been proposed.

Nucleons can interact with one another in a collective fashion to deform the nuclear shape to a cigar shape. Such large spheroidal distortions are usual for nuclei far from magic, notably with $150 \lesssim A \lesssim 190$, and $224 \lesssim$

A (the symbol < denotes less than, and ~ means that the number is approximate). In these deformed regions the collective model prescribes that orbitals be computed in a cigar-shaped potential and that the relatively low-energy rotational excitations of the tumbling motion of the cigar shape be taken into account. The collective model has been highly successful in correlating and predicting nuclear properties in deformed regions. An example of a nuclear rotational band (a series of adjacent states) is provided by the decay of the isomer hafnium-180*m* through a cascade of gamma rays down the ground rotational band.

RATES OF RADIOACTIVE TRANSITIONS

There is a vast range of the rates of radioactive decay, from undetectably slow to unmeasurably short. Before

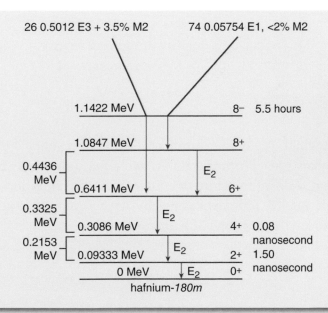

*The decay scheme of hafnium-180*m. Copyright Encyclopædia Britannica; rendering for this edition by Rosen Educational Services

considering the factors governing particular decay rates in detail, it seems appropriate to review the mathematical equations governing radioactive decay and the general methods of rate measurement in different ranges of half-life.

EXPONENTIAL-DECAY LAW

Radioactive decay occurs as a statistical exponential rate process. That is to say, the number of atoms likely to decay in a given infinitesimal time interval (dN/dt) is proportional to the number (N) of atoms present. The proportionality constant, symbolized by the Greek letter lambda, λ, is called the decay constant. Mathematically, this statement is expressed by the first-order differential equation,

$$-\frac{dN}{dt} = \lambda N. \tag{1}$$

This equation is readily integrated to give

$$N(t) = N_0 e^{-\lambda t}, \tag{2}$$

in which N_o is the number of atoms present when time equals zero. From the above two equations it may be seen that a disintegration rate, as well as the number of parent nuclei, falls exponentially with time. An equivalent expression in terms of half-life $t_{1/2}$ is

$$N(t) = N_0 (1/2)^r; \ r = t/t_{1/2}.$$

It can readily be shown that the decay constant λ and half-life ($t_{1/2}$) are related as follows: $\lambda = \log_e 2/t_{1/2} = 0.693/t_{1/2}$.

The reciprocal of the decay constant λ is the mean life, symbolized by the Greek letter tau, τ.

For a radioactive nucleus such as potassium-40 that decays by more than one process (89 percent β-, 11 percent electron capture), the total decay constant is the sum of partial decay constants for each decay mode. (The partial half-life for a particular mode is the reciprocal of the partial decay constant times 0.693.) It is helpful to consider a radioactive chain in which the parent (generation 1) of decay constant λ, decays into a radioactive daughter (generation 2) of decay constant λ_2. The case in which none of the daughter isotope (2) is originally present yields an initial growth of daughter nuclei followed by its decay. The equation giving the number (N_2) of daughter nuclei existing at time t in terms of the number $N_1(0)$ of parent nuclei present when time equals zero is

$$N_2(t) = \lambda_1 N_1(0) \frac{e^{-\lambda_1 t} - e^{-\lambda_2 t}}{\lambda_2 - \lambda_1}, \tag{3}$$

in which e represents the logarithmic constant 2.71828.

The general equation for a chain of n generations with only the parent initially present (when time equals zero) is as follows:

$$N_n(t) = N_1(0)(C_1 e^{-\lambda_1 t} + C_2 e^{-\lambda_2 t} + \cdots + C_n e^{-\lambda_n t})\lambda_1 \lambda_2 \ldots \lambda_{n-1}, \tag{4}$$

in which e represents the logarithmic constant 2.71828.

$$C_1 = 1/(\lambda_2 - \lambda_1)(\lambda_3 - \lambda_1)\ldots(\lambda_n - \lambda_1),$$
$$C_2 = 1/(\lambda_1 - \lambda_2)(\lambda_3 - \lambda_2)\ldots(\lambda_n - \lambda_2),$$
$$C_n = 1/(\lambda_1 - \lambda_n)(\lambda_2 - \lambda_n)\ldots(\lambda_{n-1} - \lambda_n).$$

These equations can readily be modified to the case of production of isotopes in the steady neutron flux of a reactor or in a star. In such cases, the chain of transformations might be mixed with some steps occurring by neutron capture and some by radioactive decay. The neutron-capture probability for a nucleus is expressed in terms of an effective cross-sectional area. If one imagines the nuclei replaced by spheres of the same cross-sectional area, the rate of reaction in a neutron flux would be given by the rate at which neutrons strike the spheres. The cross section is usually symbolized by the Greek letter sigma, σ, with the units of barns (10^{-24} cm^2) or millibarns (10^{-3} b) or microbarns (10^{-6} b). Neutron flux is often symbolized by the letters nv (neutron density, n, or number per cubic centimetre, times average speed, v) and given in neutrons per square centimetre per second.

The modification of the transformation equations merely involves substituting the product $nv\sigma_i$ in place of λ_i for any step involving neutron capture rather than radioactive decay. Reactor fluxes nv even higher than 10^{15} neutrons per square centimetre per second are available in several research reactors, but usual fluxes are somewhat lower by a factor of 1,000 or so. Tables of neutron-capture cross sections of the naturally occurring nuclei and some radioactive nuclei can be used for calculation of isotope production rates in reactors.

MEASUREMENT OF HALF-LIFE

The measurement of half-lives of radioactivity in the range of seconds to a few years commonly involves measuring the intensity of radiation at successive times over a time range comparable to the half-life. The logarithm of the decay rate is plotted against time, and a straight line is fitted to the points. The time interval for this straight-line decay curve to fall by a factor of 2 is read from the graph as the half-life, by virtue of equations (1) and (2). If there is more than one activity present in the sample, the decay curve will not be a straight line over its entire length, but it should be resolvable graphically (or by more sophisticated statistical analysis) into sums and differences of straight-line exponential terms. The general equations (4) for chain decays show a time dependence given by sums and differences of exponential terms, though special modified equations are required in the unlikely case that two or more decay constants are identically equal.

For half-lives longer than several years it is often not feasible to measure accurately the decrease in counting rate over a reasonable length of time. In such cases, a measurement of specific activity may be resorted to (i.e., a carefully weighed amount of the radioactive isotope is taken for counting measurements to determine the disintegration rate, D). Then by equation (1) the decay constant λ_i may be calculated. Alternately, it may be possible to produce the activity of interest in such a way that the number of nuclei, N, is known, and again with a measurement of D equation (1) may be used. The number of nuclei, N, might be known from counting the decay of a parent activity or from knowledge of the production rate by a nuclear reaction in a reactor or accelerator beam.

Half-lives from 100 microseconds to one nanosecond are measured electronically in coincidence experiments. The radiation yielding the species of interest is detected to provide a start pulse for an electronic clock, and the radiation by which the species decays is detected in another device to provide a stop pulse. The distribution of these time intervals is plotted semi-logarithmically, as discussed for the decay-rate treatment, and the half-life is determined from the slope of the straight line.

Half-lives in the range of 100 microseconds to one second must often be determined by special techniques. For example, the activities produced may be deposited on rapidly rotating drums or moving tapes, with detectors positioned along the travel path. The activity may be produced so as to travel through a vacuum at a known velocity and the disintegration rate measured as a function of distance; however, this method usually applies to shorter half-lives in or beyond the range of the electronic circuit.

Species with half-lives shorter than the electronic measurement limit are not considered as separate radioactivities, and the various techniques of determining their half-lives will hence not be cited here.

Alpha Decay

Alpha decay, the emission of helium ions, exhibits sharp line spectra when spectroscopic measurements of the alpha-particle energies are made. For even–even alpha emitters the most intense alpha group or line is always that leading to the ground state of the daughter. Weaker lines of lower energy go to excited states, and there are frequently numerous lines observable.

The main decay group of even–even alpha emitters exhibits a highly regular dependence on the atomic number, Z, and the energy release, Q_a. (Total alpha energy release, Q_a, is equal to alpha-particle energy, E_a, plus daughter recoil energy needed for conservation of momentum; $E_{recoil} = (m_a/[m_a + M_d])E_a$, with m_a equal to the mass of the alpha particle and M_d the mass of the daughter product.) As early as 1911 the German physicist Johannes Wilhelm Geiger, together with the British physicist John Mitchell Nuttall, noted the regularities of rates for even–even nuclei and proposed a remarkably successful equation for the decay constant, log $\lambda = a + b \log r$, in which r is the range in air, b is a constant, and a is given different values for the different radioactive series. The decay constants of odd alpha emitters (odd A or odd Z or both) are not quite so regular and may be much smaller. The values of the constant b that were used by Geiger and Nuttall implied a roughly 90th-power dependence of λ on Q_a. There is a tremendous range of known half-lives from the 2×10^{15} years of $^{144}_{60}$Nd (neodymium) with its 1.83-MeV alpha-particle energy (E_a) to the 0.3 microsecond of $^{212}_{84}$Po (polonium) with $E_a = 8.78$ MeV.

The theoretical basis for the Geiger–Nuttall empirical rate law remained unknown until the formulation of wave mechanics. A dramatic early success of wave mechanics was the quantitative theory of alpha-decay rates. One curious feature of wave mechanics is that particles may have a nonvanishing probability of being in regions of negative kinetic energy. In classical mechanics a ball that is tossed to roll up a hill will slow down until its gravitational potential energy equals its total energy, and then it will roll back toward its starting point. In quantum mechanics the ball has a certain probability of tunneling through the hill and popping out on the other side. For objects large enough to be visible to the eye, the probability of tunneling through energetically forbidden regions is unobservably small. For submicroscopic objects such as alpha particles, nucleons, or electrons, however, quantum mechanical tunneling can be an important process — as in alpha decay.

The logarithm of tunneling probability on a single collision with an energy barrier of height B and thickness D is a negative number proportional to thickness D, to the square root of the product of B and particle mass m. The size of the proportionality constant will depend on the shape of the barrier and will depend inversely on Planck's constant h.

In the case of alpha decay, the electrostatic repulsive potential between alpha particle and nucleus generates an energetically forbidden region, or potential barrier, from the nuclear radius out to several times this distance. The maximum height (B) of this alpha barrier is given approximately by the expression $B = 2Ze^2/R$, in which Z is the charge of the daughter nucleus, e is the elementary charge in electrostatic units, and R is the nuclear radius. Numerically, B is roughly equal to $2Z/A^{1/3}$, with A the mass number and B in energy units of MeV. Thus, although the height of the potential barrier for $^{212}_{84}$Po decay is nearly 28 MeV, the total energy released is $Q_a = 8.95$ MeV. The thickness of the barrier (i.e., distance of the alpha particle from the centre of the nucleus at the moment of recoil) is about twice the nuclear radius of 8.8×10^{-13} cm. The tunneling calculation for the transition probability (P) through the barrier gives approximately

$$P = \exp\left[\left(-\frac{\sqrt{2MB}\ R}{\hbar}\right)\left(\frac{\pi B^{1/2}}{Q^{1/2}} - 4\right)\right], \qquad (5)$$

in which M is the mass of the alpha particle and ℏ is Planck's constant h divided by 2π. By making simple assumptions about the frequency of the alpha particle striking the barrier, the penetration formula (5) can be used to calculate an effective nuclear radius for alpha decay. This method was one of the early ways of estimating nuclear sizes. In more sophisticated modern techniques the radius value is taken from other experiments, and alpha-decay data and penetrabilities are used to calculate the frequency factor.

The form of equation (5) suggests the correlation of decay rates by an empirical expression relating the half-life ($t_{1/2}$) of decay in seconds to the release energy (Q_a) in MeV:

$$\log t_{1/2} = \frac{a}{\sqrt{Q_a}} + b. \qquad (6)$$

SEMIEMPIRICAL CONSTANTS*		
	a	*b*
98 californium (Cf)	152.86	-52.9506
96 curium (Cm)	152.44	-53.6825
94 plutonium (Pu)	146.23	-52.0899
92 uranium (U)	147.49	-53.6565
90 thorium (Th)	144.19	-53.2644
88 radium (Ra)	139.17	-52.1476
86 radon (Rn)	137.46	-52.4597
84 polonium (Po)	129.35	-49.9229

*From correlation of ground-state decay rates of even-even nuclei with N > 126. See equation (6).

Values of the constants *a* and *b* that give best fits to experimental rates of even–even nuclei with neutron number greater than 126 are given in the table. The nuclei with 126 or fewer neutrons decay more slowly than the heavier nuclei, and constants *a* and *b* must be readjusted to fit their decay rates.

The alpha-decay rates to excited states of even–even nuclei and to ground and excited states of nuclei with odd numbers of neutrons, protons, or both may exhibit retardations from equation (6) rates ranging to factors of thousands or more. The factor by which the rate is slower than the rate formula (6) is the hindrance factor. The existence of uranium-235 in nature rests on the fact that alpha decay to the ground and low excited states exhibits hindrance factors of over 1,000. Thus the uranium-235 half-life is lengthened to 7×10^8 years, a time barely long enough compared to the age of the elements in the solar system for uranium-235 to exist in nature today.

The alpha hindrance factors are fairly well understood in terms of the orbital motion of the individual protons and neutrons that make up the emitted alpha particle. The alpha-emitting nuclei heavier than radium are considered to be cigar-shaped, and alpha hindrance factor data have been used to infer the most probable zones of emission on the nuclear surface—whether polar, equatorial, or inter-mediate latitudes.

BETA DECAY

The processes separately introduced at the beginning of this section as beta-minus decay, beta-plus decay, and orbital electron capture can be appropriately treated together. They all are processes whereby neutrons and protons may transform to one another by weak interaction. In striking contrast to alpha decay, the electrons (minus or plus charged) emitted in beta-minus and beta-plus decay do not exhibit sharp, discrete energy spectra but have distributions of electron energies ranging from zero up to the maximum energy release, Q_β. Furthermore, measurements of heat released by beta emitters (most radiation stopped in surrounding material is converted into heat energy) show a substantial fraction of the energy, Q_β, is missing. These observations, along with other considerations involving the spins or angular momenta of nuclei and electrons, led Wolfgang Pauli to postulate the simultaneous emission of the neutrino (1931). The neutrino, as a light and uncharged particle with nearly no interaction with matter, was supposed to carry off the missing heat energy. Today, neutrino theory is well accepted with the elaboration that there are six kinds of neutrinos, the electron neutrino, mu neutrino, and tau neutrino and corresponding antineutrinos of each. The electron neutrinos are involved in nuclear beta-decay transformations, the mu neutrinos are encountered in decay of muons to electrons, and the tau neutrinos are produced when a massive lepton called a tau breaks down.

Although in general the more energetic the beta decay the shorter is its half-life, the rate relationships do not show the clear regularities of the alpha-decay dependence on energy and atomic number.

The first quantitative rate theory of beta decay was given by Enrico Fermi in 1934, and the essentials of this theory form the basis of modern theory. As an example, in the simplest beta-decay process, a free neutron decays into a proton, a negative electron, and an antineutrino: $n \rightarrow p + e^- + \bar{\nu}$. The weak interaction responsible for this process, in which there is a change of species (n to p) by a nucleon with creation of electron and antineutrino, is characterized in Fermi theory by a universal constant, g. The sharing of energy between electron and antineutrino is governed by statistical probability laws giving a probability factor for each particle proportional to the square of its linear momentum (defined by mass times velocity for speeds much less than the speed of light and by a more complicated, relativistic relation for faster speeds). The overall probability law from Fermi theory gives the probability per unit time per unit electron energy interval, $P(W)$, as follows:

$$P(W) = \frac{64\pi^4 m_0^5 c^4 g^2}{h^7} W(W^2 - 1)^{1/2} (W_0 - W)^2, \qquad (7)$$

in which W is the electron energy in relativistic units ($W = 1 + E/m_o c^2$) and W_o is the maximum ($W_o = 1 + Q_\beta/m_o c^2$), m_o the rest mass of the electron, c the speed of light, and h Planck's constant. This rate law expresses the neutron beta-decay spectrum in good agreement with experiment, the spectrum falling to zero at lowest energies by the factor W and falling to zero at the maximum energy by virtue of the factor $(W_o - W)^2$.

In Fermi's original formulation, the spins of an emitted beta and neutrino are opposing and so cancel to zero. Later work showed that neutron beta decay partly proceeds with the $\frac{1}{2}$ ℏ spins of beta and neutrino adding to one unit of ℏ. The former process is known as Fermi decay (F) and the latter Gamow–Teller (GT) decay, after George Gamow and Edward Teller, the physicists who first proposed it. The interaction constants are determined to be in the ratio $g_{GT}^2/g_F^2 = 1.4$. Thus, g^2 in equation (7) should be replaced by $(g_F^2 + g_{GT}^2)$.

The scientific world was shaken in 1957 by the measurement in beta decay of maximum violation of the law of conservation of parity. The meaning of this nonconservation in the case of neutron beta decay considered earlier is that the preferred direction of electron emission is opposite to the direction of the neutron spin. By means of a magnetic field and low temperature it is possible to cause neutrons in cobalt-60 and other nuclei, or free neutrons, to have their spins set preferentially in the up direction perpendicular to the plane of the coil generating the magnetic field. The fact that beta decay prefers the down direction for spin means that the reflection of the experiment as seen in a mirror parallel to the coil represents an unphysical situation: conservation of parity, obeyed by most physical processes, demands that experiments with positions reversed by mirror reflection should also occur. Further consequences of parity violation in beta decay are that spins of emitted neutrinos and electrons are directed along the direction of flight, totally so for neutrinos and partially so by the ratio of electron speed to the speed of light for electrons.

The overall half-life for beta decay of the free neutron, measured as 12 minutes, may be related to the interaction constants g^2 (equal to $g_F^2 + g_{GT}^2$) by integrating (summing) probability expression (7) over all possible electron energies from zero to the maximum. The result for the decay constant is

$$\lambda = \frac{64\pi^4 m_0^5 c^4 g^2}{h^7} \left\{ (W_0^2 - 1)^{1/2} \left(\frac{W_0^4}{30} - \frac{3W_0^2}{20} - \frac{2}{15} \right) + \frac{W_0}{4} \ln [W_0 + (W_0^2 - 1)^{1/2}] \right\}, \quad (8)$$

in which W_0 is the maximum beta-particle energy in relativistic units ($W_0 = 1 + Q_\beta/m_0 c^2$), with m_0 the rest mass of the electron, c the speed of light, and h Planck's constant. The best g value from decay rates is approximately 10^{-49} erg per cubic centimetre. As may be noted from equation (8), there is a limiting fifth-power energy dependence for highest decay energies.

In the case of a decaying neutron not free but bound within a nucleus, the above formulas must be modified. First, as the nuclear charge Z increases, the relative probability of low-energy electron emission increases by virtue of the coulombic attraction. For positron emission, which is energetically impossible for free protons but can occur for bound protons in proton-rich nuclei, the nuclear coulomb charge suppresses lower energy positrons from the shape given by equation (7). This equation can be corrected by a factor $F(Z,W)$ depending on the daughter atomic number Z and electron energy W. The factor can be calculated quantum mechanically. The coulomb charge also affects the overall rate expression (8) such that it can no longer be expressed as an algebraic function, but tables are available for analysis of beta decay rates. The rates are analyzed in terms of a function $f(Z,Q_\beta)$ calculated by integration of equation (7) with correction factor $F(Z,W)$.

Approximate expressions for the f functions usable for decay energies Q between 0.1 MeV and 10 MeV, in which

Q is measured in MeV, and Z is the atomic number of the daughter nucleus, are as follows (the symbol $\approx$ means approximately equal to):

$$f_{\beta^-} \approx 6.0 Q^{4-0.005(Z-1)} \cdot 10^{Z/50},$$

$$f_{\beta^+} \approx 6.2 Q^4 / 10^{0.007Z} \cdot 10^{0.009Z(\log 1/3Q)^2}.$$

For electron capture, a much weaker dependence on energy is found:

$$f_{EC} \approx (Z+1)^{3.5} Q / 4 \times 10^5.$$

The basic beta decay rate expression obeyed by the class of so-called superallowed transitions, including decay of the neutron and several light nuclei is

$$\lambda_\beta = \frac{64\pi^4 m_0^5 c^4 g^2}{h^7} f_\beta. \tag{9}$$

Like the ground-to-ground alpha transitions of even–even nuclei, the superallowed beta transitions obey the basic rate law, but most beta transitions go much more slowly. The extra retardation is explained in terms of mismatched orbitals of neutrons and protons involved in the transition. For the superallowed transitions the orbitals in initial and final states are almost the same. Most of them occur between mirror nuclei, with one more or less neutron than protons (i.e., beta-minus decay of hydrogen-3, electron capture of beryllium-7 and positron emission of carbon-11, oxygen-15, neon-19, . . . titanium-43).

The nuclear retardation of beta decay rates below those of the superallowed class may be expressed in a fundamental way by multiplying the right side of equation (9) by the square of a nuclear matrix element (a quantity of quantum mechanics), which may range from unity down to zero depending on the degree of mismatch of initial and final nuclear states of internal motion. A more usual way of expressing the nuclear factor of the beta rate is the log ft value, in which f refers to the function $f(Z,Q_\beta)$. Because the half-life is inversely proportional to the decay constant λ, the product $f_\beta\, t_{1/2}$ will be a measure of (inversely proportional to) the square of the nuclear matrix element. For the log ft value, the beta half-life is taken in seconds, and the ordinary logarithm to the base 10 is used. The superallowed transitions have log ft values in the range of 3 to 3.5. Beta log ft values are known up to as large as ~ 23 in the case of indium-115. There is some correlation of log ft values with spin changes between parent and daughter nucleons, the indium-115 decay involving a spin change of four, whereas the superallowed transitions all have spin changes of zero or one.

GAMMA TRANSITION

The nuclear gamma transitions belong to the large class of electromagnetic transitions encompassing radio-frequency emission by antennas or rotating molecules, infrared emission by vibrating molecules or hot filaments, visible light, ultraviolet light, and X-ray emission by electronic jumps in atoms or molecules. The usual relations apply for connecting frequency v, wavelength λ, and photon quantum energy E with speed of light c and Planck's constant h; namely, $\lambda = c/v$ and $E = hv$. It is sometimes necessary to consider the momentum (p) of the photon given by $p = E/c$.

Classically, radiation accompanies any acceleration of electric charge. Quantum mechanically there is a probability of photon emission from higher to lower energy nuclear states, in which the internal state of motion involves acceleration of charge in the transition. Therefore, purely neutron orbital acceleration would carry no radiative contribution.

A great simplification in nuclear gamma transition rate theory is brought about by the circumstance that the nuclear diameters are always much smaller than the shortest wavelengths of gamma radiation in radioactivity (i.e., the nucleus is too small to be a good antenna for the radiation). The simplification is that nuclear gamma transitions can be classified according to multipolarity, or amount of spin angular momentum carried off by the radiation. One unit of angular momentum in the radiation is associated with dipole transitions (a dipole consists of two separated equal charges, plus and minus). If there is a change of nuclear parity, the transition is designated electric dipole (E1) and is analogous to the radiation of a linear half-wave dipole radio antenna. If there is no parity change, the transition is magnetic dipole (M1) and is analogous to the radiation of a full-wave loop antenna. With two units of angular momentum change, the transition is electric quadrupole (E2), analogous to a full-wave linear antenna of two dipoles out-of-phase, and magnetic quadrupole (M2), analogous to coaxial loop antennas driven out-of-phase. Higher multipolarity radiation also frequently occurs with radioactivity.

Transition rates are usually compared to the single-proton theoretical rate, or Weisskopf formula, named after the American physicist Victor Frederick Weisskopf, who developed it. The theoretical reference rate formulas depend on nuclear mass number A and gamma-ray energy $E\gamma$ (in MeV).

It is seen for the illustrative case of gamma energy 0.1 MeV and mass number 125 that there occurs an additional factor of 10^7 retardation with each higher multipole order. For a given multipole, magnetic radiation should be a factor of 100 or so slower than electric. These rate factors ensure that nuclear gamma transitions are nearly purely one multipole, the lowest permitted by the nuclear spin change. There are many exceptions, however; mixed M1–E2 transitions are common, because E2 transitions are often much faster than the Weisskopf formula gives and M1 transitions are generally slower. All E1 transitions encountered in radioactivity are much slower than the Weisskopf formula. The other higher multipolarities show some scatter in rates, ranging from agreement to considerable retardation. In most cases the retardations are well understood in terms of nuclear model calculations.

Though not literally a gamma transition, electric monopole (E0) transitions may appropriately be mentioned here. These may occur when there is no angular momentum change between initial and final nuclear states and no parity change. For spin-zero to spin-zero transitions, single gamma emission is strictly forbidden. The electric monopole transition occurs largely by the ejection of electrons from the orbital cloud in heavier elements and by positron–electron pair creation in the lighter elements.

APPLICATIONS OF RADIOACTIVITY

Radioactive isotopes are used in many professions. The following sections consider their use in medicine, industry, and science.

MEDICINAL

Radioisotopes have found extensive use in diagnosis and therapy, and this has given rise to a rapidly growing field called nuclear medicine. These radioactive isotopes have proven particularly effective as tracers in certain diagnostic procedures. As radioisotopes are identical chemically with stable isotopes of the same element, they can take the place of the latter in physiological processes. Moreover, because of their radioactivity, they can be readily traced even in minute quantities with such detection devices as gamma-ray spectrometers and proportional counters. Though many radioisotopes are used as tracers, iodine-131, phosphorus-32, and technetium-99*m* are among the most important. Physicians employ iodine-131 to determine cardiac output, plasma volume, and fat metabolism and particularly to measure the activity of the thyroid gland where this isotope accumulates. Phosphorus-32 is useful in the identification of malignant tumours because cancerous cells tend to accumulate phosphates more than normal cells do. Technetium-99*m*, used with radiographic scanning devices, is valuable for studying the anatomic structure of organs.

Such radioisotopes as cobalt-60 and cesium-137 are widely used to treat cancer. They can be administered selectively to malignant tumours and so minimize damage to adjacent healthy tissue.

INDUSTRIAL

Foremost among industrial applications is power generation based on the release of the fission energy of uranium. Other applications include the use of radioisotopes to measure (and control) the thickness or density of metal and plastic sheets, to stimulate the cross-linking of polymers, to induce mutations in plants in order to develop hardier species, and to preserve certain kinds of foods by killing microorganisms that cause spoilage. In tracer applications radioactive isotopes are employed, for example, to measure the effectiveness of motor oils on the wearability of alloys for piston rings and cylinder walls in automobile engines.

Scientific

Research in the Earth sciences has benefited greatly from the use of radiometric-dating techniques, which are based on the principle that a particular radioisotope (radioactive parent) in geologic material decays at a constant known rate to daughter isotopes. Using such techniques, investigators have been able to determine the ages of various rocks and rock formations and thereby quantify the geologic time scale. A special application of this type of radioactivity age method, carbon-14 dating, has proved especially useful to physical anthropologists and archaeologists. It has helped them to better determine the chronological sequence of past events by enabling them to date more accurately fossils and artifacts from 500 to 50,000 years old.

Radioisotopic tracers are employed in environmental studies, as, for instance, those of water pollution in rivers and lakes and of air pollution by smokestack effluents. They also have been used to measure deep-water currents in oceans and snow-water content in watersheds. Researchers in the biologic sciences, too, have made use of radioactive tracers to study complex processes. For example, thousands of plant metabolic studies have been conducted on amino acids and compounds of sulfur, phosphorus, and nitrogen.

CHAPTER 5
RADIATION
AND LIFE

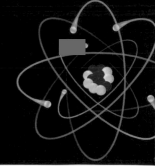

The biomedical effects of ionizing radiation have been investigated more thoroughly than those of any other environmental agent. Evidence that harmful effects may result from small amounts of such radiation has prompted growing concern about the hazards that may be associated with low-level irradiation from the fallout of nuclear weapons, medical radiography, nuclear power plants, and other sources. Assessment of the health impact of ionizing radiation requires an understanding of the interactions of radiation with living cells and the subsequent reactions that lead to injury.

HISTORICAL BACKGROUND

Within weeks after German physicist Wilhelm Röntgen revealed the first X-ray photographs in January 1896, news of the discovery spread throughout the world. Soon afterward, the penetrating properties of the rays began to be exploited for medical purposes, with no inkling that such radiation might have deleterious effects.

The first reports of X-ray injury to human tissue came later in 1896. Elihu Thomson, an American electrical engineer, deliberately exposed one of his fingers to X-rays and provided accurate observations on the burns produced. That same year, Thomas Alva Edison was engaged in developing a fluorescent X-ray lamp when he noticed that his assistant, Clarence Dally, was so "poisonously affected" by the new rays that his hair fell out and his scalp became

When developing a fluorescent X-ray lamp, Thomas Edison noticed its detrimental effects on his assistant's hair and skin. FPG/Archive Photos/ Getty Images

inflamed and ulcerated. By 1904 Dally had developed severe ulcers on both hands and arms, which soon became cancerous and caused his early death.

During the next few decades, many investigators and physicians developed radiation burns and cancer, and more than 100 of them died as a result of their exposure to X-rays. These unfortunate early experiences eventually led to an awareness of radiation hazards for professional workers and stimulated the development of a new branch of science—namely, radiobiology.

Radiations from radioactive materials were not immediately recognized as being related to X-rays. In 1906 Henri Becquerel, the French physicist who discovered radioactivity, accidentally burned himself by carrying radioactive materials in his pocket. Noting that, Pierre

Curie, the co-discoverer of radium, deliberately produced a similar burn on himself. Beginning about 1925, a number of women employed in applying luminescent paint that contained radium to clock and instrument dials became ill with anemia and lesions of the jawbones and mouth. Some subsequently developed bone cancer.

In 1933 Ernest O. Lawrence and his collaborators completed the first full-scale cyclotron at the University of California at Berkeley. This type of particle accelerator was a copious source of neutrons, which had recently been discovered by Sir James Chadwick in England. Lawrence and his associates exposed laboratory rats to fast neutrons produced with the cyclotron and found that such radiation was about two and a half times more effective in killing power for rats than were X-rays.

Considerably more knowledge about the biologic effects of neutrons had been acquired by the time the first nuclear reactor was built in 1942 in Chicago. The nuclear reactor, which has become a prime source of energy for the world, produces an enormous amount of neutrons as well as other forms of radiation. The widespread use of nuclear reactors and the development of high-energy particle accelerators, another prolific source of ionizing radiation, have given rise to health physics. This field of study deals with the hazards of radiation and protection against such hazards. Moreover, since the advent of spaceflight in the late 1950s, certain kinds of radiation from space and their effects on human health have attracted much attention. The protons in the Van Allen radiation belts (two doughnut-shaped zones of high-energy particles trapped in Earth's magnetic field), the protons and heavier ions ejected in solar flares, and similar particles near the top of the atmosphere are particularly important.

UNITS FOR MEASURING
IONIZING RADIATION

Ionizing radiation is measured in various units. The oldest unit, the roentgen (R), denotes the amount of radiation that is required to produce 1 electrostatic unit of charge in 1 cubic centimetre of air under standard conditions of pressure, temperature, and humidity. For expressing the dose of radiation absorbed in living tissue, the principal units are the gray (Gy; 1 Gy = 1 joule of radiation energy absorbed per kilogram of tissue) and the rad (1 rad = 100 ergs per gram of tissue = 0.01 Gy). The sievert (Sv) and the rem make it possible to normalize doses of different types of radiation in terms of relative biologic effectiveness (RBE), because particulate radiations tend to cause greater injury for a given absorbed dose than do X-rays or gamma rays. The dose equivalent of a given type of radiation (in Sv) is the dose of the radiation in Gy multiplied by a quality factor that is based on the RBE of the radiation. Hence, one sievert, defined loosely, is that amount of radiation roughly equivalent in biologic effectiveness to one gray of gamma rays (1 Sv = 100 rem). Because the sievert and the rem are inconveniently large units for certain applications, the milligray (mGy; 1 mGy = 1/1000 Gy) and millisievert (mSv; 1 mSv = 1/1000 Sv) are often substituted.

For expressing the collective dose to a population, the person-Sv and person-rem are the units used. These units represent the product of the average dose per person times the number of people exposed (e.g., 1 Sv to each of 100 persons = 100 person-Sv = 10,000 person-rem).

The units employed for measuring the amount of radioactivity contained in a given sample of matter are the becquerel (Bq) and the curie (Ci). One becquerel is that quantity of a radioactive element in which there is one atomic disintegration per second; one curie is that quantity in which there are 3.7×10^{10} atomic disintegrations per second (1 Bq $= 2.7 \times 10^{-11}$ Ci). The dose that will accumulate over a given period (say, 50 years) from exposure to a given source of radiation is called the committed dose, or dose commitment.

SOURCES AND LEVELS OF RADIATION IN THE ENVIRONMENT

Radiation can come from natural and artificial sources. Natural sources include radiation from both outer space and on Earth. Artificial sources, such as X-rays used in medical examinations, are a source of environmental concern.

COSMIC-RADIATION EXPOSURE	
LOCATION	MEAN DOSE IN MILLISIEVERT (mSv)* PER YEAR
sea level, temperate zone	0.20–0.40
1,500 metres	0.40–0.60
3,000 metres	0.80–1.20
12,000 metres	28
36–600 kilometres	70–150
interplanetary space	180–250
Van Allen radiation belt (protons)	<15,000
single solar flare (protons and helium)	<10,000

*Millisievert is a radiation dose-equivalent unit: it corresponds to a dose equivalent in biologic effectiveness to 10 ergs energy of gamma radiation transferred to one gram of tissue.

ESTIMATES OF AVERAGE ANNUAL DOSE EQUIVALENT TO THE WHOLE BODY FROM VARIOUS SOURCES OF IRRADIATION RECEIVED BY MEMBERS OF THE U.S. POPULATION	
SOURCE OF RADIATION	**AVERAGE DOSE RATES (mSv/YEAR)**
NATURAL	
environmental	
cosmic radiation	0.27 (0.27–1.30)*
terrestrial radiation	0.28 (0.30–1.15)**
internal radioactive isotopes	0.36
subtotal	**0.91**
MAN-MADE	
environmental	
technologically enhanced	0.04
global fallout	0.04
nuclear power	0.002
medical	
diagnostic	0.78
radiopharmaceuticals	0.14
occupational	0.01
miscellaneous	0.05
subtotal	**1.06**
total	**1.97**

*Values in parentheses indicate range over which average levels for different states vary with elevation.
**Range of variation (shown in parentheses) attributable largely to geographic differences in the content of potassium-40, radium, thorium, and uranium in the Earth's crust.

AVERAGE DOSE DUE TO NATURAL RADIOACTIVITY DEPOSITED INTERNALLY

Isotope	Radioactivity in Milli-becquerel (mBq)*	Radiation	Dose in mSv (per Year)	Critical Organ
carbon-14	$2.2(10^{-7})$ per kilogram	beta rays	0.016	gonads
potassium-40	$3.9(10^{-7})$ per kilogram	beta rays	0.165	gonads
potassium-40	$5.6(10^{-8})$ per kilogram	gamma rays	0.023	gonads
radium and daughters	$3.7(10^{-9})$ in body	alpha, beta, gamma rays	7.6	bones
radon and daughters	$1.2(10^{-2})$ per 1 in inhaled air	alpha, beta, gamma rays	20	lungs

*Millibecquerel is a unit of radioactive disintegration rate; it corresponds to that quantity of a radioactive element in which there is one disintegration every 1,000 seconds.

EXTERNAL DOSE DUE TO NATURAL RADIOACTIVITY IN SOIL OR ROCK

Source	Dose in mSv per Year
ordinary regions	0.25–1.6
active regions	
granite in France	1.8–3.5
houses in Switzerland (alum shale)	1.58–2.2
monazite alluvial deposits in Brazil	mean 5; max 10
monazite sands, Kerala, India	3.7–28

NATURAL SOURCES

From the beginning, life has evolved in the presence of natural background ionizing radiation. The principal types and sources of such radiation are cosmic rays, which impinge on Earth from outer space; terrestrial radiations, which are released by the disintegration of radium, thorium, uranium, and other radioactive minerals in Earth's crust; and internal radiations, which are emitted by the disintegration of potassium-40, carbon-14, and other radioactive isotopes normally present within living cells. The average total dose received from all three sources by a person residing at sea level is approximately 0.91 mSv per year. A dose twice this size may be received by a person residing at a higher elevation such as Denver, Colo., however, where cosmic rays are more intense, or by a person residing in a geographic region where the radium content of the soil is relatively high. In the latter type of region, the radioactive gas radon, which is formed in the decay of radium, may enter a dwelling through its floor or basement walls and accumulate in the indoor air unless the dwelling is well ventilated periodically. Occupants of such a dwelling may therefore receive a dose as high as 100 mSv per year in their lungs from inhalation of the entrapped radon and its disintegration products.

ARTIFICIAL SOURCES

In addition to natural background radiation, people are exposed to radiation from various man-made sources, the largest of which is the application of X-rays in medical diagnosis. Although the doses delivered in different types of X-ray examinations vary from a small fraction of a mGy

WORLDWIDE DOSE COMMITMENT FROM RADIOACTIVE FALLOUT FROM NUCLEAR TESTS PRIOR TO 1970*

SOURCE	ISOTOPE	HALF-LIFE	DUE TO BONE SURFACES (mGy)
external radiation	short lived (e.g., iodine-131)	8 days	360
	longer lived (e.g., cesium-137)	30 years	360
internal radiation	strontium-89 and -90	50 days	1,310
	cesium-137	28 years	210
	carbon-14**	5,730 years	160
total			2,400

*North temperate zones; doses calculated for bone surface.
**Calculated to year 2000 only.

TYPICAL DOSES TO EXPOSED TISSUE RECEIVED IN ROUTINE X-RAY DIAGNOSIS

EXAMINATION	DOSE PER EXPOSURE IN MILLIGRAY (mGy)*
X-ray photograph	
chest	0.4–10
abdominal	10
extremities	2.5–10
fluoroscopy	100–200 per minute
X-ray movies	250 per examination
CAT scan	50–100 per examination

*Milligray is a unit of absorbed radiation dose; it corresponds to 1/1,000 joule of radiation energy absorbed per kilogram of tissue.

to tens of mGy, the average annual dose per capita from medical and dental irradiation in developed countries of the world now approaches in magnitude the dose received from natural background radiation. Less significant artificial sources of radiation include radioactive minerals in crushed rock, building materials, and phosphate fertilizers; radiation-emitting components of television sets, smoke detectors, and various other consumer products; radioactive fallout from nuclear weapons; and radiation released in nuclear power production.

Most radioactivity produced in nuclear power reactors is safely contained; however, a small percentage escapes as stack gas or liquid effluent and eventually may contaminate the atmosphere and water supply. (There are similar releases from nuclear-fuel reprocessing plants.) Though nuclear plants are basically clean sources of energy, they thus contribute to the worldwide background radiation level. This problem cannot be entirely avoided by using coal instead of nuclear fuel for power production, since many sources of coal contain natural radioactivity (e.g., radium) that is released in stack gases, along with chemical pollutants.

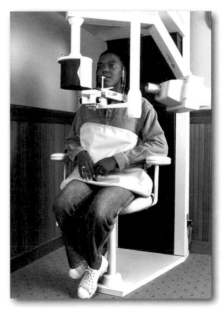

The human population is now exposed to about twice as much radiation from all sources combined as it receives from natural sources alone. Hence, it is

Mean amounts of medical and dental irradiation nearly match that received from natural background radiation. Keith Brofsky/Photodisc/Thinkstock

important to understand the possible consequences, if any, that may result from the additional exposure to radiation.

In comparison with the relatively small amounts of radiation described above, the dose typically administered to a patient in the treatment of cancer is thousands of times larger (i.e., a total dose of 50 Sv or more is usually delivered to a tumour in daily exposures over a period of four to six weeks). To protect the normal tissues of the patient against injury from such a large dose, as well as to protect medical personnel against excessive occupational exposure to stray radiation, precautions are taken to restrict exposure to the tumour itself insofar as possible. Comparable safeguards are used to minimize the exposure of workers employed in other activities involving radiation or radioactive material. Similarly, elaborate safety measures are required for disposal of radioactive wastes from nuclear reactors, in part resulting from the slow rate at which certain fission products decay. A given amount of plutonium-239, for example, still retains about one-half of its radioactivity after 25,000 years, so that reactor wastes containing this long-lived radionuclide must be safely isolated for centuries.

In the event of an atmospheric nuclear bomb explosion, large quantities of radioactivity are released, the dispersal of which depends on the prevailing weather conditions as well as on the height and nature of the blast. Although the level of contamination resulting from such an explosion or from a nuclear-power plant accident is generally highest in the immediate vicinity of the event itself, both radioactive gas and dust may be transported via air or water for many hundreds of kilometres and eventually contaminate the entire globe.

MECHANISM OF BIOLOGIC ACTION

As ionizing radiation penetrates living matter, it gives up its energy through random interactions with atoms and molecules in its path, leading to the formation of reactive ions and free radicals. It is the molecular alterations resulting from these ionizations and, in turn, the resultant biochemical changes that give rise to various types of injury. X-rays and gamma rays, for example, impart their energy to "planetary" atomic electrons, which are thereby ejected from their orbits. Such an ejection of a planetary electron results in an ion pair consisting of a free electron and the electrically charged atom from which it was ejected. The ejected electron may give rise to a highly reactive free radical, which in turn may diffuse far enough to attack a biologically important target molecule in its vicinity. This so-called indirect action process, through which radiation causes damage via radiation-induced free radicals, may be envisioned as follows:

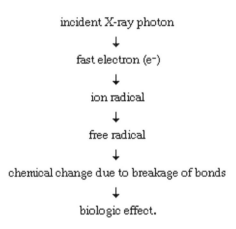

incident X-ray photon
↓
fast electron (e⁻)
↓
ion radical
↓
free radical
↓
chemical change due to breakage of bonds
↓
biologic effect.

While the initial steps in the aforementioned process occur almost instantaneously, expression of the biologic effect may take years or decades, depending on the type of injury involved. The indirect action of radiation is more important in the biologic effects of low-LET radiations than in those of high-LET radiations, but the latter have a greater capacity to cause injury through direct interaction with biologic targets.

Direct biologic actions, studied in detail between 1927 and 1947, gave rise to a target theory of radiobiology that has provided a quantitative treatment of many of the biologic effects of radiation, particularly in the field of genetics. According to this theory, a tissue or cell undergoing irradiation is likened to a field traversed by machine-gun fire, in which the production of a given effect requires one or more hits by an ionized track on a sensitive target. The probability of obtaining the effect is thus dependent on the probability of obtaining the requisite number of hits on the appropriate target or targets.

The distribution of ionizing atomic interactions along the path of an impinging radiation depends on the energy, mass, and charge of the radiation. The ionizations caused by neutrons, protons, and alpha particles are characteristically clustered more closely together than are those caused by X-rays or gamma rays. Thus, because the probability of injury depends on the concentration of molecular damage produced at a critical site, or target, in the cell (e.g., a gene or a chromosome), charged particles generally cause greater injury for a given total dose to the cell than do X-rays or gamma rays (i.e., they have a high RBE). At the same time, however, charged particles usually penetrate such a short distance in tissue that they pose relatively little hazard to tissues within the body unless they are emitted by a radionuclide, or radioactive isotope, that has been deposited internally.

RADIONUCLIDES AND RADIOACTIVE FALLOUT

Radionuclides emit various ionizing radiations (e.g., electrons, positrons, alpha particles, gamma rays, or even characteristic X-rays), the precise types of which depend on the radionuclide in question. Exposure to a radionuclide and its emissions may be external, in which case the penetrating power of the radiation is an important factor in determining the probability of injury. Alpha particles, for example, do not penetrate deeply enough into the skin to cause damage, whereas energetic beta particles or X-rays can be hazardous to the skin and deeper tissues.

ACCUMULATION IN CRITICAL ORGANS

Radionuclides can enter the body by ingestion, inhalation, or injection. Once taken into the body, their radiation effects depend on their anatomic distribution, duration of retention in the body, and rate of radioactive decay, as well as on the energies of their emitted radiations. An internally deposited radioactive element may concentrate in, and thus irradiate, certain organs more than others. Radioiodine, for example, collects in the thyroid gland, whereas radium and strontium accumulate chiefly in the bones. Different radioelements also vary in their rates of removal. Radioiodine, for instance, is normally eliminated from the thyroid rapidly enough so that its concentration is halved within days. Strontium-90, however, is retained in high concentrations in the skeleton for years.

The term *critical organ* refers to the part of the body most vulnerable to a given isotope. The critical organ for plutonium, radium, strontium, and many other fission products is bone and the adjacent bone marrow. For iodine, the critical organ is the thyroid gland. Insoluble airborne radioactive dust often settles in the alveoli of the lungs, whereas small colloidal particles may become deposited in the bone marrow, liver, or spleen. Humans can accumulate certain maximum concentrations of some radionuclides in the body without an undue risk of injury.

VALUES FOR THE MAXIMUM PERMISSIBLE CONCENTRATION (MPC) OF CERTAIN RADIONUCLIDES

Isotope	Chemical Form	Critical Organ	mBq in Body
tritium (hydrogen-3)	water		$7.4(10^{-3})$
carbon-14	carbon dioxide		$1.5(10^{-5})$
strontium-90*	water-soluble salt		$1.5(10^{-6})$
		bone	$1.5(10^{-7})$
iodine-131	water-soluble salt		$1.8(10^{-6})$
		thyroid	$2.6(10^{-8})$
cesium-137	water-soluble salt		$1.1(10^{-6})$
radon-222**	gas		
radium-226***	water-soluble salt		$7.4(10^{-8})$
		bone	$3.7(10^{-8})$
uranium	water-soluble salt		$7.4(10^{-8})$
		kidney	$1.8(10^{-10})$
plutonium-239	water-soluble salt		$1.5(10^{-8})$
		bone	$1.5(10^{-9})$

*MPC in drinking water: $3.7(10^{-9})$ micro Bq per litre.
**MPC in air: $3.7(10^{-11})$ micro Bq per litre.
***MPC in drinking water: $3.7(10^{-10})$ micro Bq per litre.

Because a radionuclide delivers radiation continuously to the surrounding tissue, the effect of such protracted continuous exposure must be distinguished from that of a single exposure or of periodically repeated exposures. From experiments with divided doses of gamma radiation or X radiation, it has been found that up to about 60 percent of the radiation effect from a single brief exposure is repaired within several hours. The body therefore is able to tolerate a larger total dose when the dose is accumulated slowly or when part of it is absorbed at a later time. There is less recovery with neutron and alpha radiation, however. (Neutrons are generally more effective agents of mutation than are X-rays: for a single brief exposure, by a factor 1 to 8; for chronic irradiation, by a factor up to 100.)

Fallout is the deposition of airborne radioactive contaminants on Earth. Radioisotopes are produced naturally in the air by cosmic radiation, and they may enter the air in stack gases from nuclear power plants or be released through industrial accidents or nuclear explosions. After 1954, nuclear bomb tests carried out by several nations produced measurable fallout on the entire surface of Earth, arousing great concern and controversy with respect to the resultant health effects. While much of the hazard from the detonation of a nuclear weapon is due to blast waves and heat, the radiation dose from fission products can be so intense that only persons remaining in underground shelters for some weeks could hope to survive. Usually the most prominent isotopes in fallout are fission products; however, all materials exposed to nuclear blasts may become radioactive.

THE HAZARDS OF LONG-LIVED RADIOISOTOPES

Several of the radioisotopes contained in fallout are especially hazardous because they remain radioactive for relatively long periods. Cesium-137, strontium-90, and plutonium-239 may be the most significant among these. Fallout material can cover external surfaces and foliage and later be washed into the soil, from which plants may absorb strontium-90, along with the chemically similar calcium, and cesium-137 with potassium. Humans take in these radioactive materials chiefly from drinking water and from plant and animal foods, including milk. Many fallout isotopes that reach the sea and inland waterways eventually end up in concentrated form in the bodies of waterborne animals and plants, becoming a source of concern when they are part of the human food chain.

The most easily detectable fallout product in humans and other animals is iodine-131, an isotope that emits beta and gamma rays and is enriched about 100 times in the thyroid gland through selective accumulation. Because of its relatively short half-life (eight days), iodine-131 is probably not the most hazardous fallout isotope. Yet, excessive amounts of radiation from this isotope can lead to metabolic disturbances and an increased incidence of thyroid cancer, especially in children.

A mixture of radioactive gases is discharged into the atmosphere in small amounts by nuclear power reactors. Reactors are thus generally placed at sites where atmospheric mixing and transport are such that the short-lived gases decay and are diluted before they can be inhaled in appreciable amounts by human populations.

Methods that have been developed for biologic protection against fallout range from measures designed to keep radioisotopes out of the body to biochemical means for rapidly eliminating such isotopes from tissues. At times of nuclear emergencies, airborne radioactive particles may be kept from the lungs by staying indoors or by wearing masks with suitable filtration. Absorption of ingested isotopes via the intestinal tract may be inhibited by certain mucoprotein substances that possess great surface affinity for adsorption of strontium and other substances. Sodium alginate prepared from seaweed kelp is such a substance. It is possible with appropriate chemicals to remove virtually all radioactive strontium from cow's milk without affecting its essential nutritive components. Certain chelates, such as EDTA (ethylenediaminetetraacetic acid), will react with strontium and "cover" this atom. As a result, the presence of EDTA in the blood reduces the deposition of strontium in bones (elimination of already deposited isotopes also is somewhat accelerated). Unfortunately, however, EDTA and most other chelating agents are not specific for strontium. They also chelate the closely related and important element calcium. Consequently, their use requires expert medical supervision and is limited in effectiveness. The uptake of radioactive iodine by the thyroid gland may be reduced by the ingestion of large amounts of stable iodine, however, which is relatively nontoxic except to those with special sensitivity.

MAJOR TYPES OF RADIATION INJURY

Any living organism can be killed by radiation if exposed to a large enough dose, but the lethal dose varies greatly from species to species. Mammals can be killed by less than 10 Gy, but fruit flies may survive 1,000 Gy. Many bacteria and viruses may survive even higher doses. In general, humans are among the most radiosensitive of all living organisms, but the effects of a given dose in a person depend on the organ irradiated, the dose, and the conditions of exposure.

The biologic effects of radiation in humans and other mammals are generally subdivided into (1) those that affect the body of the exposed individual—somatic effects—and (2) those that affect the offspring of the exposed individual—genetic, or heritable, effects. Among the somatic effects, there are those that occur within a short period of time (e.g., inhibition of cell division) and those that may not occur until years or decades after irradiation (e.g., radiation-induced cancer). In addition, there are those, called non-stochastic effects, that occur only in response to a considerable dose of radiation (e.g., ulceration of the skin) and those, termed stochastic, for which no threshold dose is known to exist (e.g., radiation-induced cancer).

Every type of biologic effect of radiation, irrespective of its precise nature, results from injury to the cell, the microscopic building block of which all living organisms are composed. It therefore seems useful to open a review of such effects with a discussion of the action of radiation on the cell.

EFFECTS ON THE CELL

The effects of radiation on the cell include interference with cell division, damage to chromosomes, damage to genes (mutations), neoplastic transformation (a change analogous to the induction of cancer), and cell death. The mechanisms through which these changes are produced are not yet fully understood, but each change is thought to be the end result of chemical alterations that are initiated by radiation as it randomly traverses the cell.

Any type of molecule in the cell can be altered by irradiation, but the DNA of the genetic material is thought to be the cell's most critical target, since damage to a single gene may be sufficient to kill or profoundly alter the cell. A dose that can kill the average dividing cell (say, 1–2 Sv) produces dozens of lesions in the cell's DNA molecules. Although most such lesions are normally reparable through the action of intracellular DNA repair processes, those that remain unrepaired or are misrepaired may give rise to permanent changes in the affected genes (i.e., mutations) or in the chromosomes on which the genes are carried, as discussed in the following text.

In general, dividing cells (such as cancer cells) are more radiosensitive than nondividing cells. As noted earlier, a dose of 1–2 Sv is sufficient to kill the average dividing cell, whereas nondividing cells can usually withstand many times as much radiation without overt signs of injury. It is when cells attempt to divide for the first time after irradiation that they are most apt to die as a result of radiation injury to their genes or chromosomes.

The percentage of human cells retaining the ability to multiply generally decreases exponentially with increasing radiation dose, depending on the type of cell exposed and the conditions of irradiation. With X-rays and gamma rays, traversal by two or more radiation tracks in swift succession are usually required to kill the cell. Hence, the survival curve is typically shallower at low doses and low dose rates than at high doses and high dose rates. The reduced killing effectiveness of a given dose when it is delivered in two or more widely spaced fractions is attributed to the repair of sublethal damage between successive exposures. With densely ionizing particulate radiations, however, the survival curve is characteristically steeper than with X-rays or gamma rays, and its slope is relatively unaffected by the dose or the dose rate, implying that the death of the cell usually results from a single densely ionizing particle track and that the injury produced by such a track is of a relatively irreparable type.

Damage to Genes (Mutations)

Gene mutations resulting from radiation-induced damage to DNA have been produced experimentally in many types of organisms. In general, the frequency of a given mutation increases in proportion to the dose of radiation in the low-to-intermediate dose range. At higher doses, however, the frequency of mutations induced by a given dose may be dependent on the rate at which the dose is accumulated, tending to be lower if the dose is accumulated over a long period of time.

In human white blood cells (lymphocytes), as in mouse spermatogonia and oocytes, the frequency of radiation-induced mutations approximates 1 mutation per 100,000 cells per genetic locus per Sv. This rate of increase is not large enough to detect with existing methodology in the children of the atomic-bomb survivors of Hiroshima and Nagasaki, owing to their limited numbers and the comparatively small average dose of radiation received by their parents. Accordingly, it is not surprising that heritable effects of irradiation have not been observable thus far in this population or in any other irradiated human population, in spite of exhaustive efforts to detect them.

The observed proportionality between the frequency of induced mutations and the radiation dose has important health implications for the human population, since it implies that even a small dose of radiation given to a large number of individuals may introduce mutant genes into the population, provided that the individuals are younger than reproductive age at the time of irradiation. The effect on a population of a rise in its mutation rate depends, however, on the role played by mutation in determining the characteristics of the population. Although deleterious genes enter the population through mutations, they tend to be eliminated because they reduce the fitness of their carriers. Thus, a genetic equilibrium is reached at the point where the entry of deleterious genes into the population through mutation is counterbalanced by their loss through reduction in fitness. At the point of equilibrium, an increase of the mutation rate by a given percentage causes a proportionate increase in the gene-handicapped fraction in the population. The full increase is not manifested immediately, however, but only when genetic equilibrium is again established, which requires several generations.

The capacity of radiation to increase the frequency of mutations is often expressed in terms of the mutation-rate doubling dose, which is the dose that induces as large an additional rate of mutations as that which occurs spontaneously in each generation. The more sensitive the genes are to radiation, the lower is the doubling dose. The doubling dose for high-intensity exposure in several different organisms has been found experimentally to lie between about 0.3 and 1.5 Gy. For seven specific genes in the mouse, the doubling dose of gamma radiation for spermatogonia is about 0.3 Gy for high-intensity exposure and about 1.0 Gy for low-intensity exposure. Little is known about the doubling dose for human genes, but most geneticists assume that it is about the same as the doubling dose for those of mice. Studies of the children of atomic-bomb survivors are consistent with this view, as previously noted.

From the results of experiments with mice and other laboratory animals, the dose required to double the human mutation rate is estimated to lie in the range of 0.2–2.5 Sv, implying that less than 1 percent of all genetically related diseases in the human population is attributable to natural background irradiation. Although natural background irradiation therefore appears to make only a relatively small contribution to the overall burden of genetic illness in the world's population, millions of individuals may be thus affected in each generation.

Notwithstanding the fact that most mutations are decidedly harmful, those induced by irradiation in seeds are of interest to horticulturists as a means of producing new and improved varieties of plants. Mutations produced in this manner can affect such properties of the plant as early ripening and resistance to disease, with the result that economically important varieties of a number of species have been produced by irradiation. In their effects on plants, fast neutrons and heavy particles have been found to be up to about 100 times more mutagenic than X-rays. Radioactive elements taken up by plants also can be strongly mutagenic. In the choice of a suitable dose for the production of mutations, a compromise has to be made between the mutagenic effects and damaging effects of the radiation. As the number of mutations increases, so also does the extent of damage to the plants. In the irradiation of dry seeds by X-rays, a dose of 10 to 20 Gy is usually given.

DAMAGE TO CHROMOSOMES

By breaking both strands of the DNA molecule, radiation also can break the chromosome fibre and interfere with the normal segregation of duplicate sets of chromosomes to daughter cells at the time of cell division, thereby altering the structure and number of chromosomes in the cell. Chromosomal changes of this kind may cause the affected cell to die when it attempts to divide, or they may alter its properties in various other ways.

Chromosome breaks often heal spontaneously, but a break that fails to heal may cause the loss of an essential part of the gene complement. This loss of genetic material is called gene deletion. A germ cell thus affected may be capable of taking part in the fertilization process, but the resulting zygote may be incapable of full development and may therefore die in an embryonic state.

When adjoining chromosome fibres in the same nucleus are broken, the broken ends may join together in such a way that the sequence of genes on the chromosomes is changed. For example, one of the broken ends of chromosome A may join onto a broken end of chromosome B, and vice versa in a process called translocation. A germ cell carrying such a chromosome structural change may be capable of producing a zygote that can develop into an adult individual, but the germ cells produced by the resulting individual may include many that lack the normal chromosome complement and so yield zygotes that are incapable of full development. An individual affected in this way is termed semisterile. Because the number of his descendants is correspondingly lower than normal, such chromosome structural changes tend to die out in successive generations.

As would be expected from target theory consider-ations, X-rays and gamma rays given at high doses and high dose rates induce more two-break chromosome aberrations per unit dose than are produced at low doses and low dose rates. With densely ionizing radiation, by comparison, the yield of two-break aberrations for a given dose is higher than with sparsely ionizing radiation and is proportional to the dose irrespective of the dose rate. From these comparative dose-response relationships, it is inferred that a single X-ray track rarely deposits enough energy at any one point to break two adjoining chromo-somes simultaneously, whereas the two-break aberrations that are induced by high-LET irradiation result prepon-derantly from single particle tracks.

In irradiated human lymphocytes, the frequency of chromosome aberrations varies so predictably with the dose of radiation that it is used as a crude biologic dosim-eter of exposure in radiation workers and other exposed persons. What effect, if any, an increase in the frequency of chromosome aberrations may have on the health of an affected individual is uncertain. Only a small percentage of all chromosome aberrations is attributable to natural background radiation. Most result from other causes, including certain viruses, chemicals, and drugs.

EFFECTS ON ORGANS OF THE BODY (SOMATIC EFFECTS)

A wide variety of reactions occur in response to irradiation in the different organs and tissues of the body. Some reactions occur quickly, and others occur slowly. The killing of cells in affected tissues, for example, may be detectable within minutes after exposure, whereas degenerative changes such as scarring and tissue breakdown may not appear until months or years afterward.

In general, dividing cells are more radiosensitive than nondividing cells, with the result that radiation injury tends to appear soonest in those organs and tissues in which cells proliferate rapidly. Such tissues include the skin, the lining of the gastrointestinal tract, and the bone marrow, where progenitor cells multiply continually to replace the mature cells that are constantly being lost through normal aging. The early effects of radiation on these organs largely result from the destruction of the progenitor cells and the consequent interference with the replacement of the mature cells, a process essential for the maintenance of normal tissue structure and function. The damaging effects of radiation on an organ are generally limited to that part of the organ directly exposed. Accordingly, irradiation of only a part of an organ generally causes less impairment in the function of the organ than does irradiation of the whole organ.

SKIN

Radiation can cause various types of injury to the skin, depending on the dose and conditions of exposure. The earliest outward reaction of the skin is transitory reddening (erythema) of the exposed area, which may appear within hours after a dose of 6 Gy or more. This reaction typically lasts only a few hours and is followed two to four weeks later by one or more waves of deeper and more prolonged reddening in the same area. A larger dose may cause subsequent blistering and ulceration of the skin and loss of hair, followed by abnormal pigmentation months or years later.

BONE MARROW

The blood-forming cells of the bone marrow are among the most radiosensitive cells in the body. If a large percentage of such cells are killed, as can happen when intensive irradiation of the whole body occurs, the normal replacement of circulating blood cells is impaired. As a result, the blood cell count may become depressed and, ultimately, infection, hemorrhage, or both may ensue. A dose less than 0.5–1 Sv generally causes only a mild, transitory depletion of blood-forming cells; however, a dose more than 8 Sv delivered rapidly to the whole body usually causes a fatal depression of blood-cell formation.

GASTROINTESTINAL TRACT

The response of the gastrointestinal tract is comparable in many respects to that of the skin. Proliferating cells in the mucous membrane that lines the tract are easily killed by irradiation, resulting in the denudation and ulceration of the mucous membrane. If a substantial portion of the small intestine is exposed rapidly to a dose in excess of 10 Gy, as may occur in a radiation accident, a fatal dysentery-like reaction results within a very short period of time.

REPRODUCTIVE ORGANS

Although mature spermatozoa are relatively resistant to radiation, immature sperm-forming cells (spermatogonia) are among the most radiosensitive cells in the body. Hence, rapid exposure of both testes to a dose as low as 0.15 Sv may interrupt sperm-production temporarily, and a dose in excess of 4 Sv may be sufficient to cause permanent sterility in a certain percentage of men.

In the human ovary, oocytes of intermediate maturity are more radiosensitive than those of greater or lesser maturity. A dose of 1.5–2.0 Sv delivered rapidly to both ovaries may thus cause only temporary sterility, whereas a dose exceeding 2–3 Sv is likely to cause permanent sterility in an appreciable percentage of women.

LENS OF THE EYE

Irradiation can cause opacification of the lens, the severity of which increases with the dose. The effect may not become evident, however, until many months after exposure. During the 1940s, some physicists who worked with the early cyclotrons developed cataracts as a result of occupational neutron irradiation, indicating for the first time the high relative biologic effectiveness of neutrons for causing lens damage. The threshold for a progressive, vision-impairing opacity, or cataract, varies from 5 Sv delivered to the lens in a single exposure to as much as 14 Sv delivered in multiple exposures over a period of months.

BRAIN AND SENSORY ORGANS

Generally speaking, humans do not sense a moderate radiation field. However, small doses of radiation (less than 0.01 Gy) can produce phosphene, a light sensation on the dark-adapted retina. American astronauts on the first spacecraft that landed on the Moon (Apollo 11, July 20, 1969) observed irregular light flashes and streaks during their flight, which resulted from single heavy cosmic-ray particles striking the retina. In various food-preference tests, rats, when given the choice, avoid radiation fields of even a few mGy. A dose of 0.03 Gy is sufficient to arouse a slumbering rat, probably through effects on the olfactory system, and a dose of the same order of magnitude can accelerate seizures in genetically susceptible mice. The mature brain and nervous system are relatively resistant to radiation injury, but the developing brain is radiosensitive to damage.

RADIATION SICKNESS

The signs and symptoms resulting from intensive irradiation of a large portion of the bone marrow or gastrointestinal tract constitute a clinical picture known as radiation sickness, or the acute radiation syndrome. Early manifestations of this condition typically include loss of appetite, nausea, and vomiting within the first few hours after irradiation, followed by a symptom-free interval that lasts until the main phase of the illness.

The main phase of the intestinal form of the illness typically begins two to three days after irradiation, with abdominal pain, fever, and diarrhea, which progress rapidly in severity and lead within several days to dehydration, prostration, and a fatal, shocklike state. The main phase of the hematopoietic form of the illness characteristically begins in the second or third week after irradiation, with fever, weakness, infection, and hemorrhage. If damage to the bone marrow is severe, death from overwhelming infection or hemorrhage may ensue four to six weeks after exposure unless corrected by transplantation of compatible unirradiated bone marrow cells.

The higher the dose received, the sooner and more profound are the radiation effects. Following a single dose of more than 5 Gy to the whole body, survival is improbable. A dose of 50 Gy or more to the head may cause immediate and discernible effects on the central nervous system, followed by intermittent stupor and incoherence alternating with hyperexcitability, epileptiform seizures, and death within several days (the cerebral form of the acute radiation syndrome).

SYMPTOMS OF ACUTE RADIATION SICKNESS (HEMATOPOIETIC FORM)			
TIME AFTER EXPOSURE	SUPRALETHAL DOSE RANGE (6–10 Gy)	MIDLETHAL DOSE RANGE (2.5–5 Gy)	SUBLETHAL DOSE RANGE (1–2 Gy)
several hours	no definite symptoms	nausea and vomiting	
first week	diarrhea, vomiting, inflammation of throat	no definite symptoms	
second week	fever, rapid emaciation leading to death for 100 percent of the population		
third week		loss of hair begins; loss of appetite; general malaise; fever, hemorrhages, pallor leading to rapid emaciation and death for 50 percent of the population	loss of appetite; sore throat; pallor and diarrhea; recovery begins (no deaths in absence of complications)

When the dose to the whole body is between 6 and 10 Gy, the earliest symptoms are loss of appetite, nausea, and vomiting, followed by prostration, watery and bloody diarrhea, abhorrence of food, and fever. The blood-forming tissues are profoundly injured, and the white blood cell count may decrease within 15–30 days from about 8,000 per cubic millimetre to as low as 200. As a result of these effects, the body loses its defenses against microbial infection, and the mucous membranes lining the gastrointestinal tract may become inflamed.

Furthermore, internal or external bleeding may occur because of a reduction in blood platelets. Return of the early symptoms, frequently accompanied by delirium or coma, presage death. However, symptoms may vary significantly from individual to individual. Complete loss of hair within 10 days has been taken as an indication of a lethally severe exposure.

In the dose range of 1.5–5.0 Gy, survival is possible (though in the upper range improbable), and the symptoms appear as described earlier but in milder form and generally following some delay. Nausea, vomiting, and malaise may begin on the first day and then disappear, and a latent period of relative well-being follows. Anemia and leukopenia set in gradually. After three weeks, internal hemorrhages may occur in almost any part of the body, but particularly in mucous membranes. Susceptibility to infection remains high, and some loss of hair occurs. Lassitude, emaciation, and fever may persist for many weeks before recovery or death occurs.

Moderate doses of radiation can severely depress the immunologic defense mechanisms, resulting in enhanced sensitivity to bacterial toxins, greatly decreased fixation of antigens, and reduced efficiency of antibody formation. Antibiotics, unfortunately, are of limited effectiveness in combating postirradiation infections. Hence, plastic isolators that allow antiseptic isolation of a person from his environment are considerably valuable, because they provide protection against infection from external sources during the period critical for recovery.

Below a dose of 1.5 Gy, irradiated people are generally able to survive intensive whole-body irradiation. The symptoms following exposure in this dose range are similar to those already described but milder and delayed. With a dose less than 1 Gy, the symptoms may be so mild that exposed people can continue their normal occupations in spite of measurable depression of their bone marrow. Some persons, however, suffer subjective discomfort from doses as low as 0.3 Gy. Although such doses may cause no immediate reactions, they may produce delayed effects that appear years later.

Effects on the Growth and Development of the Embryo

The tissues of the embryo, like others composed of rapidly proliferating cells, are highly radiosensitive. The types and frequencies of radiation effects, however, depend heavily on the stage of development of the embryo or fetus at the time it is exposed. For example, when exposure occurs while an organ is forming, malformation of the organ may result. Exposure earlier in embryonic life is more likely to kill the embryo than cause a congenital malformation, whereas exposure at a later stage is more likely to produce a functional abnormality in the offspring than a lethal effect or a malformation.

A wide variety of radiation-induced malformations have been observed in experimentally irradiated rodents. Many of these are malformations of the nervous system, including microcephaly (reduced size of brain), exencephaly (part of the brain formed outside the skull), hydrocephalus (enlargement of the head due to excessive fluid), and anophthalmia (failure of the eyes to develop). Such effects may follow a dose of 1–2 Gy given at an appropriate stage of development. Functional abnormalities produced in laboratory animals by prenatal irradiation include abnormal reflexes, restlessness, and hyperactivity, impaired learning ability, and susceptibility to externally induced seizures. The abnormalities induced by radiation are similar to those that can be caused by certain virus infections, neurotropic drugs, pesticides, and mutagens.

Abnormalities of the nervous system, which occur in 1–2 percent of human infants, were found with greater frequency among children born to women who were pregnant and residing in Hiroshima or Nagasaki at the time of the atomic explosions. The incidence of reduced head size and mental retardation in such children was increased by about 40 percent per Gy when exposure occurred between the eighth and 15th week of gestation, the age of greatest susceptibility to radiation.

The period of maximal sensitivity for each developing organ is sharply circumscribed in time, with the result that the risk of malformation in a particular organ depends heavily on the precise stage of development at which the embryo is irradiated. The risk that a given dose will produce a particular malformation is thus much smaller if the dose is spread out over many days or weeks than if it is received during the few hours of the critical period itself. It also would appear that the induction of a malformation generally requires injury to many cells in a developing organ, so that there is little likelihood of such an effect resulting from the low doses and dose rates characteristic of natural background radiation.

EFFECTS ON THE INCIDENCE OF CANCER

Atomic-bomb survivors, certain groups of patients exposed to radiation for medical purposes, and some groups of radiation workers have shown dose-dependent increases in the incidence of certain types of cancer. The induced cancers have not appeared until years after exposure, however, and they have shown no distinguishing features by which they can be identified individually as having resulted from radiation, as opposed to some other cause. With few exceptions, moreover, the incidence of cancer has not been increased detectably by doses of less than 0.01 Sv.

Because the carcinogenic effects of radiation have not been documented over a wide enough range of doses and dose rates to define the shape of the dose-incidence curve precisely, the risk of radiation-induced cancer at low levels of exposure can be estimated only by extrapolation from observations at higher dose levels, based on assumptions about the relation between cancer incidence and dose. For most types of cancer, information about the dose-incidence relationship is rather meagre. The most extensive data available are for leukemia and cancer of the female breast.

The overall incidence of all forms of leukemia other than the chronic lymphatic type has been observed to increase roughly in proportion to dose during the first 25 years after irradiation. Different types of leukemia, however, vary in the magnitude of the radiation-induced increase for a given dose, the age at which irradiation occurs, and the time after exposure. The total excess of all types besides chronic lymphatic leukemia, averaged over all ages, amounts to approximately one to three additional cases of leukemia per year per 10,000 persons at risk per sievert to the bone marrow.

Cancer of the female breast also appears to increase in incidence in proportion to the radiation dose. Furthermore, the magnitude of the increase for a given dose appears to be essentially the same in women whose breasts were irradiated in a single, brief exposure (e.g., atomic-bomb survivors), as in those who were irradiated over a period of years (e.g., patients subjected to

multiple fluoroscopic examinations of the chest or workers assigned to coating watch and clock dials with paint
containing radium), implying that even small exposures
widely separated in time exert carcinogenic effects on the
breast that are fully additive and cumulative. Although
susceptibility decreases sharply with age at the time of
irradiation, the excess of breast cancer averaged over all
ages amounts to three to six cases per 10,000 women per
sievert each year.

Additional evidence that carcinogenic effects can be
produced by a relatively small dose of radiation is provided by the increase in the incidence of thyroid tumours
that has been observed to result from a dose of 0.06–2.0
Gy of X-rays delivered to the thyroid gland during infancy
or childhood, and by the association between prenatal
diagnostic X irradiation and childhood leukemia. The latter association implies that exposure to as little as 10–50
mGy of X radiation during intrauterine development may
increase the subsequent risk of leukemia in the exposed
child by as much as 40–50 percent.

Although some, but not all, other types of cancer
have been observed to occur with greater frequency in
irradiated populations, the data do not suffice to indicate whether the risks extend to low doses. It is apparent,
however, that the dose-incidence relationship varies from
one type of cancer to another. From the existing evidence,
the overall excess of all types of cancer combined may be
inferred to approximate 0.6–1.8 cases per 1,000 persons
per sievert per year when the whole body is exposed to
radiation, beginning two to 10 years after irradiation. This
increase corresponds to a cumulative lifetime excess of
roughly 20–100 additional cases of cancer per 1,000 persons per sievert, or to an 8–40 percent per sievert increase
in the natural lifetime risk of cancer.

ESTIMATED LIFETIME CANCER RISKS ATTRIBUTED TO LOW-LEVEL IRRADIATION	
SITE IRRADIATED	CANCERS PER 10,000 PERSON-Sv*
bone marrow (leukemia)	15–20
thyroid	25–120
breast (women only)	40–200
lung	25–140
stomach	
liver	5–60 (each)
colon	
bone	
esophagus	
small intestine	5–30 (each)
urinary bladder	
pancreas	
lymphatic tissue	
skin	10–20
total (both sexes)	**125–1,000**

*The unit person-Sv represents the product of the average dose per person times the number of people exposed (1 sievert to each of 10,000 persons = 10,000 person-Sv); all values provided here are rounded.

Source: National Academy of Sciences Advisory Committee on the Biological Effects of Ionizing Radiation, *The Effects on Populations of Exposure to Low Levels of Ionizing Radiation* (1972, 1980); United Nations Scientific Committee on the Effects of Atomic Radiation, *Sources and Effects of Ionizing Radiation* (1977 report to the General Assembly, with annexes).

The risk estimates previously cited imply that no more than 1–3 percent of all cancers in the general population result from natural background ionizing radiation. At the same time, however, the data suggest that up to 20 percent of lung cancers in nonsmokers may be attributable to inhalation of radon and other naturally occurring radionuclides present in air.

Shortening of the Life Span

Laboratory animals whose entire bodies are exposed to radiation in the first half of life suffer a reduction in longevity that increases in magnitude with increasing dose. This effect was mistakenly interpreted by early investigators as a manifestation of accelerated or premature aging. The shortening of life in irradiated animals, however, has since been observed to be attributable largely, if not entirely, to the induction of benign and malignant growths. In keeping with this observation is the finding that mortality from diseases other than cancer has not been increased detectably by irradiation among atomic-bomb survivors.

PROTECTION AGAINST EXTERNAL RADIATION

A growing number of substances have been found to provide some protection against radiation injury when administered prior to irradiation. Many of them apparently act by producing anoxia or by competing for oxygen with normal cell constituents and radiation-produced radicals. All of the protective compounds tried thus far, however, are toxic, and anoxia itself is hazardous. As a consequence, their administration to humans is not yet practical.

SOME CHEMICALS THAT EXERT RADIOPROTECTIVE EFFECTS IN LABORATORY ANIMALS		
CLASS	SPECIFIC CHEMICAL	EFFECTIVE DOSE (IN MILLIGRAMS PER KILOGRAM OF TISSUE)
sulfur compounds	glutathione	1,000
	cysteine	1,000
	cysteamine	150
	AET*	350
hormones	estradiolbenzoate	12
	ACTH	25 for 7 days
enzyme inhibitors	sodium cyanide	5
	carbon monoxide	by inhalation
	mercaptoethylamine (MEA)	235
	para-aminopropiophenone (PAPP)	30
metabolites	formic acid	90
vasoconstrictors	serotonin	50
nervous system drugs	amphetamine	1
	chlorpromazine	20

*Aminoethylisothiuronium bromide hydrobromide.

Diurnal changes in the radiosensitivity of rodents indicate that the factors responsible for daily biologic rhythms may also alter the responses of tissues to radiation. Such factors include the hormone thyroxine, a normal secretion of the thyroid gland. Other sensitizers at the cellular level include nucleic-acid analogues (e.g., 5-fluorouracil) as well as certain compounds that selectively radiosensitize hypoxic cells such as metronidazole.

Radiosensitivity is also under genetic control to some degree, susceptibility varying among different inbred mouse strains and increasing in the presence of inherited deficiencies in capacity for repairing radiation-induced damage to DNA. Germ-free mice, which spend their entire lives in a sterile environment, also exhibit greater resistance to radiation than do animals in a normal microbial environment owing to elimination of the risk of infection.

For many years it was thought that radiation disease was irreversible once a lethal dose had been received. It has since been found that bone-marrow cells administered soon after irradiation may enable an individual to survive an otherwise lethal dose of X-rays, because these cells migrate to the marrow of the irradiated recipient, where they proliferate and repopulate the blood-forming tissues. Under these conditions bone-marrow transplantation is feasible even between histo-incompatible individuals, because the irradiated recipient has lost the ability to develop antibodies against the injected "foreign" cells. After a period of some months, however, the transplanted tissue may eventually be rejected, or it may develop an immune reaction against the irradiated host, which also can be fatal. The transplantation of bone-marrow cells has been helpful in preventing radiation deaths among the victims of reactor accidents, as, for example, those injured in 1986 at the Chernobyl nuclear power plant in Ukraine, then in the Soviet Union. It should be noted, however, that cultured or stored marrow cells cannot yet be used for this purpose.

CONTROL OF RADIATION RISKS

In view of the fact that radiation is now assumed to play a role in mutagenic or carcinogenic activity, any procedure

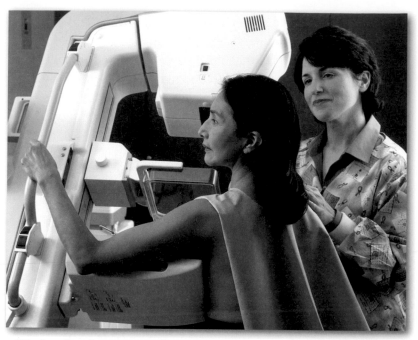

The benefits of some types of irradiation, such as cancer-detecting mammograms, far outweigh the risks. Rhoda Baer/National Cancer Institute

involving radiation exposure is considered to entail some degree of risk. At the same time, however, the radiation-induced risks associated with many activities are negligibly small in comparison with other risks commonly encountered in daily life. Nevertheless, such risks are not necessarily acceptable if they can be easily avoided or if no measurable benefit is to be gained from the activities with which they are associated. Consequently, systematic efforts are made to avoid unnecessary exposure to ionizing radiation in medicine, science, and industry. Toward this end, limits have been placed on the amounts of radioactivity and on the radiation doses that the different tissues of the body are permitted to accumulate in radiation workers or members of the public at large.

Although most activities involving exposure to radiation for medical purposes are highly beneficial, the benefits cannot be assumed to outweigh the risks in situations where radiation is used to screen large segments of the population for the purpose of detecting an occasional person with an asymptomatic disease. Examples of such applications include the "annual" chest X-ray examination and routine mammography. Each use of radiation in medicine (and dentistry) is now evaluated for its merits on a case-by-case basis.

Other activities involving radiation also are assessed with care in order to assure that unnecessary exposure is avoided and that their presumed benefits outweigh their calculated risks. In operating nuclear power plants, for example, much care is taken to minimize the risk to surrounding populations. Because of such precautions, the total impact on health of generating a given amount of electricity from nuclear power is usually estimated to be smaller than that resulting from the use of coal for the same purpose, even after allowances for severe reactor accidents such as the one at Chernobyl.

CHAPTER 6
NUCLEAR FISSION

The subdivision of a heavy atomic nucleus, such as that of uranium or plutonium, into two fragments of roughly equal mass is called nuclear fission. The process is accompanied by the release of a large amount of energy.

In nuclear fission the nucleus of an atom breaks up into two lighter nuclei. The process may take place spontaneously in some cases or may be induced by the excitation of the nucleus with a variety of particles (e.g., neutrons, protons, deuterons, or alpha particles) or with electromagnetic radiation in the form of gamma rays. In the fission process, a large quantity of energy is released, radioactive products are formed, and several neutrons are emitted. These neutrons can induce fission in a nearby nucleus of fissionable material and release more neutrons that can repeat the sequence, causing a chain reaction in which a large number of nuclei undergo fission and an enormous amount of energy is released. If controlled in a nuclear reactor, such a chain reaction can provide power for society's benefit. If uncontrolled, as in the case of the so-called atomic bomb, it can lead to an explosion of awesome destructive force.

The discovery of nuclear fission opened a new era—the "Atomic Age." The potential of nuclear fission for good or evil and the risk/benefit ratio of its applications have not only provided the basis of many sociological, political, economic, and scientific advances but grave concerns as well. Even from a purely scientific perspective, the process of nuclear fission has given rise to many puzzles and complexities, and a complete theoretical explanation is still not at hand.

HISTORY OF FISSION RESEARCH AND TECHNOLOGY

The term *fission* was first used by the German physicists Lise Meitner and Otto Frisch in 1939 to describe the disintegration of a heavy nucleus into two lighter nuclei of approximately equal size. The conclusion that such an unusual nuclear reaction can in fact occur was the culmination of a truly dramatic episode in the history of science, and it set in motion an extremely intense and productive period of investigation.

The story of the discovery of nuclear fission actually began with the discovery of the neutron in 1932 by James Chadwick in England. Shortly thereafter, Enrico Fermi and his associates in Italy undertook an extensive investigation of the nuclear reactions produced by the bombardment of various elements with this uncharged particle. In particular, these workers observed (1934) that at least four different radioactive species resulted from the bombardment of uranium with slow neutrons. These newly discovered species emitted beta particles and were thought to be isotopes of unstable "transuranium elements" of atomic numbers 93, 94, and perhaps higher. There was, of course, intense interest in examining the properties of these elements, and many radiochemists participated in the studies. The results of these investigations, however, were extremely perplexing, and confusion persisted until 1939 when Otto Hahn and Fritz Strassmann in Germany, following a clue provided by Irène Joliot-Curie and Pavle Savić in France (1938), proved definitely that the so-called transuranic elements were in fact radioisotopes of barium, lanthanum, and other elements in the middle of the periodic table.

That lighter elements could be formed by bombarding heavy nuclei with neutrons had been suggested earlier (notably by the German chemist Walter Noddack in 1934), but the idea was not given serious consideration because it entailed such a broad departure from the accepted views of nuclear physics and was unsupported by clear chemical evidence. Armed with the unequivocal results of Hahn and Strassmann, however, Meitner and Frisch invoked the recently formulated liquid-drop model of the nucleus to give a qualitative theoretical interpretation of the fission process and called attention to the large energy release that should accompany it. There was almost immediate confirmation of this reaction in dozens of laboratories throughout the world, and within a year more than 100 papers describing most of the important features of the process were published. These experiments confirmed the formation of extremely energetic heavy particles and extended the chemical identification of the products.

The chemical evidence that was so vital in leading Hahn and Strassmann to the discovery of nuclear fission was obtained by the application of carrier and tracer techniques. Because invisible amounts of the radioactive species were formed, their chemical identity had to be deduced from the manner in which they followed known carrier elements, present in macroscopic quantity, through various chemical operations. Known radioactive species were also added as tracers and their behaviour was compared with that of the unknown species to aid in the identification of the latter. Over the years, these radiochemical techniques have been used to isolate and identify some 34 elements from zinc (atomic number 30) to gadolinium (atomic number 64) that are formed as fission products. The wide range of radioactivities produced in fission makes this reaction a rich source of tracers for chemical, biologic, and industrial use.

Although the early experiments involved the fission of ordinary uranium with slow neutrons, it was rapidly established that the rare isotope uranium-235 was responsible for this phenomenon. The more abundant isotope uranium-238 could be made to undergo fission only by fast neutrons with energy exceeding 1 MeV. The nuclei of other heavy elements, such as thorium and protactinium, also were shown to be fissionable with fast neutrons; and other particles, such as fast protons, deuterons, and alphas, along with gamma rays, proved to be effective in inducing the reaction.

In 1939, Frédéric Joliot-Curie, Hans von Halban, and Lew Kowarski found that several neutrons were emitted in the fission of uranium-235, and this discovery led to the possibility of a self-sustaining chain reaction. Fermi and his coworkers recognized the enormous potential of such a reaction if it could be controlled. On Dec. 2, 1942, they succeeded in doing so, operating the world's first nuclear reactor. Known as a "pile," this device consisted of an array of uranium and graphite blocks and was built on the campus of the University of Chicago.

The secret Manhattan Project, established not long after the United States entered World War II, developed

Soon after entering Word War II, the United States commenced the Manhattan Project, developing and testing an atomic bomb in locations such as New Mexico. Joe Raedle/Getty Images

the atomic bomb. Once the war had ended, efforts were made to develop new reactor types for large-scale power generation, giving birth to the nuclear power industry.

FUNDAMENTALS OF THE FISSION PROCESS

How does fission work? The fission process may be best understood through a consideration of the structure and stability of nuclear matter.

STRUCTURE AND STABILITY OF NUCLEAR MATTER

Nuclei consist of nucleons (neutrons and protons), the total number of which is equal to the mass number of the nucleus. The actual mass of a nucleus is always less than the sum of the masses of the free neutrons and protons that constitute it, the difference being the mass equivalent of the energy of formation of the nucleus from its constituents. The conversion of mass to energy follows Einstein's equation, $E = mc^2$, where E is the energy equivalent of a mass, m, and c is the velocity of light. This difference is known as the mass defect and is a measure of the total binding energy (and, hence, the stability) of the nucleus. This binding energy is released during the formation of a nucleus from its constituent nucleons and would have to be supplied to the nucleus to decompose it into its individual nucleon components.

In the curve illustrating the average binding energy per nucleon as a function of the nuclear mass number, the largest binding energy (highest stability) occurs near mass number 56—the mass region of the element iron. This indicates that any nucleus heavier than mass number 56 would become a more stable system by breaking into

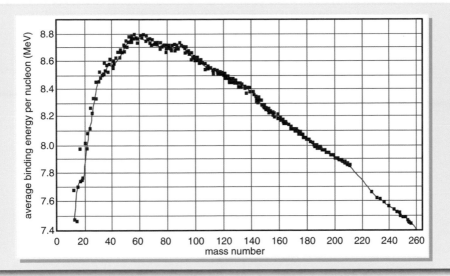

The average binding energy per nucleon as a function of the mass number, A. The line connects the odd-A points. Copyright Encyclopædia Britannica; rendering for this edition by Rosen Educational Services

lighter nuclei of higher binding energy with the difference in binding energy being released in the process. (It should be noted that nuclei lighter than mass number 56 can gain in stability by fusing to produce a heavier nucleus of greater mass defect—again, with the release of the energy equivalent of the mass difference. It is the fusion of the lightest nuclei that provides the energy released by the Sun and constitutes the basis of the hydrogen, or fusion, bomb. Efforts to harness fusion reaction for power production are being actively pursued.)

On the basis of energy considerations alone, it would seem that all matter should seek its most stable configuration, becoming nuclei of mass number near 56. However, this does not happen, because barriers to such a spontaneous conversion are provided by other factors. A good qualitative understanding of the nucleus is achieved by treating it as analogous to a uniformly charged liquid drop. The strong attractive nuclear force between pairs of nucleons is of short range and acts only between the closest neighbours. Since nucleons near the surface of the drop have fewer close neighbours than those in the interior, a surface tension is developed, and the nuclear drop assumes a spherical shape in order to minimize this surface energy. (The smallest surface area enclosing a given volume is provided by a sphere.) The protons in the nucleus exert a long-range, repulsive (Coulomb) force on each other due to their positive charge. As the number of nucleons in a nucleus increases beyond about 40, the number of protons must be diluted with an excess of neutrons to maintain relative stability.

If the nucleus is excited by some stimulus and begins to oscillate (i.e., deform from its spherical shape), the surface forces will increase and tend to restore it to a sphere, where the surface tension is at a minimum. Conversely,

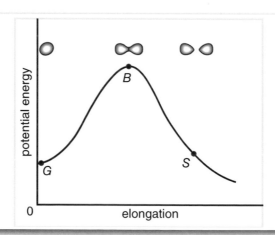

The potential energy as a function of elongation of a fissioning nucleus. G is the ground state of the nucleus; B is the top of the barrier to fission (called the saddle point); and S is the scission point. The nuclear shape at these points is shown at the top. Copyright Encyclopædia Britannica; rendering for this edition by Rosen Educational Services

the Coulomb repulsion decreases as the drop deforms and the protons are positioned farther apart. These opposing tendencies set up a barrier in the potential energy of the system.

The potential energy rises initially with elongation, because the strong, short-range nuclear force that gives rise to the surface tension increases. The Coulomb repulsion between protons decreases faster with elongation than the surface tension increases, and the two are in balance at a point that represents the height of the barrier to fission. (This point is called the "saddle point" because, in a three-dimensional view of the potential energy surface, the shape of the pass over the barrier resembles a saddle.) Beyond the saddle point, the Coulomb repulsion between the protons drives the nucleus into further elongation until at some point called the scission point, the nucleus breaks in two. Qualitatively, at least, the fission process is thus seen to be a consequence of the Coulomb repulsion between protons.

INDUCED FISSION

The height and shape of the fission barrier are dependent on the particular nucleus being considered. Fission can be induced by exciting the nucleus to an energy equal to or greater than that of the barrier. This can be done by gamma-ray excitation (photofission) or through excitation of the nucleus by the capture of a neutron, proton, or other particle (particle-induced fission). The binding energy of a particular nucleon to a nucleus will depend on—in addition to the factors considered above—the odd–even character of the nucleus. Thus, if a neutron is added to a nucleus having an odd number of neutrons, an even number of neutrons will result, and the binding energy will be greater than for the addition of a neutron that makes the total number of neutrons odd. This "pairing energy" accounts in part for the difference in behaviour of nuclides in which fission can be induced with slow (low-energy) neutrons and those that require fast (higher-energy) neutrons. Although the heavy elements are unstable with respect to fission, the reaction takes place to an appreciable extent only if sufficient energy of activation is available to surmount the fission barrier. Most nuclei that are fissionable with slow neutrons contain an odd number of neutrons (e.g., uranium-233, uranium-235, or plutonium-239), whereas most of those requiring fast neutrons (e.g., thorium-232 or uranium-238) have an even number. The addition of a neutron in the former case liberates sufficient binding energy to induce fission. In the latter case, the binding energy is less and may be insufficient to surmount the barrier and induce fission. Additional energy must then be supplied in the form of the kinetic energy of the incident neutron. (In the case of thorium-232 or uranium-238, a neutron having about 1 MeV of kinetic energy is required.)

SPONTANEOUS FISSION

The laws of quantum mechanics deal with the probability of a system such as a nucleus or atom being in any of its possible states or configurations at any given time. A fissionable system (uranium-238, for example) in its ground state (i.e., at its lowest excitation energy and with an elongation small enough that it is confined inside the fission barrier) has a small but finite probability of being in the energetically favoured configuration of two fission fragments. In effect, when this occurs, the system has penetrated the barrier by the process of quantum mechanical tunneling. This process is called spontaneous fission because it does not involve any outside influences. In the case of uranium-238, the process has a very low probability, requiring more than 10^{15} years for half of the material to be transformed (its so-called half-life) by this reaction. Moreover, the probability for spontaneous fission increases dramatically for the heaviest nuclides known and becomes the dominant mode of decay for some—those having half-lives of only fractions of a second. In fact, spontaneous fission becomes the limiting factor that may prevent the formation of still heavier (super-heavy) nuclei.

THE PHENOMENOLOGY OF FISSION

When a heavy nucleus undergoes fission, a variety of fragment pairs may be formed, depending on the distribution of neutrons and protons between the fragments. This leads to probability distribution of both mass and nuclear charge for the fragments. The probability of formation of a particular fragment is called its fission yield and is expressed as the percentage of fissions leading to it.

The separated fragments experience a large Coulomb repulsion due to their nuclear charges, and they recoil from each other with kinetic energies determined by the fragment charges and the distance between the charge centres at the time of scission. Variations in these parameters lead to a distribution of kinetic energies, even for the same mass split.

The initial velocities of the recoiling fragments are too fast for the outer (atomic) electrons of the fissioning atom to keep pace, and many of them are stripped away. Thus, the nuclear charge of the fragment is not fully neutralized by the atomic electrons, and the fission fragments fly apart as highly charged atoms. As the nucleus of the fragment adjusts from its deformed shape to a more stable configuration, the deformation energy (i.e., the energy required to deform it) is recovered and converted into internal excitation energy, and neutrons and prompt gamma rays (an energetic form of electromagnetic radiation given off nearly coincident with the fission event) may be evaporated from the moving fragment. The fast-moving, highly charged atom collides with the atoms of the medium through which it is moving, and its kinetic energy is transferred to ionization and heating of the medium as it slows down and comes to rest. The range of fission fragments in air is only a few centimetres.

During the slowing-down process, the charged atom picks up electrons from the medium and becomes neutral by the time it stops. At this stage in the sequence of events, the atom produced is called a fission product to distinguish it from the initial fission fragment formed at scission. Because a few neutrons may have been lost in the transition from fission fragment to fission product, the two may not have the same mass number. The fission product is still not a stable species but is radioactive, and it finally reaches stability by undergoing a series of beta decays, which may vary over a time scale of fractions of a second to many years. The beta emission consists of electrons and antineutrinos, often accompanied by gamma rays and X-rays.

The distributions in mass, charge, and kinetic energy of the fragments have been found to be dependent on the fissioning species as well as on the excitation energy at which the fission act occurs. Many other aspects of fission have been observed, adding to the extensive phenomenology of the process and providing an intriguing set of problems for interpretation. These include the systematics of fission cross sections (a measure of the probability for fission to occur); the variation of the number of prompt neutrons emitted as a function of the fissioning species and the particular fragment mass split; the angular distribution of the fragments with respect to the direction of the beam of particles inducing fission; the systematics of spontaneous fission half-lives; the occurrence of spontaneous fission isomers (excited states of the nucleus); the emission of light particles (hydrogen-3, helium-3, helium-4, etc.) in small but significant numbers in some fission events; the presence of delayed neutron emitters among the fission products; the time scale on which the various stages of the process take place; and the distribution of the energy release in fission among the particles and radiations produced.

A detailed discussion of all these facets of fission and how the data were obtained is not possible here, but a few of them are treated to provide some insight into this field of study and a taste of its fascination.

FISSION FRAGMENT MASS DISTRIBUTIONS

The distribution of the fragment masses formed in fission is one of the most striking features of the process. It is dependent on the mass of the fissioning nucleus and the excitation energy at which the fission occurs. At low excitation energy, the fission of such nuclides as uranium-235 or plutonium-239 is asymmetric (i.e., the fragments are formed in a two-humped probability or yield distribution favouring an unequal division in mass). As will be noted, the light group of fragment masses shifts to higher mass numbers as the mass of the fissioning nucleus increases, whereas the position of the heavy group remains nearly stationary. As the excitation energy of the fission increases, the probability for a symmetric mass split increases, while

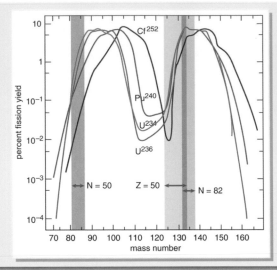

The light mass group shifts to higher masses as the mass of the fissioning nucleus increases, while the heavy group remains nearly stationary. The shaded areas show the location of the closed shells of 50 protons, 50 neutrons, and 82 neutrons.

Mass distributions (or fission-yield curves) for the thermal-neutron fission of uranium-233, uranium-235, and plutonium-239 and the spontaneous fission of californium-252. From A.C. Wahl, *Symposium on Physics and Chemistry of Fission* (1965); International Atomic Energy Agency, Vienna; rendering for this edition by Rosen Educational Services

that for asymmetric division decreases. Thus, the valley between the two peaks increases in probability (yield of formation), and at high excitations the mass distribution becomes single-humped, with the maximum yield at symmetry. Radium isotopes show interesting triple-humped mass distributions, and nuclides lighter than radium show a single-humped, symmetric mass distribution. (These nuclides, however, require a relatively high activation energy to undergo fission.) For very heavy nuclei in the region of fermium-260, the mass-yield curve becomes symmetric (single-humped) even for spontaneous fission, and the kinetic energies of the fragments are unusually high. An understanding of these mass distributions has been one of the major puzzles of fission, and a complete, theoretical interpretation is still lacking, albeit much progress has been made.

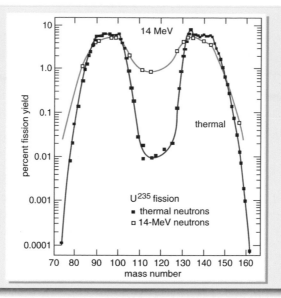

Mass distribution dependence on the energy excitation in the fission of uranium-235. At still higher energies, the curve becomes single-humped, with a maximum yield for symmetric mass splits. Copyright Encyclopædia Britannica; rendering for this edition by Rosen Educational Services

FISSION DECAY CHAINS AND CHARGE DISTRIBUTION

To maintain stability, the neutron-to-proton (*n/p*) ratio in nuclei must increase with increasing proton number. The ratio remains at unity up to the element calcium, with 20 protons. It then gradually increases until it reaches a value of about 1.5 for the heaviest elements. When a heavy nucleus fissions, a few neutrons are emitted. However, this still leaves too high an *n/p* ratio in the fission fragments to be consistent with stability for them. They undergo radioactive decay and reach stability by successive conversions of neutrons to protons with the emission of a negative electron (called a beta particle, β⁻) and an antineutrino. The mass number of the nucleus remains the same, but the nuclear charge (atomic number) increases by one, and a new element is formed for each such conversion. The successive beta decays constitute an isobaric, fission-product decay chain for each mass number. The half-lives for the decay of the radioactive species generally increase as they approach the stable isobar of the chain. (Species of the same element characterized by the same nuclear charge, Z [number of protons], but differing in their number of neutrons [and therefore in mass number A] are called isotopes. Species that have the same mass number, A, but differ in Z are known as isobars.)

For a typical mass split in the neutron-induced fission of uranium-235, the complementary fission-product masses of 93 and 141 may be formed following the emission of two neutrons from the initial fragments. The division of charge (i.e., protons) between the fragments represents an important parameter in the fission process. Thus, for the mass numbers 93 and 141, the following isobaric fission-product decay chains would be formed (the half-lives for the beta-decay processes are indicated above the arrows):

$$^{93}_{36}\text{Kr} \xrightarrow[\beta^-]{1.3\ \text{sec}} {}^{93}_{37}\text{Rb} \xrightarrow[\beta^-]{6\ \text{sec}} {}^{93}_{38}\text{Sr} \xrightarrow[\beta^-]{7.5\ \text{min}} {}^{93}_{39}\text{Y} \xrightarrow[\beta^-]{10\ \text{hr}} {}^{93}_{40}\text{Zr} \xrightarrow[]{1.5 \times 10^6\ \text{yr}} {}^{93m}_{41}\text{Nb}$$

$$\beta^- \searrow \quad {}^{93}_{41}\text{Nb (stable)} \quad \downarrow 13\ \text{yr}$$

$$^{141}_{54}\text{Xe} \xrightarrow[\beta^-]{1.7\ \text{sec}} {}^{141}_{55}\text{Cs} \xrightarrow[\beta^-]{25\ \text{sec}} {}^{141}_{56}\text{Ba} \xrightarrow[\beta^-]{18\ \text{min}} {}^{141}_{57}\text{La} \xrightarrow[\beta^-]{3.9\ \text{hr}} {}^{141}_{58}\text{Ce} \xrightarrow[\beta^-]{32.5\ \text{d}} {}^{141}_{59}\text{Pr (stable)}$$

(The left subscript on the element symbol denotes Z, while the superscript denotes A.) The 92 protons of the uranium nucleus must be conserved, and complementary fission-product pairs, such as krypton-36 with barium-56, rubidium-37 with cesium-55, or strontium-38 with xenon-54, would be possible.

The percentage of fissions in which a particular nuclide is formed as a primary fission product (i.e., as the direct descendant of an initial fragment following its de-excitation) is called the independent yield of that product. The total yield for any nuclide in the isobaric decay chain is the sum of its independent yield and the independent yields of all of its precursors in the chain. The total yield for the entire chain is called the cumulative yield for that mass number.

Extensive radiochemical investigations have suggested that the most probable charge division is one that is displaced from stability about the same distance in both chains. This empirical observation is called the equal charge displacement (ECD) hypothesis, and it has been confirmed by several physical measurements. In the preceding example the ECD would predict the most probable charges at about rubidium-37 and cesium-55. A strong shell effect modifies the ECD expectations for fragments having 50 protons. The dispersion of the charge formation probability about the most probable charge (Z_p) is rather narrow and approximately Gaussian in shape and is nearly independent of the mass split as well as of the fissioning species. The most probable charge for an isobaric chain is a useful concept in the description of the charge dispersion, and it need not have an integral value. As the energy of fission increases, the charge division tends toward maintaining the n/p ratio in the fragments the same as that in the fissioning nucleus. This is referred to as an unchanged charge distribution.

PROMPT NEUTRONS IN FISSION

The average number of neutrons emitted per fission (represented by the symbol v) varies with the fissioning nucleus. It is about 2.0 for the spontaneous fission of uranium-238 and 4.0 for that of fermium-257. In the thermal-neutron induced fission of uranium-235, $v = 2.4$.

The actual number of neutrons emitted, however, varies with each fission event, depending on the mass split. Although there is still controversy regarding the number of neutrons emitted at the instant of scission, it is generally agreed that most of the neutrons are given off by the recoiling fission fragments soon after scission occurs. The number of neutrons emitted from each fragment depends on the amount of energy the fragment possesses. The energy can be in the form of internal excitation (heat) energy or stored as energy of deformation of the fragment to be released when the fragment returns to its stable equilibrium shape.

The number of neutrons emitted per fragment graphed as a function of the fragment mass number yields a "sawtooth" neutron emission curve that is typical of many fissioning systems at low excitation energy. It is directly correlated with the fragment deformations at scission.

Delayed Neutrons in Fission

A few of the fission products have beta-decay energies that exceed the binding energy of a neutron in the daughter nucleus. This is likely to happen when the daughter nucleus contains one or two neutrons more than a closed shell of 50 or 82 neutrons, since these "extra" neutrons are more loosely bound. The beta decay of the precursor may take place to an excited state of the daughter from which a neutron is emitted. The neutron emission is "delayed" by the beta-decay half-life of the precursor. Six such delayed neutron emitters have been identified, with half-lives varying from about 0.5 to 56 seconds. The yield of the delayed neutrons is only about 1 percent of that of the prompt neutrons, but they are very important for the control of the chain reaction in a nuclear reactor.

ENERGY RELEASE IN FISSION

The total energy release in a fission event may be calculated from the difference in the rest masses of the reactants (e.g., $^{235}U + n$) and the final stable products (e.g., $^{93}Nb + {}^{141}Pr + 2n$). The energy equivalent of this mass difference is given by the Einstein relation, $E = mc^2$. The total energy release depends on the mass split, but a typical fission event would have the total energy release distributed approximately as follows for the major components in the thermal neutron-induced fission of uranium-235:

Energy component	number per fission	total energy
Kinetic energy of fission fragments	2	170 MeV
Kinetic energy of prompt neutrons	2.5	5
Binding energy from capture of prompt neutrons	2.5	~12
Prompt gamma rays	8	8

Total = 195 MeV

(The energy release from the capture of the prompt neutrons depends on how they are finally stopped, and some will escape the core of a nuclear reactor.)

This energy is released on a time scale of about 10^{-12} second and is called the prompt energy release. It is largely converted to heat within an operating reactor and is used for power generation. Also, there is a delayed release of energy from the radioactive decay of the fission products varying in half-life from fractions of a second to many years. The shorter-lived species decay in the reactor, and their energy adds to the heat generated. However, the longer-lived species remain radioactive and pose a problem in the handling and disposition of the reactor fuel elements when they need to be replaced. The antineutrinos that accompany the beta decay of the fission products are unreactive, and their kinetic energy (about 10 MeV per fission) is not recovered. Overall, about 200 MeV of energy per fission may be recovered for power applications.

FISSION THEORY

Nuclear fission is a complex process that involves the rearrangement of hundreds of nucleons in a single nucleus to produce two separate nuclei. A complete theoretical understanding of this reaction would require a detailed knowledge of the forces involved in the motion of each of the nucleons through the process. Since such knowledge is still not available, it is necessary to construct simplified models of the actual system to simulate its behaviour and gain as accurate a description as possible of the steps in the process. The successes and failures of the models in accounting for the various observations of the fission process can provide new insights into the fundamental physics governing the behaviour of real nuclei, particularly at the large nuclear deformations encountered in a nucleus undergoing fission.

The framework for understanding nuclear reactions is analogous to that for chemical reactions and involves the concept of a potential-energy surface on which the reaction occurs. The driving force for physical or chemical reactions is the tendency to lower the potential energy and increase the stability of the system. Thus, for example, a stone at the top of a hill will roll down the hill, converting its potential energy at the top to kinetic energy of motion, and will come to rest at the bottom in a more stable state of lower potential energy. The potential energy is calculated as a function of various parameters of the system being studied. In the case of fission, the potential energy may be calculated as a function of the shape of the system as it proceeds over the barrier to the scission point, and the path of lowest potential energy may be determined.

As has been pointed out, an exact calculation of the nuclear potential energy is not yet possible, and it is to approximate this calculation that various models have been constructed to simulate the real system. Some of the models were developed to address aspects of nuclear structure and spectroscopy as well as features of nuclear reactions, and they also have been employed in attempts to understand the complexity of nuclear fission. The models are based on different assumptions and approximations of the nature of the nuclear forces and the dynamics of the path to scission. No one model can account for all of the extensive phenomenology of fission, but each addresses different aspects of the process and provides a foundation for further development toward a complete theory.

Fission is perhaps best understood in comparison to the conversion of potential to kinetic energy of a stone rolling down a hill and finally coming to rest. Shutterstock.com

NUCLEAR MODELS
AND NUCLEAR FISSION

The nucleus exhibits some properties that reflect the collective motion of all its constituent nucleons as a unit, as well as other properties that are dependent on the motion and state of the individual nucleons.

The analogy of the nucleus to a drop of an incompressible liquid was first suggested by George Gamow in 1935 and later adapted to a description of nuclear reactions (by Niels Bohr [1936]; and Bohr and Fritz Kalckar [1937]) and to fission (Bohr and John A. Wheeler [1939]; and Yakov Frenkel [1939]). Bohr proposed the so-called compound nucleus description of nuclear reactions, in which the excitation energy of the system formed by the absorption of a neutron or photon, for example, is distributed among a large number of degrees of freedom of the system. This excited state persists for a long time relative to the periods of motion of nucleons across the nucleus and then decays by emission of radiation, the evaporation of neutrons or other particles, or by fission. The liquid-drop model of the nucleus accounts quite well for the general collective behaviour of nuclei and provides an understanding of the fission process on the basis of the competition between the cohesive nuclear force and the disruptive Coulomb repulsion between protons. It predicts, however, a symmetric division of mass in fission, whereas an asymmetric mass division is observed. Moreover, it does not provide an accurate description of fission barrier systematics or of the ground-state masses of nuclei. The liquid-drop model is particularly useful in describing the behaviour of highly excited nuclei, but it does not provide an accurate description for nuclei in their ground or low-lying excited states. Many versions of the liquid-drop model employing improved sets of parameters have been developed. However, investigators have found that mass asymmetry and certain other features in fission cannot be adequately described on the basis of the collective behaviour posited by such models alone.

A preference for the formation of unequal masses (i.e., an asymmetric division) was observed early in fission research, and it has remained the most puzzling feature of the process to account for. Investigators have invoked various models other than that of the liquid drop in an attempt to address this question. Dealing with the mutual interaction of all the nucleons in a nucleus has been simplified by treating it as if it were equivalent to the interaction of one particle with an average, spherical static potential field that is generated by all the other nucleons. The methods of quantum mechanics provide the solution for the motion of a nucleon in such a potential. A characteristic set of energy levels for neutrons and protons is obtained, and, analogous to the set of levels of the electrons in an atom, the levels group themselves into shells at certain so-called magic numbers of nucleons. (For both neutrons and protons, these numbers are 2, 8, 20, 28, 50, 82, and 126.) Shell closures at these nuclear numbers are marked by especially strong binding, or extra stability. This constitutes the essence of the spherical-shell model (sometimes called the independent-particle, or single-particle, model), as developed by Maria Goeppert Mayer and J. Hans D. Jensen and their colleagues (1949). It accounts well for ground-state masses and spins, and for the existence of isomeric nuclear states (excited states having measurable half-lives) that occur when nuclear levels of widely differing spins lie relatively close to each other. The agreement with observations is excellent for spherical nuclei with nucleon numbers near the magic shell numbers. The spherical-shell model, however, does not agree well with the properties of nuclei that have other nucleon numbers (e.g., the nuclei of the lanthanide and actinide elements, with nucleon numbers between the magic numbers).

In the lanthanide and actinide nuclei, the ground state is not spherical but rather deformed into a prolate spheroidal shape—that of a football or watermelon. For such nuclei, the allowed states of motion of a nucleon must be calculated in a potential having a symmetry corresponding to a spheroid rather than a sphere. This was first done by Aage Bohr, Ben R. Mottelson, and Sven G. Nilsson in 1955, and the level structure was calculated as a function of the deformation of the nucleus. A spheroid has three axes of symmetry, and it can rotate in space as a unit about any one of them. The rotation can occur independent of the internal state of excitation of the individual nucleons. Various modes of vibration of the spheroid also may take place. Because this deformed shell model has components of both the independent-particle motion and the collective motion of the nucleus as a whole (i.e., rotations and vibrations), it is sometimes referred to as the unified model.

In Aage Bohr's application of the unified model to the fission process, the sequence of potential-energy surfaces for the excited states of the system are considered to be functions of a deformation parameter (i.e., elongation) characterizing the motion toward fission and evaluated at the saddle point. As the system passes over the saddle point, most of its excitation energy is used up in deforming the nucleus, and the system remains "cold" (i.e., it manifests little excitation, or heat, energy). Thus, only the low-lying excited states are available to the system. The spin and parity of the particular state (or channel) in which the system exists as it passes over the saddle point are then expected to determine the fission properties. In this channel (or transition-state) analysis of fission, a number of characteristics of the process are qualitatively accounted for. Hence, fission thresholds would depend on the spin and parity of the compound nuclear state, the fission fragment angular distribution would be governed by the collective rotational angular momentum of the state, and asymmetry in the mass distribution would result from passage over the barrier in a state of negative parity (which does not possess reflection symmetry). This model gives a good qualitative interpretation of many fission phenomena, but it must assume that at least some of the properties of the transition state at the saddle point are not altered by dynamical considerations in the descent of the system to the scission point. It is the only model that provides a satisfactory interpretation of the angular distributions of fission fragments, and it has attractive features that must be included in any complete theory of fission.

The first application of the spherical-shell model to fission was the recognition that the positions of the peaks in the fission mass distribution correlated fairly well with the magic numbers and suggested a qualitative interpretation of the asymmetric mass division. Thus, a preference for the formation of nuclei with neutron numbers close to 82 would favour the formation of nuclides near the peak in the heavy group and would thus determine the mass split for the fissioning system. Some extra stability for nuclear configurations of 50 protons would also be expected, but this is not particularly evident. In fact, the so-called doubly magic nucleus tin-132, with 50 protons and 82 neutrons, has a rather low yield in low-energy fission.

A more quantitative application of the spherical-shell model to fission was undertaken by Peter Fong in the United States in 1956. He related the probability of formation of a given pair of fragments to the available density of states for that pair of fragments at the scission point in a statistical-model approach. A model of this sort predicts that the system, in its random motions, will experience all possible configurations and so will have a greater probability of being in the region where the greatest number of such configurations (or states) is concentrated. The model assumes that the potential energy at the saddle point is essentially all converted to excitation energy and that a statistical equilibrium among all possible states is established at the scission point. The extra binding energy for closed-shell nuclei leads to a higher density of states at a given excitation energy than is present for other nuclei and, hence, leads to a higher probability of formation. An asymmetric mass distribution in good agreement with that observed for the neutron-induced fission of uranium-235 is obtained. Moreover, the changes in the mass distribution with an increased excitation energy of fission (e.g., an increase in the probability of symmetric fission relative to asymmetric fission) are accounted for by the decrease in importance of the shell effects as the excitation energy increases. Other features of the fission process also are qualitatively explained. However, extensive changes in the parameters of the model are required to obtain agreement with experiments for other fissionable nuclides. Then, too, there are fundamental problems concerning the validity of some of the basic assumptions of the model.

The fundamental question as to the validity of models that evaluate the properties of the system at the scission point (the so-called scission-point models of fission) is whether the system remains long enough at this point on the steep decline of the potential-energy surface for a quasi-equilibrium condition to be established. There is some evidence that such a condition may indeed prevail, but it is not clearly established. Nonetheless, such models have proved quite useful in interpreting observations of mass, charge, and kinetic energy distributions, as well as of neutron emission dependence on fragment mass. It seems quite likely that the fragment shell structure plays a significant role in determining the course of the fission process.

Although the single-particle models provide a good description of various aspects of nuclear structure, they are not successful in accounting for the energy of deformation

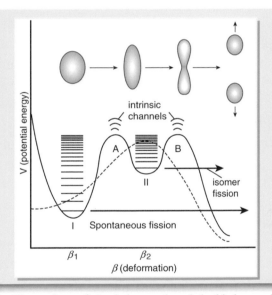

Schematic illustrations of single-humped and double-humped fission barriers. The former are represented by the dashed line and the latter by the continuous line. Intrinsic excitations in the first and second wells at deformations β_1 and β_2 are designated class I and class II states, respectively. Intrinsic channels at the two barriers also are illustrated. The transition in the shape of the nucleus as a function of deformation is schematically represented in the upper part of the figure. Spontaneous fission of the ground state and isomeric state occurs from the lowest energy class I and class II states, respectively. Copyright Encyclopædia Britannica; rendering for this edition by Rosen Educational Services

of nuclei (i.e., surface energy), particularly at the large deformations encountered in the fission process. A major breakthrough occurred when a hybrid model incorporating shell effects as a correction to the potential energy of the liquid-drop model was proposed by the Russian physicist V.M. Strutinskii in 1967. This approach retains the dominant collective surface and Coulomb effects while adding shell and pairing corrections that depend on deformation. Shell corrections of several million electron volts are calculated, and these can have a significant effect on a liquid-drop barrier of about 5 MeV. The nucleon numbers at which the shells appear depend on the deformation and may differ from the spherical model magic numbers. In the vicinity of the fission barrier, the shells introduce structure in the liquid-drop potential-energy curve. The relative heights and widths of the two peaks vary with the mass and charge of the fissioning system.

The double-humped barrier provides a satisfactory explanation for a number of puzzling observations in fission. The existence of short-lived, spontaneous fission isomers, for example, is understood as the consequence of the population of states in the second well (class II). These isomers have a much smaller barrier to penetrate and so exhibit a much shorter spontaneous fission half-life. The change in shape associated with these states, as compared to class I states, also hinders a rapid return to the ground state by gamma emission. (Class II states are also called shape isomers.) The systematics of neutron-induced fission cross sections and structure in some fission-fragment angular distributions also find an interpretation in the implications of the double-humped barrier.

The Strutinskii procedure provided a strong stimulus for calculations of the potential-energy surfaces appropriate to fissioning systems, because it provided a consistent and useful prescription for treating both the macroscopic (liquid-drop) and microscopic (single-particle) effects in deformed nuclei. Many calculations of the potential-energy surface employing different model potentials and parameters have been carried out as functions of the shapes of the system. The work of the American nuclear physicists W.J. Swiatecki, James R. Nix, and their collaborators has been particularly noteworthy in such studies, which also include some attempts to treat the dynamical evolution of the fission process.

Calculations for the actinide elements indicate that, at deformations corresponding to the second barrier, the potential energy for asymmetric mass splits is lower than that for symmetric ones. Hence, the former are favoured at that stage of the process. For larger deformations, however, a single potential does not represent the incipient formation of two fragments very well. In fact, a discontinuity occurs at the scission point, and the results of the calculation depend on whether the scission configuration is treated as one nucleus or as two separate nuclei.

A two-centre potential may also be used to represent the nature of the forces at work in a fissioning nucleus. In such a model, the potential energy surfaces are represented by two overlapping spheres or spheroids. It is equivalent to a one-centre potential when there is a complete overlap at small deformations, and it has the correct asymptotic behaviour as the nascent fragments separate. This approach indicates a preformation of the final shell structure of the fragments early in the process.

Although the validity of the assumptions inherent in scission-point models may be in question, the results obtained with them are in excellent agreement with observation. Representative of such a model is the Argonne Scission-Point model, which uses a macroscopic-microscopic calculation with deformed fragment shell and pairing corrections to determine the potential energy of a system of two nearly touching spheroids and which includes their interaction in terms of a neck connecting them. Models of this kind provide a simple approach to a highly quantitative and detailed study of the dependence of the probability of formation of a given fragment pair on the neutron and proton number and on the deformation in each fragment. They account very well for the mass, charge, and kinetic-energy distributions and the neutron-emission dependence on mass number for a broad range of fissioning nuclei. The scission-point models, however, do not address questions of fission probability or the angular distributions of the fragments. As the fission-excitation energy increases, the shell correction diminishes and the macroscopic (liquid-drop) behaviour dominates.

Nuclides in the region of fermium-264 have been observed to undergo symmetric fission with unusually high fragment kinetic energies. This appears to be the consequence of the stability for the magic number configurations of 50 protons and 82 neutrons. The formation of two doubly magic fragments of tin-132 is strongly favoured energetically, whereas the formation of only one such fragment in the low-energy fission of uranium or plutonium isotopes is not. The fragments of tin-132 are spherical rather than deformed, and a more compact configuration at the scission point (with the charge centres closer together) leads to higher fragment kinetic energies.

It is evident that shell effects, both in the fissioning system at the saddle point and in the deformed fragments near the scission point, are important in interpreting many of the features of the fission process. The stage of the process at which the various fragment distributions are determined is, however, not clearly established. All the components of a reasonable understanding of fission seem to be at hand, but they have yet to be synthesized into a complete, dynamic theory.

Considerations of the dynamics of the descent of the system on the potential-energy surface from the saddle point to the scission point involve two extreme points of view. An "adiabatic" approximation may be valid if the collective motion of the system is considered to be so slow or the coupling between the collective and internal single-particle degrees of freedom (i.e., between macroscopic and microscopic behaviour) so weak that the fast single-particle motions can readily adjust to the changes in shape of the fissioning nucleus as it progresses toward scission. In this case, the changes in the system take place without the gain or loss of heat energy. The decrease in potential energy between the saddle and scission points will then appear primarily in the collective degrees of freedom at scission and be associated with the kinetic energy of the relative motion of the nascent fragments (referred to as pre-scission kinetic energy). Yet, if the collective motion toward scission is relatively fast or the coupling-to-particle motion stronger, collective energy can be transformed into internal excitation (heat) energy of the nucleons. (This is analogous to heating in the motion of a viscous fluid.) In such a "non-adiabatic" process the mixing among the single-particle degrees of freedom may be sufficiently complete that a statistical model may be applicable at the scission point. Either extreme represents an approximation of complex behaviour, and some experimental evidence in support of either interpretation may be advanced. As in most such instances in nature, the truth probably lies somewhere between the extremes, with both playing some role in the fission process.

FISSION CHAIN REACTIONS AND THEIR CONTROL

The emission of several neutrons in the fission process leads to the possibility of a chain reaction if at least one of the fission neutrons induces fission in another fissile nucleus, which in turn fissions and emits neutrons to continue the chain. If more than one neutron is effective in inducing fission in other nuclei, the chain multiplies more rapidly. The condition for a chain reaction is usually expressed in terms of a multiplication factor, k, which is defined as the ratio of the number of fissions produced in one step (or neutron generation) in the chain to the number of fissions in the preceding generation. If k is less than unity, a chain reaction cannot be sustained. If $k = 1$, a steady-state chain reaction can be maintained; and if k is greater than 1, the number of fissions increases at each step, resulting in a divergent chain reaction. The term *critical assembly* is applied to a configuration of fissionable material for which $k = 1$; if $k > 1$, the assembly is said to be supercritical. A critical assembly might consist of the fissile material in the form of a metal or oxide, a moderator to slow the fission neutrons, and a reflector to scatter neutrons that would otherwise be lost back into the assembly core.

In a fission bomb it is desirable to have k as large as possible and the time between steps in the chain as short as possible so that many fissions occur and a large amount of energy is generated within a brief period ($\sim 10^{-7}$ second) to produce a devastating explosion. If one kilogram of uranium-235 were to fission, the energy released would be equivalent to the explosion of 20,000 tons of the chemical explosive trinitrotoluene (TNT). In a controlled nuclear reactor, k is kept equal to unity for steady-state operation.

A practical reactor, however, must be designed with k somewhat greater than unity. This permits power levels to be increased if desired, as well as allowing for the following: the gradual loss of fuel by the fission process, the buildup of "poisons" among the fission products being formed that absorb neutrons and lower the k value, and the use of some of the neutrons produced for research studies or the preparation of radioactive species for various applications. The value of k is controlled during the operation of a reactor by the positioning of movable rods made of a material that readily absorbs neutrons (i.e., one with a high neutron-capture cross section), such as boron, cadmium, or hafnium. The delayed-neutron emitters among the fission products increase the time between successive neutron generations in the chain reaction and make the control of the reaction easier to accomplish by the mechanical movement of the control rods.

Fission reactors can be classified by the energy of the neutrons that propagate the chain reaction. The most common type, called a thermal reactor, operates with thermal neutrons (those having the same energy distribution as gas molecules at ordinary room temperatures). In such a reactor the fission neutrons produced (with an average kinetic energy of more than 1 MeV) must be slowed down to thermal energy by scattering from a moderator, usually consisting of ordinary water, heavy water (D_2O), or graphite. In another type termed an intermediate reactor the chain reaction is maintained by neutrons of intermediate energy, and a beryllium moderator may be used. In a fast reactor fast fission neutrons maintain the chain reaction, and no moderator is needed. All reactor types require a coolant to remove the heat generated; water, a gas, or a liquid metal may be used for this purpose, depending on the design needs.

USES OF FISSION REACTORS
AND FISSION PRODUCTS

A nuclear reactor is essentially a furnace used to produce steam or hot gases that can provide heat directly or drive turbines to generate electricity. Nuclear reactors are employed for commercial electric-power generation throughout much of the world and as a power source for propelling submarines and certain kinds of surface vessels. Another important use for reactors is the utilization of their high neutron fluxes for studying the structure and properties of materials and for producing a broad range of radionuclides, which, along with a number of fission products, have found many different applications. Heat generated by radioactive decay can be converted into electricity through the thermoelectric effect in semiconductor materials and thereby produce what is termed an atomic battery. When powered by either a long-lived, beta-emitting fission product (e.g., strontium-90, calcium-144, or promethium-147) or one that emits alpha particles (plutonium-238 or curium-244), these batteries are a particularly useful source of energy for cardiac pacemakers and for instruments employed in remote, unmanned facilities, such as those in outer space, the polar regions of Earth, or the open seas. There are many practical uses for other radionuclides.

CHAPTER 7
NUCLEAR FUSION

Nuclear fusion is the process by which nuclear reactions between light elements form heavier elements (up to iron). In cases where the interacting nuclei belong to elements with low atomic numbers (e.g., hydrogen [atomic number 1] or its isotopes deuterium and tritium), substantial amounts of energy are released. The vast energy potential of nuclear fusion was first exploited in thermonuclear weapons, or hydrogen bombs, which were developed in the decade immediately following World War II. Meanwhile, the potential peaceful applications of nuclear fusion, especially in view of the essentially limitless supply of fusion fuel on Earth, have encouraged an immense effort to harness this process for the production of power.

THE FUSION REACTION

Fusion reactions constitute the fundamental energy source of stars, including the Sun. The evolution of stars can be viewed as a passage through various stages as thermonuclear reactions and nucleosynthesis cause compositional changes over long time spans. Hydrogen (H) "burning" initiates the fusion energy source of stars and leads to the formation of helium (He). Generation of fusion energy for practical use also relies on fusion reactions between the lightest elements that burn to form helium. In fact, the heavy isotopes of hydrogen—deuterium (D) and tritium (T)—react more efficiently with each other, and, when they do undergo fusion, they yield more energy per reaction than do two hydrogen nuclei. (The hydrogen nucleus consists of a single proton. The deuterium nucleus has one proton and one neutron, while tritium has one proton and two neutrons.)

Fusion reactions between light elements, like fission reactions that split heavy elements, release energy because of a key feature of nuclear matter called the binding energy, which can be released through fusion or fission. The binding energy of the nucleus is a measure of the efficiency with which its constituent nucleons are bound together. Take, for example, an element with Z protons and N neutrons in its nucleus. The element's atomic weight A is $Z + N$, and its atomic number is Z. The binding energy B is the energy associated with the mass difference between the Z protons and N neutrons considered separately and the nucleons bound together $(Z + N)$ in a nucleus of mass M. The formula is

$$B = (Zm_p + Nm_n - M)c^2,$$

where m_p and m_n are the proton and neutron masses and c is the speed of light. It has been determined experimentally that the binding energy per nucleon is a maximum of about 1.4×10^{-12} joule at an atomic mass number of approximately 60—that is, approximately the atomic mass number of iron. Accordingly, the fusion of elements lighter than iron or the splitting of heavier ones generally leads to a net release of energy.

Two Types of Fusion Reactions

Fusion reactions are of two basic types: (1) those that preserve the number of protons and neutrons and (2) those that involve a conversion between protons and neutrons. Reactions of the first type are most important for practical fusion energy production, whereas those of the second type are crucial to the initiation of star burning. An arbitrary element is indicated by the notation $^A_Z X$, where Z is the charge of the nucleus and A is the atomic weight. An important fusion reaction for practical energy generation is that between deuterium and tritium (the D-T fusion reaction). It produces helium (He) and a neutron (n) and is written

$$D + T \to He + n.$$

To the left of the arrow (before the reaction) there are two protons and three neutrons. The same is true on the right.

The other reaction, that which initiates star burning, involves the fusion of two hydrogen nuclei to form deuterium (the H-H fusion reaction):

$$H + H \to D + \beta^+ + \nu,$$

where β^+ represents a positron and ν stands for a neutrino. Before the reaction there are two hydrogen nuclei (that is, two protons). Afterward there are one proton and one neutron (bound together as the nucleus of deuterium) plus a positron and a neutrino (produced as a consequence of the conversion of one proton to a neutron).

Both of these fusion reactions are exoergic and so yield energy. The German-born physicist Hans Bethe proposed in the 1930s that the H-H fusion reaction could occur with a net release of energy and provide, along with subsequent reactions, the fundamental energy source sustaining the stars. However, practical energy generation requires the D-T reaction for two reasons: first, the rate of reactions between deuterium and tritium is much higher than that between protons; second, the net energy release from the D-T reaction is 40 times greater than that from the H-H reaction.

ENERGY RELEASED IN FUSION REACTIONS

Energy is released in a nuclear reaction if the total mass of the resultant particles is less than the mass of the initial reactants. To illustrate, suppose two nuclei, labeled X and a, react to form two other nuclei, Y and b, denoted

$$X + a \rightarrow Y + b.$$

The particles a and b are often nucleons, either protons or neutrons, but in general can be any nuclei. Assuming that none of the particles is internally excited (i.e., each is in its ground state), the energy quantity called the Q-value for this reaction is defined as

$$Q = (m_x + m_a - m_b - m_y)c^2,$$

where the m-letters refer to the mass of each particle and c is the speed of light. When the energy value Q is positive, the reaction is exoergic; when Q is negative, the reaction is endoergic (i.e., absorbs energy). When both the total proton number and the total neutron number are preserved before and after the reaction (as in D-T reactions), then the Q-value can be expressed in terms of the binding energy B of each particle as

$$Q = B_y + B_b - B_x - B_a.$$

The D-T fusion reaction has a positive Q-value of 2.8×10^{-12} joule. The H-H fusion reaction is also exoergic, with a Q-value of 6.7×10^{-14} joule. To develop a sense for these figures, one might consider that one metric ton (1,000 kg, or almost 2,205 pounds) of deuterium would contain roughly 3×10^{32} atoms. If one ton of deuterium were to be consumed through the fusion reaction with tritium, the energy released would be 8.4×10^{20} joules. This can be compared with the energy content of one ton of coal—namely, 2.9×10^{10} joules. In other words, one ton of deuterium has the energy equivalent of approximately 29 billion tons of coal.

Rate and Yield of Fusion Reactions

The energy yield of a reaction between nuclei and the rate of such reactions are both important. These quantities have a profound influence in scientific areas such as nuclear astrophysics and the potential for nuclear production of electrical energy.

When a particle of one type passes through a collection of particles of the same or different type, there is a measurable chance that the particles will interact. The particles may interact in many ways, such as simply scattering, which means that they change direction and exchange energy, or they may undergo a nuclear fusion reaction. The measure of the likelihood that particles will interact is called the cross section, and the magnitude of the cross section depends on the type of interaction and the state and energy of the particles. The product of the cross section and the atomic density of the target particle is called the macroscopic cross section. The inverse of the macroscopic cross section is particularly noteworthy as it gives the mean distance an incident particle will travel before interacting with a target particle. This inverse measure is called the mean free path. Cross sections are measured by producing a beam of one particle at a given energy, allowing the beam to interact with a (usually thin) target made of the same or a different material, and measuring deflections or reaction products. In this way it is possible to determine the relative likelihood of one type of fusion reaction versus another, as well as the optimal conditions for a particular reaction.

The cross sections of fusion reactions can be measured experimentally or calculated theoretically, and they have been determined for many reactions over a wide range of particle energies. They are well known for practical fusion energy applications and are reasonably well known, though with gaps, for stellar evolution. Fusion reactions between nuclei, each with a positive charge of one or more, are the most important for both practical applications and the nucleosynthesis of the light elements in the burning stages of stars. Yet, it is well known that two positively charged nuclei repel each other electrostatically (i.e., they experience a repulsive force inversely proportional to the square of the distance separating them). This repulsion is called the Coulomb barrier. It is highly unlikely that two positive nuclei will approach each other closely enough to undergo a fusion reaction unless they have sufficient energy to overcome the Coulomb barrier. As a result, the cross section for fusion reactions between charged particles is small unless the energy of the particles is high, at least 10^4 electron volts ($1 \, eV \cong 1.602 \times 10^{-19}$ joule) and often more than 10^5 or 10^6 eV. This explains why the centre of a star must be hot for the fuel to burn and why fuel for practical fusion energy systems must be heated to at least 50,000,000 kelvins (K; 90,000,000 °F). Only then will a reasonable fusion reaction rate and power output be achieved.

The phenomenon of the Coulomb barrier also explains a fundamental difference between energy generation by nuclear fusion and nuclear fission. While fission of heavy elements can be induced by either protons or neutrons, generation of fission energy for practical applications is dependent on neutrons to induce fission reactions in uranium or plutonium. Having no electric charge, the neutron is free to enter the nucleus even if its energy corresponds to room temperature. Fusion energy, relying as it does on the fusion reaction between light nuclei, occurs only when the particles are sufficiently energetic to overcome the Coulomb repulsive force. This requires the production and heating of the gaseous reactants to the high temperature state known as the plasma state.

THE PLASMA STATE

Typically, a plasma is a gas that has had some substantial portion of its constituent atoms or molecules ionized by the dissociation of one or more of their electrons. These free electrons enable plasmas to conduct electric charges, and a plasma is the only state of matter in which thermonuclear reactions can occur in a self-sustaining manner. Astrophysics and magnetic fusion research, among other

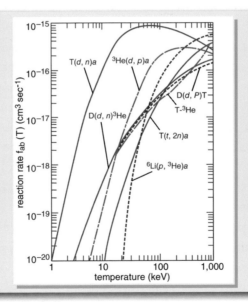

The reaction rate as a function of plasma temperature, expressed in kiloelectron volts (keV; 1 keV is equivalent to a temperature of 11,000,000 K). The rate of reaction between deuterium and tritium is seen to be higher than all others and is substantial, even at temperatures in the 5-to-10-keV range. Copyright Encyclopædia Britannica; rendering for this edition by Rosen Educational Services

fields, require extensive knowledge of how gases behave in the plasma state. The stars, the solar wind, and much of interstellar space are examples where the matter present is in the plasma state. Very high-temperature plasmas are fully ionized gases, which means that the ratio of neutral gas atoms to charged particles is small. For example, the ionization energy of hydrogen is 13.6 eV, while the average energy of a hydrogen ion in a plasma at 50,000,000 K is 6,462 eV. Thus, essentially all of the hydrogen in this plasma would be ionized.

A reaction-rate parameter more appropriate to the plasma state is obtained by accounting for the fact that the particles in a plasma, as in any gas, have a distribution of energies. That is to say, not all particles have the same energy. In simple plasmas this energy distribution is given by the Maxwell-Boltzmann distribution law, and the temperature of the gas or plasma is, within a proportionality constant, two-thirds of the average particle energy (i.e., the relationship between the average energy $\overline{E}$ and temperature T is $\overline{E} = 3kT/2$, where k is the Boltzmann constant, 8.62×10^{-5} eV per kelvin). The intensity of nuclear fusion reactions in a plasma is derived by averaging the product of the particles' speed and their cross sections over a distribution of speeds corresponding to a Maxwell-Boltzmann distribution. The cross section for the reaction depends on the energy or speed of the particles. The averaging process yields a function for a given reaction that depends only on the temperature and can be denoted $f(T)$. The rate of energy released (i.e., the power released) in a reaction between two species, a and b, is $P_{ab} = n_a n_b f_{ab}(T) U_{ab}$, where n_a and n_b are the density of species a and b in the plasma, respectively, and U_{ab} is the energy released each time a and b undergo a fusion reaction. The parameter P_{ab} properly takes into account both the rate of a given reaction and the energy yield per reaction.

FUSION REACTIONS IN STARS

Fusion reactions are the primary energy source of stars and the mechanism for the nucleosynthesis of the light elements. In the late 1930s Hans Bethe first recognized that the fusion of hydrogen nuclei to form deuterium is exoergic (i.e., there is a net release of energy) and, together with subsequent nuclear reactions, leads to the synthesis of helium. The formation of helium is the main source of energy emitted by normal stars, such as the Sun, where the burning-core plasma has a temperature of less than 15,000,000 K. However, because the gas from which a star is formed often contains some heavier elements, notably carbon (C) and nitrogen (N), it is important to include nuclear reactions between protons and these nuclei. The reaction chain between protons that ultimately leads to helium is the proton-proton cycle. When protons also induce the burning of carbon and nitrogen, the CN cycle must be considered. And when oxygen (O) is included, still another alternative scheme, the CNO bi-cycle, must be accounted for.

The proton-proton nuclear fusion cycle in a star containing only hydrogen begins with the reaction $H + H \rightarrow D + \beta^+ + \nu$; $Q = 1.44$ MeV, where the Q-value assumes annihilation of the positron by an electron. The deuterium could react with other deuterium nuclei, but, because there is so much hydrogen, the D/H ratio is held to very low values, typically 10^{-18}. Thus, the next step is $H + D \rightarrow {}^3He + \gamma$; $Q = 5.49$ MeV, where γ indicates that gamma rays carry off some of the energy yield. The burning of the helium-3 isotope then gives rise to ordinary helium and hydrogen via the last step in the chain: ${}^3He + {}^3He \rightarrow {}^4He + 2(H)$; $Q = 12.86$ MeV.

At equilibrium, helium-3 burns predominantly by reactions with itself because its reaction rate with hydrogen is small, while burning with deuterium is negligible because of the very low deuterium concentration. Once helium-4 builds up, reactions with helium-3 can lead to the production of still-heavier elements, including beryllium-7, beryllium-8, lithium-7, and boron-8, if the temperature is greater than about 10,000,000 K.

The stages of stellar evolution are the result of compositional changes over very long periods. The size of a star, on the other hand, is determined by a balance between the pressure exerted by the hot plasma and the gravitational

A star's size is determined by the balance between the pressure put forth by the searing plasma and the gravitational force of its mass. NASA, ESA, and H. Bond (STScI)

force of the star's mass. The energy of the burning core is transported toward the surface of the star, where it is radiated at an effective temperature. The effective temperature of the Sun's surface is about 6,000 K, and significant amounts of radiation in the visible and infrared wavelength ranges are emitted.

FUSION REACTIONS FOR CONTROLLED POWER GENERATION

Reactions between deuterium and tritium are the most important fusion reactions for controlled power generation because the cross sections for their occurrence are high, the practical plasma temperatures required for net energy release are moderate, and the energy yield of the reactions are high—17.58 MeV for the basic D-T fusion reaction.

It should be noted that any plasma containing deuterium automatically produces some tritium and helium-3 from reactions of deuterium with other deuterium ions. Other fusion reactions involving elements with an atomic number above 2 can be used, but only with much greater difficulty. This is because the Coulomb barrier increases with increasing charge of the nuclei, leading to the requirement that the plasma temperature exceed 1,000,000,000 K if a significant rate is to be achieved. Some of the more interesting reactions are:

(1) $H + {}^{11}B \rightarrow 3({}^4He)$; $Q = 8.68$ MeV;

(2) $H + {}^6Li \rightarrow {}^3He + {}^4He$; $Q = 4.023$ MeV;

(3) ${}^3He + {}^6Li \rightarrow H + 2({}^4He)$; $Q = 16.88$ MeV; and

(4) ${}^3He + {}^6Li \rightarrow D + {}^7Be$; $Q = 0.113$ MeV.

Reaction (2) converts lithium-6 to helium-3 and ordinary helium. Interestingly, if reaction (2) is followed by reaction (3), then a proton will again be produced and be available to induce reaction (2), thereby propagating the process. Unfortunately, it appears that reaction (4) is 10 times more likely to occur than reaction (3).

METHODS OF ACHIEVING FUSION ENERGY

Practical efforts to harness fusion energy involve two basic approaches to containing a high-temperature plasma of elements that undergo nuclear fusion reactions: magnetic confinement and inertial confinement. A much less likely but nevertheless interesting approach is based on fusion catalyzed by muons. Research on this topic is of intrinsic interest in nuclear physics.

MAGNETIC CONFINEMENT

In magnetic confinement the particles and energy of a hot plasma are held in place using magnetic fields. A charged particle in a magnetic field experiences a Lorentz force that is proportional to the product of the particle's velocity and the magnetic field. This force causes electrons and ions to spiral about the direction of the magnetic line of force, thereby confining the particles. When the topology of the magnetic field yields an effective magnetic well and the pressure balance between the plasma and the field is stable, the plasma can be confined away from material boundaries. Heat and particles are transported both along and across the field, but energy losses can be prevented in two ways. The first is to increase the strength of the magnetic field at two locations along the field line. Charged particles contained between these points can be made to reflect back and forth, an effect called magnetic mirroring. In a basically

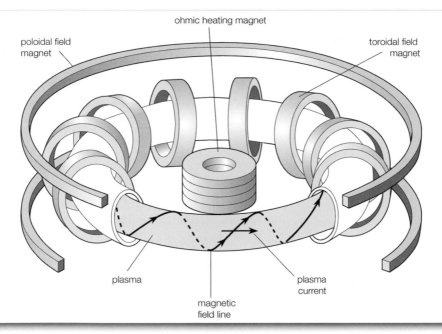

ohmic heating magnet

poloidal field
magnet

toroidal field
magnet

plasma

plasma
current

magnetic
field line

Tokamak magnetic confinement. Encyclopædia Britannica, Inc.

straight system with a region of intensified magnetic field
at each end, particles can still escape through the ends due
to scattering between particles as they approach the mirroring points. Such end losses can be avoided altogether
by creating a magnetic field in the topology of a torus (i.e.,
configuration of a doughnut or inner tube).

External magnets can be arranged to create a magnetic
field topology for stable plasma confinement, or they can
be used in conjunction with magnetic fields generated
by currents induced to flow in the plasma itself. The late
1960s witnessed a major advance by the Soviet Union in
harnessing fusion reactions for practical energy production. Soviet scientists achieved a high plasma temperature
(about 3,000,000 K), along with other physical parameters, in a machine referred to as a tokamak. A tokamak
is a toroidal magnetic confinement system in which the

plasma is kept stable both by an externally generated, doughnut-shaped magnetic field and by electric currents flowing within the plasma. Since the late 1960s the tokamak has been the major focus of magnetic fusion research worldwide, though other approaches such as the stellarator, the compact torus, and the reversed field pinch (RFP) have also been pursued. In these approaches, the magnetic field lines follow a helical, or screwlike, path as the lines of magnetic force proceed around the torus. In the tokamak the pitch of the helix is weak, so the field lines wind loosely around the poloidal direction (through the central hole) of the torus. In contrast, RFP field lines wind much tighter, wrapping many times in the poloidal direction before completing one loop in the toroidal direction (around the central hole).

Magnetically confined plasma must be heated to temperatures at which nuclear fusion is vigorous, typically greater than 75,000,000 K (equivalent to an energy of 4,400 eV). This can be achieved by coupling radio-frequency waves or microwaves to the plasma particles, by injecting energetic beams of neutral atoms that become ionized and heat the plasma, by magnetically compressing the plasma, or by the ohmic heating (also known as Joule heating) that occurs when an electric current passes through the plasma.

Employing the tokamak concept, scientists and engineers in the United States, Europe, and Japan began in the mid-1980s to use large experimental tokamak devices to attain conditions of temperature, density, and energy confinement that now match those necessary for practical fusion power generation. The machines employed to achieve these results include the Joint European Torus (JET) of the European Union, the Japanese Tokamak-60 (JT-60), and, until 1997, the Tokamak Fusion Test Reactor

(TFTR) in the United States. Indeed, in both the TFTR and the JET devices, experiments using deuterium and tritium produced more than 10 megawatts of fusion power and essentially energy breakeven conditions in the plasma itself. Plasma conditions approaching those achieved in tokamaks were also achieved in large stellarator machines in Germany and Japan during the 1990s.

INERTIAL CONFINEMENT FUSION (ICF)

In this approach, a fuel mass is compressed rapidly to densities 1,000 to 10,000 times greater than normal by generating a pressure as high as 10^{17} pascals (10^{12} atmospheres) for periods as short as a nanosecond (10^{-9} second). Near the end of this time period, the implosion speed exceeds about 3×10^{5} metres per second. At maximum compression of the fuel, which is now in a cool plasma state, the energy in converging shock waves is sufficient to heat the very centre of the fuel to temperatures high enough to induce fusion reactions (greater than an equivalent energy of about 4,400 eV). If the mass of this highly compressed fuel material is large enough, energy will be generated through fusion reactions before this hot plasma ball disassembles. Under proper conditions, much more energy can be released than is required to compress and shock heat the fuel to thermonuclear burning conditions.

The physical processes in ICF bear a relationship to those in thermonuclear weapons and in star formation—namely, collapse, compression heating, and the onset of nuclear fusion. The situation in star formation differs in one respect: gravity is the cause of the collapse, and a collapsed star begins to expand again due to heat from exoergic nuclear fusion reactions. The expansion is ultimately arrested by the gravitational force associated with the enormous mass of the star, at which point a state of equilibrium in both size and temperature is achieved. In contrast, the fuel in a thermonuclear weapon or ICF completely disassembles. In the ideal ICF case, however, this does not occur until about 30 percent of the fusion fuel has burned.

Over the decades, very significant progress has been made in developing the technology and systems for high-energy, short-time-pulse drivers that are necessary to

When scientists at the National Ignition Facility at the Lawrence Livermore National Laboratory in Livermore, California, aimed 192 lasers at a hydrogen-filled target (hohlraum), a very symmetrical compression of simulated fuel capsules resulted, which will allow for the necessary fusion ignition and energy gain for ignition experiments. Bloomberg via Getty Images

implode the fusion fuel. The most common driver is a high-power laser, though particle accelerators capable of producing beams of high-energy ions are also used. Lasers that produce more than 100,000 joules in pulses of about one nanosecond are now used in experiments, and the power available in short bursts exceeds 10^{14} watts.

Two lasers capable of delivering more than 1,000,000 joules in equally short bursts, generating a power level on the fusion targets in excess of 5×10^{14} watts, are operational. One facility is the Laser MegaJoule in Bordeaux, France. The other is the National Ignition Facility at the Lawrence Livermore National Laboratory in Livermore, Calif., U.S.

MUON-CATALYZED FUSION

The need in traditional schemes of nuclear fusion to confine very high-temperature plasmas has led some researchers to explore alternatives that would permit fusion reactants to approach each other more closely at much lower temperatures. One method involves substituting muons (μ) for the electrons that ordinarily surround the nucleus of a fuel atom. Muons are negatively charged subatomic particles similar to electrons, except that their mass is a little more than 200 times the electron mass and they are unstable, having a half-life of about 2.2×10^{-6} second. In fact, fusion has been observed in liquid and gas mixtures of deuterium and tritium at cryogenic temperatures when muons were injected into the mixture.

Muon-catalyzed fusion is the name given to the process of achieving fusion reactions by causing a deuteron (deuterium nucleus, D^+), a triton (tritium nucleus, T^+), and a muon to form what is called a muonic molecule. Once a muonic molecule is formed, the rate of fusion reactions is approximately 3×10^{-8} second. However, the formation of a muonic molecule is complex, involving a series of atomic, molecular, and nuclear processes.

In schematic terms, when a muon enters a mixture of deuterium and tritium, the muon is first captured by one of the two hydrogen isotopes in the mixture, forming either atomic D^+-μ or T^+-μ, with the atom now in an excited state. The excited atom relaxes to the ground state through a cascade collision process, in which the muon may be transferred from a deuteron to a triton or vice versa. More important, it is also possible that a muonic molecule (D^+-μ-T^+) will be formed. Although a much rarer reaction, once a muonic molecule does form, fusion takes place almost immediately, releasing the muon in the mixture to be captured again by a deuterium or tritium nucleus and allowing the process to continue. In this sense the muon acts as a catalyst for fusion reactions within the mixture. The key to practical energy production is to generate enough fusion reactions before the muon decays.

The complexities of muon-catalyzed fusion are many and include generating the muons (at an energy expenditure of about five billion electron volts per muon) and immediately injecting them into the deuterium-tritium mixture. In order to produce more energy than what is required to initiate the process, about 300 D-T fusion reactions must take place within the half-life of a muon.

Cold Fusion and Bubble Fusion

Two disputed fusion experiments merit mention. In 1989 two chemists, Martin Fleischmann of the University of Utah and Stanley Pons of the University of Southampton in England, announced that they had produced fusion reactions at essentially room temperature. Their system consisted of electrolytic cells containing heavy water (deuterium oxide, D_2O) and palladium rods that absorbed the deuterium from the heavy water. Efforts to give a theoretical explanation of the results failed, as did worldwide efforts to reproduce the claimed cold fusion.

In 2002 Rusi Taleyarkhan and colleagues at Purdue University in Lafayette, Ind., claimed to have observed a statistically significant increase in nuclear emissions of products of fusion reactions (neutrons and tritium) during acoustic cavitation experiments with chilled deuterated (bombarded with deuterium) acetone. Their experimental setup was based on the known phenomenon of sonoluminescence. In sonoluminescence a gas bubble is imploded with high-pressure sound waves. At the end of the implosion process, and for a short time afterward, conditions of high density and temperature are achieved that lead to light emission. By starting with larger, millimetre-sized cavitations (bubbles) that had been deuterated in the acetone liquid, the researchers claimed to have produced densities and temperatures sufficient to induce fusion reactions just before the bubbles broke up. As with cold fusion, attempts to replicate their results have failed.

CONDITIONS FOR PRACTICAL FUSION YIELD

Two conditions must be met to achieve practical energy yields from fusion. First, the plasma temperature must be high enough that fusion reactions occur at a sufficient rate. Second, the plasma must be confined so that the energy released by fusion reactions, when deposited in the plasma, maintains its temperature against loss of energy by such phenomena as conduction, convection, and radiation. When these conditions are achieved, the plasma is said to be ignited. In the case of stars, or some approaches to fusion by magnetic confinement, a steady state can be achieved, and no energy beyond what is supplied from fusion reactions is needed to sustain the system. In other cases, such as the ICF approach, there is a large temperature excursion once fuel ignition is achieved. The energy yield can far exceed the energy required to attain plasma ignition conditions, but this energy is released in a burst, and the process has to be repeated roughly once every second for practical power to be produced.

The conditions for plasma ignition are readily derived. When fusion reactions occur in a plasma, the power released is proportional to the square of plasma ion density, n^2. The plasma loses energy when electrons scatter from positively charged ions, accelerating and radiating in the process. Such radiation is called bremsstrahlung and is proportional to $n^2 T^{1/2}$, where T is the plasma temperature. Other mechanisms by which heat can escape the plasma lead to a characteristic energy-loss time denoted by τ. The energy content of the plasma at temperature T is $3nkT$, where k is the Boltzmann constant. The rate of energy loss by mechanisms other than bremsstrahlung is thus simply $3nkT/\tau$. The energy balance of the plasma is the balance between the fusion energy heating the plasma and the energy-loss rate, which is the sum of $3nkT/\tau$ and the bremsstrahlung. The condition satisfying this balance is called the ignition condition. An equation relates the product of density and energy confinement time, denoted $n\tau$, to a function that depends only on the plasma temperature and the type of fusion reaction. For example, when the plasma is composed of deuterium and tritium, the smallest value of $n\tau$ required to achieve ignition is about 2×10^{20} particles per cubic metre times seconds, and the required temperature corresponds to an energy of about 25,000 eV. If the only energy losses are due to bremsstrahlung escaping from the plasma (meaning τ is infinite), the ignition temperature decreases to an energy level of

4,400 eV. Hence, the keys to generating usable amounts of fusion energy are to attain a sufficient plasma temperature and a sufficient confinement quality, as measured by the product $n\tau$. At a temperature equivalent to 10,000 eV, the $n\tau$ product must be about 3×10^{20} particles per cubic metre times seconds.

Magnetic fusion energy generally creates plasmas with a density of about 3×10^{20} particles per cubic metre, which is about 10^{-8} of normal density. Hence, the characteristic time for heat to escape must be greater than about one second. This is a measure of the required degree of magnetic insulation for the heat content. Under these conditions the plasma remains in energy balance and can operate continuously if the ash of the nuclear fusion, namely helium, is removed (otherwise it will quench the plasma) and fuel is replenished.

ICF creates plasmas of much higher density, generally between 10^{31} and 10^{32} particles per cubic metre, or 1,000 to 10,000 times the normal density. As such, the confinement time, or minimum burn time, can be as short as 20×10^{-12} second. The objective in ICF is to achieve a temperature equivalent of 4,400 eV at the centre of the highly compressed fuel mass, while still having sufficient mass left around the centre so that the disassembly time will exceed the minimum burn time.

HISTORY OF FUSION ENERGY RESEARCH

The fusion process has been studied in order to understand nuclear matter and forces, to learn more about the nuclear physics of stellar objects, and to develop thermonuclear weapons. During the late 1940s and early '50s, research programs in the United States, United Kingdom, and the Soviet Union began to yield a better understanding of nuclear fusion, and investigators embarked on ways of exploiting the process for practical energy production. Fusion reactor research focused primarily on using magnetic fields and electromagnetic forces to contain the extremely hot plasmas needed for thermonuclear fusion.

Researchers soon found, however, that it is exceedingly difficult to contain plasmas at fusion reaction temperatures because the hot gases tend to expand and escape from the enclosing magnetic structure. Plasma physics theory in the 1950s was incapable of describing the behaviour of the plasmas in many of the early magnetic confinement systems.

The undeniable potential benefits of practical fusion energy led to an increasing call for international cooperation. American, British, and Soviet fusion programs were strictly classified until 1958, when most of their research programs were made public at the Second Geneva Conference on the Peaceful Uses of Atomic Energy, sponsored by the United Nations. Since that time, fusion research has been characterized by international collaboration. In addition, scientists have also continued to study and measure fusion reactions between the lighter elements so as to arrive at a more accurate determination of reaction rates. The formulas developed by nuclear physicists for predicting the rate of fusion energy generation have been adopted by astrophysicists to derive new information about the structure and evolution of stars.

Work on the other major approach to fusion energy, inertial confinement fusion (ICF), was begun in the early 1960s. The initial idea was proposed in 1961, only a year after the reported invention of the laser, in a then-classified proposal to employ large pulses of laser energy (which no one then quite knew how to achieve) to implode and shock-heat matter to temperatures at which nuclear fusion would proceed vigorously. Aspects of inertial confinement fusion were declassified in the 1970s and, especially, in the early 1990s to reveal important aspects of the design of the targets containing fusion fuels. Very painstaking and sophisticated work to design and develop short-pulse, high-power lasers and suitable millimetre-sized targets continues, and significant progress has been made.

Although practical fusion reactors have not been built yet, the necessary conditions of plasma temperature and heat insulation have been largely achieved, suggesting that fusion energy for electric-power production is now a serious possibility. Commercial fusion reactors promise an inexhaustible source of electricity for countries worldwide. From a practical viewpoint, however, the initiation of nuclear fusion in a hot plasma is but the first step in a whole sequence of steps required to convert fusion energy to electricity. In the end, successful fusion power systems must be capable of producing electricity safely and in a cost-effective manner, with a minimum of radioactive waste and environmental impact. The quest for practical fusion energy remains one of the great scientific and engineering challenges of humankind.

CONCLUSION

The 20th-century revolution changed many ideas about atoms that had apparently been firmly established by Newtonian physics during the 18th and 19th centuries. Closer examination of 19th-century physics shows that Newtonian ideas were already being undermined in many areas and that the program of mechanical explanation was openly challenged by several influential physicists toward the end of the century. Yet, there was no agreement as to what the foundations of a new physics might be.

The discovery of radioactivity by the French physicist Henri Becquerel in 1896 is generally taken to mark the beginning of 20th-century physics. Ernest Rutherford proposed that radioactivity involves a transmutation of one element into another. This proposal called into question one of the basic assumptions of 19th-century chemistry: that the elements consist of qualitatively different substances. It implied a return to the ideas of the ancient atomists — namely, that everything in the world is composed of only one or a few basic substances.

Transmutation was governed by certain empirical rules. Using these rules, Rutherford and his colleagues could determine the atomic numbers and atomic weights of many substances formed by radioactive decay, even though the substances decayed so quickly into others that these properties could not be measured directly. The atomic number of an element determines its place in Mendeleyev's periodic table.

Although the products of radioactive decay are determined by simple rules, the decay process itself seems to occur at random. All one can say is that there is a certain probability that an atom of a radioactive substance will decay during a certain time interval, or, equivalently, that half of the atoms of the sample will have decayed after a certain time (i.e., the half-life of the material).

On the basis of an experiment in which alpha particles were scattered by a thin film of metal, Rutherford proposed a nuclear model of the atom. In this model, the atom consists mostly of empty space, with a tiny, positively charged nucleus that contains most of the mass, surrounded by one or more negatively charged electrons.

During the 1920s physicists thought that the nucleus was composed of two particles: the proton (the positively charged nucleus of hydrogen) and the electron. In 1932 English physicist James Chadwick discovered the neutron, a particle with about the same mass as the proton but no electric charge. Since there were technical difficulties with the proton–electron model of the nucleus, physicists were willing to accept Heisenberg's hypothesis that it consists instead of protons and neutrons. The atomic number is then simply the number of protons in the nucleus. The mass number, the integer closest to the atomic weight, is equal to the total number of neutrons and protons.

In 1938 German physicists found that, when uranium is bombarded by neutrons, lighter elements are produced. This phenomenon was interpreted as a breakup, or fission, of the uranium nucleus into smaller nuclei. The U.S. Manhattan Project did eventually produce

James Chadwick's toolbox held paraffin as well as aluminium and silver foils, which he used with his neutron detector. SSPL via Getty Images

atomic bombs based on fission, and these were used against Japan in August 1945. Later, even more powerful bombs based on the fusion of hydrogen atoms were developed. Thus nuclear physics, the study of the inside of the atom, began to play a major role in world history.

CHAPTER 8
BIOGRAPHIES

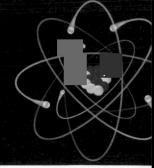

In this section, biographies of some of the notable men and women who studied the atom are presented. These biographies span thousands of years from the earliest speculations of Democritus to the experiments of 20th-century physicists like Marie Curie and Ernest Rutherford.

CLASSICAL WORLD: PHILOSOPHERS

For more than two thousand years, atoms were mere speculation. They were the subject of philosophy and not science.

DEMOCRITUS
(b. *c.* 460 BCE — d. *c.* 370 BCE)

The Greek philosopher Democritus was a central figure in the development of the atomic theory of the universe.

Knowledge of Democritus's life is largely limited to untrustworthy tradition: it seems that he was a wealthy citizen of Abdera, in Thrace; he traveled widely in the East; and he lived to a great age. According to Diogenes Laërtius, his works numbered 73. Only a few hundred fragments have survived, mostly from his treatises on ethics.

Democritus's physical and cosmological doctrines were an elaborated and systematized version of those of his teacher, Leucippus. To account for the world's changing physical phenomena, Democritus asserted that space, or the Void, had an equal right with reality, or Being, to be considered existent. He conceived of the Void as a vacuum, an infinite space in which moved an infinite number of atoms that made up Being (i.e., the physical world). These atoms are eternal and invisible; absolutely small, so small that their size cannot be diminished (hence the name *atomon,* or "indivisible"); absolutely full and incompressible, as they

Greek philosopher Democritus expounded upon the atomic theory of the universe. Hulton Archive/ Getty Images

are without pores and entirely fill the space they occupy; and homogeneous, differing only in shape, arrangement, position, and magnitude. But, while atoms thus differ in quantity, differences of quality are only apparent, owing to the impressions caused on our senses by different configurations and combinations of atoms. A thing is hot or cold, sweet or bitter, or hard or soft only by convention. The only things that exist in reality are atoms and the Void. Thus, the atoms of water and iron are the same, but those of water, being smooth and round and therefore unable to hook onto one another, roll over and over like small globes. Yet, those of iron, being rough, jagged, and uneven, cling together and form a solid body. Because all phenomena are composed of the same eternal atoms, it may be said that nothing comes into being or perishes in the absolute sense of the words, although the compounds made out of the atoms are liable to increase and decrease, explaining a thing's appearance and disappearance, or "birth" and "death."

Just as the atoms are uncaused and eternal, so too, according to Democritus, is motion. Democritus posited the fixed and "necessary" laws of a purely mechanical system, in which there was no room for an intelligent cause working with a view to an end. He explained the origin of the universe as follows. The original motion of the atoms was in all directions—it was a sort of "vibration." Hence there resulted collisions and, in particular, a whirling movement, whereby similar atoms were brought together and united to form larger bodies and worlds. This happened not as the result of any purpose or design but rather merely as the result of "necessity" (i.e., it is the normal manifestation of the nature of the atoms themselves). Atoms and void being infinite in number and extent, and motion having always existed, there must always have been an infinite number of worlds, all consisting of similar atoms in various stages of growth and decay.

Democritus devoted considerable attention to perception and knowledge. He asserted, for example, that sensations are changes produced in the soul by atoms emitted from other objects that impinge on it. The atoms of the soul can be affected only by the contact of other atoms. But sensations such as sweet and bitter are not as such inherent in the emitted atoms, for they result from effects caused merely by the size and shape of the atoms. For example, sweet taste is caused by round and not excessively small atoms. Democritus also was the first to attempt to explain colour, which he thought resulted from the "position" (which he differentiated from shape) of the constituent atoms of compounds. The sensation of white, for instance, is caused by atoms that are smooth and flat so as to cast no shadow. The sensation of black is caused by rough, uneven atoms.

Democritus attributed popular belief in the gods to a desire to explain extraordinary phenomena (thunder, lightning, earthquakes) by reference to superhuman agency. His ethical system, founded on a practical basis, posited an ultimate good ("cheerfulness") that was "a state in which the soul lives peacefully and tranquilly, undisturbed by fear or superstition or any other feeling."

LEUCIPPUS

(fl. 5th century BCE, probably at Miletus, on the west coast of Asia Minor)

The Greek philosopher Leucippus was credited by Aristotle and by Theophrastus with having originated the theory of atomism. It has been difficult to distinguish his contribution from that of his most famous pupil, Democritus. Only fragments of Leucippus' writings remain, but two works believed to have been written by him are *The Great World System* and *On the Mind*. His theory stated that matter is homogeneous but consists of an infinity of small indivisible particles. These atoms are constantly in motion, and through their collisions and regroupings form various compounds. A cosmos is formed by the collision of atoms that gather together into a "whirl," and the drum-shaped Earth is located in the centre of man's cosmos.

18TH AND 19TH CENTURIES: BEGINNINGS OF ATOMIC THEORY

Atomic theory emerged from chemistry with investigations of the nature of molecules. The study of the atom in the 18th and 19th century culminated with Mendeleyev's periodic table of the elements.

Amedeo Avogadro

(b. Aug. 9, 1776, Turin, in the Kingdom of Sardinia and Piedmont—
d. July 9, 1856, Turin, Italy)

The Italian mathematical physicist Amedeo Avogadro showed in what became known as Avogadro's law that, under controlled conditions of temperature and pressure, equal volumes of gases contain an equal number of molecules.

Avogadro was the son of Filippo Avogadro, conte di Quaregna e Cerreto, a distinguished lawyer and senator in the Piedmont region of northern Italy. Avogadro graduated in jurisprudence in 1792 but did not practice law until after receiving his doctorate in ecclesiastical law four years later. In 1801 he became secretary to the prefecture of Eridano.

Beginning in 1800 Avogadro privately pursued studies in mathematics and physics, and he focused his early research on electricity. In 1804 he became a corresponding member of the Academy of Sciences of Turin, and in 1806 he was appointed to the position of demonstrator at the academy's college. Three years later he became professor of natural philosophy at the Royal College of Vercelli, a post he held until 1820 when he accepted the first chair of mathematical physics at the University of Turin. Following civil disturbances in the Piedmont, the university was closed, and Avogadro lost his chair in July 1822. After the chair was reestablished in 1832, it was offered to the French mathematical physicist Augustin-Louis Cauchy. A year later Cauchy left for Prague, and on Nov. 28, 1834, Avogadro was reappointed.

Avogadro is chiefly remembered for his molecular hypothesis, first stated in 1811, in which he claimed that equal volumes of all gases at the same temperature and pressure contain the same number of molecules. He used this hypothesis further to explain the French chemist

Joseph-Louis Gay-Lussac's law of combining volumes of gases (1808) by assuming that the fundamental units of elementary gases may actually divide during chemical reactions. It also allowed for the calculation of the molecular weights of gases relative to some chosen standard. Avogadro and his contemporaries typically used the density of hydrogen gas as the standard for comparison. Thus, the following relationship was shown to exist:

$$\frac{\text{Weight of 1 volume of gas or vapour}}{\text{Weight of 1 volume of hydrogen}} = \frac{\text{Weight of 1 molecule of gas or vapour}}{\text{Weight of 1 molecule of hydrogen}}$$

To distinguish between atoms and molecules of different kinds, Avogadro adopted terms including *molécule intégrante* (the molecule of a compound), *molécule constituante* (the molecule of an element), and *molécule élémentaire* (atom). Although his gaseous elementary molecules were predominantly diatomic, he also recognized the existence of monatomic, triatomic, and tetratomic elementary molecules. In 1811 he provided the correct molecular formula for water, nitric and nitrous oxides, ammonia, carbon monoxide, and hydrogen chloride. Three years later he described the formulas for carbon dioxide, carbon disulfide, sulfur dioxide, and hydrogen sulfide. He also applied his hypothesis to metals and assigned atomic weights to 17 metallic elements based upon analyses of particular compounds that they formed. However, his references to *gaz métalliques* may have actually delayed chemists' acceptance of his ideas. In 1821 he offered the correct formula for alcohol (C_2H_6O) and for ether ($C_4H_{10}O$).

Priority over who actually introduced the molecular hypothesis of gases was disputed throughout much of the 19th century. Avogadro's claim rested primarily upon his repeated statements and applications. Others attributed this hypothesis to the French natural philosopher André-Marie Ampère, who published a similar idea in 1814. Many factors account for the fact that Avogadro's hypothesis was generally ignored until after his death. First, the distinction between atoms and molecules was not generally understood. Furthermore, as similar atoms were thought to repel one another, the existence of polyatomic elementary molecules seemed unlikely. Avogadro also mathematically represented his findings in ways more familiar to physicists than to chemists. Consider, for example, his proposed relationship between the specific heat of a compound gas and its chemical constituents:

$$c^2 = p_1 c_1^{\,2} + p_2 c_2^{\,2} + \text{etc.}$$

(Here c, c_1, c_2, etc., represent the specific heats at constant volume of the compound gas and its constituents; p_1, p_2, etc., represent the numbers of molecules of each component in the reaction.) Based on experimental evidence, Avogadro determined that the specific heat of a gas at constant volume was proportional to the square root of its attractive power for heat. In 1824 he calculated the "true affinity for heat" of a gas by dividing the square of its specific heat by its density. The results ranged from 0.8595 for oxygen to 10.2672 for hydrogen, and the numerical order of the affinities coincided with the electrochemical series, which listed the elements in the order of their chemical reactivities. Mathematically dividing an element's affinity for heat by that of his selected standard, oxygen, resulted in what he termed the element's "affinity number." Between 1843 and his retirement in 1850, Avogadro wrote four memoirs on atomic volumes and designated affinity numbers for the elements using atomic volumes according to a method "independent of all chemical considerations"—a claim that held little appeal for chemists.

Avogadro married Felicita Mazzé of Biella in 1815, and together they had six children. Home-loving, industrious, and modest, he rarely left Turin. His minimal contact with prominent scientists and his habit of citing his own results increased his isolation. Although he argued in 1845 that his molecular hypothesis for determining atomic weights was widely accepted, considerable confusion still existed over the concept of atomic weights at that time. Avogadro's hypothesis began to gain broad appeal among chemists only after his compatriot and fellow scientist Stanislao Cannizzaro demonstrated its value in 1858, two years after Avogadro's death. Many of Avogadro's pioneering ideas and methods anticipated later developments in physical chemistry. His hypothesis is now regarded as a law, and the value known as Avogadro's number ($6.02214179 \times 10^{23}$), the number of molecules in a gram molecule, or mole, of any substance, has become a fundamental constant of physical science.

JOHANN JAKOB BALMER
(b. May 1, 1825, Lausanne, Switz.—d. March 12, 1898, Basel)

Johann Jakob Balmer was a Swiss mathematician who discovered a formula basic to the development of atomic theory and the field of atomic spectroscopy. A secondary-school teacher in Basel from 1859 until his death, Balmer also lectured (1865–90) on geometry at the University of Basel. In 1885 he announced a simple formula representing the wavelengths of the spectral lines of hydrogen—the "Balmer series." Why the formula held true, however, was not explained until 1913, when Niels Bohr found that it fit into and supported his theory of discrete energy states within the hydrogen atom.

JÖNS JACOB BERZELIUS

(b. Aug. 20, 1779, near Linköping, Sweden—d. Aug. 7, 1848, Stockholm)

Jöns Jacob Berzelius was one of the founders of modern chemistry. He is especially noted for his determination of atomic weights, the development of modern chemical symbols, his electrochemical theory, the discovery and isolation of several elements, the development of classical analytical techniques, and his investigation of isomerism and catalysis, phenomena that owe their names to him. He was a strict empiricist and insisted that any new theory be consistent with the sum of chemical knowledge.

Berzelius studied medicine at Uppsala University from 1796 to 1802, and from 1807 to 1832 he served as a professor of medicine and pharmacy at the Karolinska Institute. He became a member of the Royal Swedish Academy of Sciences in 1808, serving from 1818 as its principal functionary, the perpetual secretary. In recognition of his growing international reputation, Berzelius was elevated to a position of nobility in 1818 on the coronation of King Charles XIV John. He was awarded a baronetcy in 1835 upon his marriage to Elizabeth Poppius. Together they had no children.

Berzelius was an early Swedish supporter of the new chemistry proposed a generation earlier by the renowned French chemist Antoine Lavoisier, and he remained a forceful exponent of enlightenment science and progressive politics even as romanticism pervaded Sweden and Europe. After initially aspiring to a career in physiological, especially animal, chemistry, he shifted his interests toward inorganic chemistry, the field in which he made his chief contributions. He eventually devoted considerable time to organic chemistry as well.

In addition to his qualitative specification of chemicals, Berzelius investigated their quantitative relationships as well. As early as 1806, he began to prepare an up-to-date Swedish chemistry textbook and read widely on the subject of chemical combination. Finding little information on the subject, he decided to undertake further investigations. His pedagogical interest focused his attention on inorganic chemistry. Around 1808 he launched what became a vast and enduring program in the laboratory analysis of inorganic matter. To this end, he created most of his apparatuses and prepared his own reagents. Through precise experimental trials, supported by extraordinary interpretive acumen, he established the atomic weights of the elements, the formulas of their oxides, sulfides, and salts, and the formulas of virtually all known inorganic compounds, many of which he was the first to prepare or characterize.

Berzelius's experiments led to a more complete depiction of the principles of chemical combining proportions, an area of investigation that the German chemist Jeremias Benjamin Richter named "stoichiometry" in 1792. Richter, the French chemist Joseph-Louis Proust, and the English chemist John Dalton, despite their theoretical insights, had contributed little empirical evidence toward elucidating the principles of chemical combination. By showing how compounds conformed to the laws of constant, multiple, and equivalent proportions as well as to a series of semiempirical rules devised to cover specific classes of compounds, Berzelius established the quantitative specificity by which substances combined. These results, when viewed alongside his qualitative identification of electrically opposing constituents, allowed Berzelius to specify more completely the combining properties of all known chemicals. He reported his analytical results in a series of famous publications, most prominently his *Essai sur la théorie des proportions chimiques et sur l'influence chimique de l'électricité* (1819; "Essay on the Theory of Chemical Proportions and on the Chemical Influence of Electricity"), and the atomic weight tables that appeared in the 1826 German translation of his *Lärbok i kemien* (*Textbook of Chemistry*). He continued his analytical work until 1844, reporting in specialized articles and new editions of his textbook both new results, such as his extensive analysis of the compounds of the platinum metals in 1827–28, together with refinements of his earlier experimental findings.

The project of specifying substances had several important consequences. In order to establish and display the laws of stoichiometry, Berzelius invented and perfected more exacting standards and techniques of analysis. His generalization of the older acid/base chemistry led him to extend chemical nomenclature that Lavoisier had introduced to cover the bases (mostly metallic oxides), a change that allowed Berzelius to name any compound consistently with Lavoisier's chemistry. For this purpose, he bypassed the French names that Lavoisier and his colleagues had devised as well as their translations into Swedish introduced by Berzelius's colleagues at Uppsala, Pehr Afzelius and Anders Gustav Ekeberg. Instead, Berzelius created a Latin template for translation into diverse vernacular languages.

The project of specifying substances also led Berzelius to develop a new system of notation that could portray the composition of any compound both qualitatively (by showing its electrochemically opposing ingredients) and quantitatively (by showing the proportions in which the ingredients were united). His system abbreviated the Latin names of the elements with one or two letters and applied superscripts to designate the number of atoms of each element present in both the acidic and basic ingredient. In his own work, however, Berzelius preferred to indicate the proportions of oxygen with dots placed over the letters of the oxidized elements, but most chemists rejected that practice. Instead, they followed Berzelius's younger German colleagues, who replaced his superscripts with subscripts and thus created the system still used today. Berzelius's new nomenclature and notation were prominently displayed in his 1819 *Essai*, which presented a coherent, compelling system of chemical theory backed by a vast body of analytical results that rested on improved, highly precise laboratory methods.

Berzelius had a profound influence on chemistry, stemming in part from his substantial achievements and in part from his ability to enhance and project his authority. Among Berzelius's other accomplishments were his improvements of laboratory apparatuses and techniques used for chemical and mineral analysis, especially solvent extraction, elemental analysis, quantitative wet chemistry, and qualitative mineral analysis. Berzelius also characterized and named two new concepts: "isomerism," in which chemically diverse substances possess the same composition; and "catalysis," in which certain chemical reactions are facilitated by the presence of substances that are themselves unaffected. He also coined the term *protein* while attempting to apply a dualistic organic chemistry to the constituents of living things.

ROBERT BROWN

(b. Dec. 21, 1773, Montrose, Angus, Scot.—d. June 10, 1858, London, Eng.)

Robert Brown was a Scottish botanist best known for his description of the natural continuous motion of minute particles in solution, which came to be called Brownian movement. In addition, he recognized the fundamental distinction between the conifers and their allies (gymnosperms) and the flowering plants (angiosperms), recognized and named the nucleus as a constant constituent of living cells in most plants, and improved the natural classification of plants by establishing and defining new families and genera. He also contributed substantially to knowledge of plant morphology, embryology, and geography, in particular by his original work on the flora of Australia.

Brown was the son of a Scottish Episcopalian clergyman. He studied medicine at the universities of Aberdeen and Edinburgh and spent five years in the British army serving in Ireland as an ensign and assistant surgeon (1795–1800). A visit to London in 1798 brought Brown to the notice of Sir Joseph Banks, president of the Royal Society. Banks recommended Brown to the Admiralty for the post of naturalist aboard a ship (the *Investigator*) for a surveying voyage along the northern and southern coasts of Australia under the command of Matthew Flinders.

Brown sailed with the expedition in July 1801. The *Investigator* reached King George's Sound, Western Australia, an area of great floral richness and diversity, in December 1801. Until June 1803, and while the ship circumnavigated Australia, Brown made extensive plant collections. Returning to England in October 1805, Brown devoted his time to classifying the approximately 3,900 species he had gathered, almost all of which were new to science. The results of his Australian trip were partially published in 1810 as his *Prodromus Florae Novae Hollandiae . . . ,* a classic of systematic botany and Brown's major work, in which he laid the foundations for Australian botany while refining the prevailing systems of plant classification. Disappointed by its small sale, however, he published only one volume. Brown's close observation of minute but significant details was also shown in his publication on *Proteaceae,* in which he demonstrated how the study of pollen-grain characters could assist in the classification of plants into new genera. In 1810 Banks appointed Brown as his librarian and in 1820 bequeathed him a life interest in his extensive botanical collection and library. Brown transferred them to the British Museum in 1827, when he became keeper of its newly formed botanical department.

In 1828 he published a pamphlet, *A Brief Account of Microscopical Observations* . . . , in which he recorded that, after having noticed moving particles suspended in the fluid within living pollen grains of *Clarkia pulchella,* he examined both living and dead pollen grains of many other plants and observed a similar motion in the particles of all fresh pollen. Brown's experiments with organic and inorganic substances, reduced to a fine powder and suspended in water, then revealed such motion to be a general property of matter in that state. This phenomenon has long been known as Brownian motion. In 1831, while dealing with the fertilization of *Orchidaceae* and *Asclepiadaceae,* he noted the existence of a structure within the cells of orchids as well as many other plants that he termed the "nucleus" of the cell. These observations testify to the range and depth of his pioneering microscopical work and his ability to draw far-reaching conclusions from isolated data or selected structures. Brown was elected a fellow of the Royal Society in 1810.

ROBERT WILHELM BUNSEN

(b. March 31, 1811, Göttingen, Westphalia [Germany]—d. Aug. 16, 1899, Heidelberg, Baden)

Robert Wilhelm Bunsen was a German chemist who, with Gustav Kirchhoff, about 1859 observed that each element emits a light of characteristic wavelength. These studies opened the field of spectrum analysis, which became of great importance in the study of the Sun and stars and also led Bunsen almost immediately to his discovery of two alkali-group metals, cesium and rubidium.

After taking his Ph.D. in chemistry at the University of Göttingen (1830), Bunsen taught at the universities of Marburg and Breslau and elsewhere. As professor at Heidelberg (1852–99), he built up an excellent school of chemistry. Never married, he lived for his students, with whom he was very popular, and his laboratory. He chiefly concerned himself with experimental and analytical work.

Although famous for his association with the Bunsen burner, Robert Wilhelm Bunsen was more involved in the invention of the carbon-zinc electric cell known by his name. SSPL via Getty Images

He found an antidote to arsenic poisoning in freshly precipitated, hydrated ferric oxide (1834). In 1837 he began his only notable venture into organic chemistry with a study of the highly toxic, arsenic-containing compound cacodyl. During six years of work with it, he lost the sight in one eye from an explosion and nearly killed himself from arsenic poisoning. His research led to profitable studies of organometallic compounds by his student Edward Frankland. Eventually, Bunsen barred organic research in his laboratory.

Bunsen's studies of the composition of gases given off from blast furnaces showed that 50 to 80 percent or more of the heat was wasted and led to elaboration of his methods of measuring volumes of gases in his only publication, *Gasometrische Methoden* (1857).

In 1841 he invented the carbon-zinc electric cell known by his name. To measure the light produced by it, he developed the grease-spot photometer (1844). He was the first to obtain magnesium in the metallic state and study its physical and chemical properties, demonstrating the brilliance and reaction-producing (actinic) qualities of the flame when magnesium is burned in air.

Bunsen also invented the filter pump (1868), the ice calorimeter (1870), and the vapour calorimeter (1887). Though he is generally credited with the invention of the Bunsen burner, he seems to have contributed to its development only in a minor way.

STANISLAO CANNIZZARO

(b. July 13, 1826, Palermo, Sicily, Kingdom of the Two Sicilies [Italy]—d. May 10, 1910, Rome, Italy)

Italian chemist Stanislao Cannizzaro was closely associated with a crucial reform movement in science. Cannizzaro, the son of a magistrate, studied medicine at the universities in Palermo and Naples and then proceeded to Pisa to study organic chemistry with Raffaele Piria, the finest chemist then working in Italy. In 1849 Cannizzaro traveled to Paris, where he joined Michel Chevreul in his laboratory at the Muséum National d'Histoire Naturelle. Two years later, with some fine published work to his credit, Cannizzaro was appointed professor of physics and chemistry at the Collegio Nazionale in Alessandria, Piedmont (now part of Italy). Then, in 1855, he was called to a professorship in Genoa.

Cannizzaro's chemical interests centred on natural products and on reactions of aromatic compounds. In 1853 he discovered that when benzaldehyde is treated with concentrated base, both benzoic acid and benzyl alcohol are produced—a phenomenon known today as the Cannizzaro reaction. Despite the fact that Cannizzaro struggled through much of his career with inadequate laboratory facilities, his published research was important and influential. In 1861 he returned to his native Palermo, where he taught for 10 years, making the local university the centre of chemical education and research in Italy. Among his students in Palermo was Wilhelm Körner, a German chemist who made his subsequent career in Italy and whose "absolute" method of determining the structure of aromatic derivatives solved a problem that had bedeviled organic chemists for many years. Cannizzaro's last move, in 1871, was to the University of Rome, where he spent the rest of his long and distinguished career.

Cannizzaro's historical significance is most closely associated with a long letter he wrote on March 12, 1858, to his friend Sebastiano de Luca, professor of chemistry at Pisa, and subsequently published as "Sunto di un corso di filosofia chimica fatto nella R. Università de Genova" ("Sketch of a Course in Chemical Philosophy at the Royal University of Genoa"). To make clear the significance of this pamphlet, it is necessary to describe something of the state of chemical theory at the time.

The English scientist John Dalton published his atomic theory in 1808, and certain of his central ideas were soon thereafter adopted by most chemists. However, uncertainty persisted for half a century about how atomic theory was to be configured and applied to concrete situations. Lacking a way to directly weigh particles as small as atoms and molecules, and having no means to unambiguously determine the formulas of compounds, chemists in different countries developed several different incompatible atomistic systems. A paper that suggested a way out of this difficult situation was published as early as 1811 by the Italian physicist Amedeo Avogadro, who used vapour densities to infer the relative weights of atoms and molecules and suggested that elementary gases must consist of molecules with more than one atom.

Despite their apparent promise, Avogadro's ideas were distressingly abstract and burdened by some anomalies, which delayed their adoption by chemists. An additional barrier to acceptance was the fact that many chemists were reluctant to adopt physical methods (such as vapour-density determinations) to solve their problems. By mid-century, however, some leading figures had begun to view the chaotic multiplicity of competing systems of atomic weights and molecular formulas as intolerable. Moreover, purely chemical evidence began to mount that suggested Avogadro's approach might be right after all. During the 1850s, younger chemists, such as Alexander Williamson in England, Charles Gerhardt and Adolphe Wurtz in France, and August Kekulé in Germany, began to advocate reforming theoretical chemistry to make it consistent with Avogadrian theory.

In his 1858 pamphlet, Cannizzaro showed that a complete return to the ideas of Avogadro could be used to construct a consistent and robust theoretical structure that fit nearly all of the available empirical evidence. The few remaining anomalies, he argued, could easily be understood as minor (and legitimate) exceptions to general rules. For instance, he pointed to evidence that suggested that not all elementary gases consist of two atoms per molecule—some were monoatomic, most were diatomic, and a few were even more complex. Another point of contention had been the formulas for compounds of the alkali metals (such as sodium) and the alkaline-earth metals (such as calcium), which, in view of their striking chemical analogies, most chemists had wanted to assign to the same formula type. Cannizzaro argued that placing these metals in different categories had the beneficial result of eliminating certain anomalies when using their physical properties to deduce atomic weights.

Cannizzaro's striking summary from this careful and perceptive analysis was that "the conclusions drawn from [Avogadro's theory] are invariably in accordance with all physical and chemical laws hitherto discovered." This meant (to Cannizzaro, at least) that it was possible and desirable to construct a single "true" atomistic system that should immediately replace the chaos of competing conventional systems of the 1850s. Unfortunately, Cannizzaro's pamphlet was published initially only in Italian and had little immediate impact.

The real breakthrough came with an international chemical congress held in the German town of Karlsruhe in September 1860, at which most of the leading European chemists were present. The Karlsruhe Congress had been arranged by Kekule, Wurtz, and a few others who shared Cannizzaro's sense of the direction chemistry should go. Speaking in French (as everyone there did), Cannizzaro's eloquence and logic made an indelible impression on the assembled body. Moreover, his friend Angelo Pavesi (a professor at Pavia) distributed Cannizzaro's pamphlet to attendees at the end of the meeting. More than one chemist later wrote of the decisive impression the reading of this document provided. Cannizzaro thus played a crucial role in winning the battle for reform. The system advocated by him, and soon thereafter adopted by most leading chemists, is substantially identical to what is still used today.

JOHN DALTON

(b. Sept. 5 or 6, 1766, Eaglesfield, Cumberland, Eng. — d. July 27, 1844, Manchester)

English meteorologist and chemist John Dalton was a pioneer in the development of modern atomic theory. Dalton was born into a Quaker family of tradesmen. His grandfather Jonathan Dalton was a shoemaker, and his father, Joseph, was a weaver. Joseph married Deborah Greenup in 1755, herself from a prosperous local Quaker family. Dalton was the youngest of their three offspring who survived to adulthood. He attended John Fletcher's Quaker grammar school in Eaglesfield. When John was only 12 years old, Fletcher turned the school over to John's older brother, Jonathan, who called upon the younger Dalton to assist him with teaching. Two years later the brothers purchased a school in Kendal, where they taught approximately 60 students, some of them boarders.

In 1793 Dalton moved to Manchester to teach mathematics at a dissenting academy, the New College. Soon after his arrival at Manchester, Dalton was elected a member of the Manchester Literary and Philosophical Society. His first contribution to this society was a description of the defect he had discovered in his own and his brother's vision. This paper was the first publication on colour blindness, which for some time thereafter was known as Daltonism.

By far Dalton's most influential work in chemistry was his atomic theory. Attempts to trace precisely how Dalton developed this theory have proved futile; even Dalton's own recollections on the subject are incomplete. He based his theory of partial pressures on the idea that only like atoms in a mixture of gases repel one another, whereas unlike atoms appear to react indifferently toward each other. This conceptualization explained why each gas in a mixture behaved independently. Although this view was later shown to be erroneous, it served a useful purpose in allowing him to abolish the idea, held by many previous atomists from the Greek philosopher Democritus to the 18th-century mathematician and astronomer Ruggero Giuseppe Boscovich, that atoms of all kinds of matter are alike. Dalton claimed that atoms of different elements vary in size and mass, and indeed this claim is the cardinal feature of his atomic theory. His argument that each element had its own kind of atom was counterintuitive to those who believed that having so many different fundamental particles would destroy the simplicity of nature, but Dalton dismissed their objections as fanciful. Instead, he focused on determining the relative masses of each different kind of atom, a process that could be accomplished, he claimed, only by considering the number of atoms of each element present in different chemical compounds. Although Dalton had taught chemistry for several years, he had not yet performed actual research in this field.

In a memoir read to the Manchester Literary and Philosophical Society on Oct. 21, 1803, he claimed: "An inquiry into the relative weights of the ultimate particles of bodies is a subject, as far as I know, entirely new; I have lately been prosecuting this inquiry with remarkable success." He described his method of measuring the masses of various elements, including hydrogen, oxygen, carbon, and nitrogen, according to the way they combined with fixed masses of each other. If such measurements were to be meaningful, the elements had to combine in fixed proportions. Dalton took the fixed proportions for granted, disregarding the contemporary controversy between French chemists Joseph-Louis Proust and Claude-Louis Berthollet over that very proposition. Dalton's measurements, crude as they were, allowed him to formulate the Law of Multiple Proportions: When two elements form more than one compound, the masses of one element that combine with a fixed mass of the other are in a ratio of small whole numbers. Thus, taking the elements as A and B, various combinations between them naturally occur according to the mass ratios $A:B = x:y$ or $x:2y$ or $2x:y$, and so on. Different compounds were formed by combining atomic building blocks of different masses. As the Swedish chemist Jöns Jacob Berzelius wrote to Dalton: "The law of multiple proportions is a mystery without the atomic theory." And Dalton provided the basis for this theory.

The problem remained, however, that a knowledge of ratios was insufficient to determine the actual number of elemental atoms in each compound. For example, methane was found to contain twice as much hydrogen as ethylene. Following Dalton's rule of "greatest simplicity," namely, that AB is the most likely combination for which he found a meretricious justification in the geometry of close-packed spheres, he assigned methane a combination of one carbon and two hydrogen atoms and ethylene a combination of one carbon and one hydrogen atom. This, we now know, is incorrect, for the methane molecule is chemically symbolized as CH_4 and the ethylene molecule as C_2H_4. Nevertheless, Dalton's atomic theory triumphed over its weaknesses because his foundational argument was correct. However, overcoming the defects of Dalton's theory was a gradual process, finalized in 1858 only after the Italian chemist Stanislao Cannizzaro pointed out the utility of Amadeo Avogadro's hypothesis in determining molecular masses. Since then, chemists have shown the theory of Daltonian atomism to be a key factor underlying further advances in their field. Organic chemistry in particular progressed rapidly once Dalton's theory gained acceptance. Dalton's atomic theory earned him the sobriquet "father of chemistry."

After the age of 50, Dalton performed little scientific work of distinction, although he continued to pursue research in various fields. When faced with the Royal Society's rejection of his 1838 paper "On the Arseniates and Phosphates," he had it printed privately, noting bitterly that Britain's chemistry elites, "Cavendish, Davy, Wollaston, and Gilbert are no more." His atomic theory eventually began to prove its worth, and its author gained widespread recognition.

Joseph Loschmidt

(b. May 15, 1821, Putschin, Bohemia, Austrian Empire [now in Czech Republic]—d. July 8, 1895, Vienna, Austria)

Johann Joseph Loschmidt was a German chemist who made advances in the study of aromatic hydrocarbons. The son of poor peasants, Loschmidt gained an education through the help of his village priest, and by 1839 he was a student at the German University in Prague. Moving to Vienna in 1841, he completed his university studies in 1843 but was unable to obtain a teaching post. His attempts to succeed in business ended in bankruptcy in 1854, and he decided to return to his studies in the natural sciences. In 1856 Loschmidt qualified as a teacher and obtained a post at the Vienna Realschule. He turned to research in chemistry and theoretical physics and soon began publishing scientific papers. He was appointed an assistant professor of physical chemistry at the University of Vienna in 1868 and went on to become an important figure in Vienna's scientific community.

Loschmidt was the first to use double and triple lines to graphically represent the double and triple bonds in organic molecules. He recognized that most "aromatic compounds" (i.e., aromatic hydrocarbons, so called because they were obtained from pleasantly fragrant substances) could be derived from benzene by replacing one or more hydrogen substituents by other atoms or groups. The term "aromatic" thus came to be applied to any hydrocarbon that has the benzene ring as part of its structure, regardless of the question of aroma. Loschmidt was the first to state that in alcohols containing several OH groups, each OH group is attached to a different carbon atom. He partly explained the structures of several organic and inorganic compounds, among them benzene, toluene, and ozone, and he also recognized that an element could have several valences. Loschmidt made perhaps the first accurate calculations of the size of air molecules and of the number of molecules in a gram-mole (the quantity now commonly called the Avogadro constant). He arrived at a size of somewhat less than 10^{-7} cm for the diameter of the molecules in air, which is relatively close to the accepted figure of 0.5×10^{-7} cm.

DMITRY IVANOVICH MENDELEYEV

(b. Jan. 27 [Feb. 8, New Style], 1834, Tobolsk, Siberia, Russian Empire—d. Jan. 20 [Feb. 2], 1907, St. Petersburg, Russia)

Russian chemist Dmitry Ivanovich Mendeleyev developed the periodic classification of the elements. Mendeleyev was born in the small Siberian town of Tobolsk as the last of 14 surviving children (or 13, depending on the source) of Ivan Pavlovich Mendeleyev, a teacher at the local gymnasium, and Mariya Dmitriyevna Kornileva. Dmitry's father became blind in the year of Dmitry's birth and died in 1847. To support the family, his mother turned to operating a small glass factory owned by her family in a nearby town. The factory burned down in December 1848, and Dmitry's mother took him to St. Petersburg, where he enrolled in the Main Pedagogical Institute. His mother died soon after, and Mendeleyev graduated in 1855.

He got his first teaching position at Simferopol in Crimea. He stayed there only two months and, after a short time at the lyceum of Odessa, decided to go back to St. Petersburg to continue his education. He received a master's degree in 1856 and began to conduct research in organic chemistry. Financed by a government fellowship, he went to study abroad for two years at the University of Heidelberg. Instead of working closely with the prominent chemists of the university, including Robert Bunsen, Emil Erlenmeyer, and August Kekulé, he set up a laboratory in his own apartment. In September 1860 he attended the International Chemistry Congress in Karlsruhe, convened to discuss such crucial issues as atomic weights, chemical symbols, and chemical formulas. There he met and established contacts with many of Europe's leading chemists. In later years Mendeleyev would especially remember a paper circulated by the Italian chemist Stanislao Cannizzaro that clarified the notion of atomic weights.

In 1861 Mendeleyev returned to St. Petersburg, where he obtained a professorship at the Technological Institute in 1864. After the defense of his doctoral dissertation in 1865 he was appointed professor of chemical technology at the University of St. Petersburg (now St. Petersburg State University). He became professor of general chemistry in 1867 and continued to teach there until 1890.

As he began to teach inorganic chemistry, Mendeleyev could not find a textbook that met his needs. Because he had already published a textbook on organic chemistry in 1861 that had been awarded the prestigious Demidov Prize, he set out to write another one. The result was *Osnovy Khimii* (1868–71; *The Principles of Chemistry*), which became a classic, running through many editions and many translations. When Mendeleyev began to compose the chapter on the halogen elements (chlorine and its analogs) at the end of the first volume, he compared the properties of this group of elements to those of the group of alkali metals such as sodium. Within these two groups of dissimilar elements, he discovered similarities in the progression of atomic weights, and he wondered if other groups of elements exhibited similar properties. After studying the alkaline earths, Mendeleyev established that the order of atomic weights could be used not only to arrange the elements within each group but also to arrange the groups themselves. Thus, in his effort to make sense of the extensive knowledge that already existed of the chemical and physical properties of the chemical elements and their compounds, Mendeleyev discovered the periodic law.

His newly formulated law was announced before the Russian Chemical Society in March 1869 with the statement "elements arranged according to the value of their atomic weights present a clear periodicity of properties." Mendeleyev's law allowed him to build up a systematic table of all the 70 elements then known. He had such faith in the validity of the periodic law that he proposed changes to the generally accepted values for the atomic weight of a few elements and predicted the locations within the table of unknown elements together with their properties. At first the periodic system did not raise interest among chemists. However, with the discovery of the predicted elements, notably gallium in 1875, scandium in 1879, and germanium in 1886, it began to win wide acceptance. Gradually, the periodic law and table became the framework for a great part of chemical theory. By the time Mendeleyev died in 1907, he enjoyed international recognition and had received distinctions and awards from many countries.

Because Mendeleyev is best known today as the discoverer of the periodic law, his chemical career is often viewed as a long process of maturation of his main discovery. Indeed, in the three decades following his discovery, Mendeleyev offered many recollections suggesting that there had been a remarkable continuity in his career, from his early dissertations on isomorphism and specific volumes (for graduation and his master's degree), which involved the study of the relations between various properties of chemical substances, to the periodic law itself. In this account, Mendeleyev mentioned the Karlsruhe congress as the major event that led him to the discovery of the relations between atomic weights and chemical properties.

However, this retrospective impression of a continuous research program is misleading, because one striking feature of Mendeleyev's long career is the diversity of his activities. In the field of chemical science, Mendeleyev made various contributions. In the field of physical chemistry, for instance, he conducted a broad research program throughout his career that focused on gases and liquids. In 1860, while working in Heidelberg, he defined the "absolute point of ebullition" (the point at which a gas in a container will condense to a liquid solely by the application of pressure). In 1864 he formulated a theory (subsequently discredited) that solutions are chemical combinations in fixed proportions. In 1871, as he published the final volume of the first edition of his *Principles of Chemistry*, he was investigating the elasticity of gases and gave a formula for their deviation from Boyle's law (now also known as the Boyle-Mariotte law, the principle that the volume of a gas varies inversely with its pressure). In the 1880s he studied the thermal expansion of liquids.

LOTHAR MEYER

(b. Aug. 19, 1830, Varel, Oldenburg [Germany]—d. April 11, 1895, Tübingen)

Julius Lothar Meyer was a German chemist who, independently of Dmitry Mendeleyev, developed a periodic classification of the chemical elements. Though originally educated as a physician, he was chiefly interested in chemistry and physics.

In 1859 Meyer began his career as a science educator, holding various appointments before serving as professor of chemistry at the University of Tübingen (1876–95). His book *Die modernen Theorien der Chemie* (1864; "Modern Chemical Theory"), a lucid treatise on the fundamental principles of chemical science, contained a preliminary scheme for the arrangement of elements by atomic weight and discussed the relation between the atomic weights and the properties of the elements. This influential work was often enlarged and went into many editions. In about 1868 Meyer prepared an expanded table, similar in many ways to Mendeleyev's table published in 1869. It was not until 1870, however, that Meyer published his own table, a graph relating atomic volume and atomic number and clearly showing the periodic relationships of the elements. He did not claim priority for his achievement, and he admitted that he had been reluctant to predict the existence of undiscovered elements as Mendeleyev had done.

Meyer worked in several areas of chemistry, but much of his activity grew out of his preoccupation with the classification of the elements. He worked on recalculating a number of atomic weights and made use of the periodic table for predicting and studying related elements' chemical properties.

JEAN PERRIN
(b. Sept. 30, 1870, Lille, France—d. April 17, 1942, New York, N.Y., U.S.)

French physicist Jean-Baptiste Perrin, in his studies of the Brownian motion of minute particles suspended in liquids, verified Albert Einstein's explanation of this phenomenon and thereby confirmed the atomic nature of matter. For this achievement he was honoured with the Nobel Prize for Physics in 1926.

Educated at the École Normale Supérieure, Paris, Perrin joined the faculty of the University of Paris (1898) where he became professor of physical chemistry (1910–40). In 1895 he established that cathode rays are negatively charged particles (electrons). His attempt to determine the mass of these particles was soon anticipated by the work of J.J. Thomson.

About 1908 Perrin began to study Brownian motion, the erratic movement of particles suspended in a liquid. Einstein's mathematical analysis (1905) of this phenomenon suggested that the particles were being jostled by the randomly moving water molecules around them. Using the newly developed ultra-microscope, Perrin carefully observed the manner of sedimentation of these particles and provided experimental

Jean Perrin. H. Roger-Viollet

confirmation of Einstein's equations. His observations also enabled him to estimate the size of water molecules and atoms as well as their quantity in a given value. This was the first time the size of atoms and molecules could be reliably calculated from actual visual observations. Perrin's work helped raise atoms from the status of useful hypothetical objects to observable entities whose reality could no longer be denied.

JOSEPH-LOUIS PROUST

(b. Sept. 26, 1754, Angers, France—d. July 5, 1826, Angers)

French chemist Joseph-Louis Proust proved that the relative quantities of any given pure chemical compound's constituent elements remain invariant, regardless of the compound's source. This is known as Proust's law, or the law of definite proportions (1793), and it is the fundamental principle of analytical chemistry. Proust also carried out important applied research in metallurgy, explosives, and nutritional chemistry.

The son of an apothecary, Proust prepared for the same occupation, first with his father in Angers and then in Paris, where he also studied chemistry with Hilaire-Martin Rouelle. In 1776 Proust was appointed a pharmacist at the Salpêtrière Hospital in Paris. This position was short-lived, however, for in 1778 Proust abandoned pharmacy to take a professorship of chemistry at the recently established Seminario Patriótico Vascongado in Vergara, Spain. This school was the creation of the Real Sociedad Económica Vascongada de Amigos del País, the first and most important of the "enlightened" provincial societies in Spain.

In 1780 Proust returned to Paris, where he taught chemistry at the Musée, a private teaching institution founded by scientific impresario Jean-François Pilâtre de Rozier. Part of this association involved Proust with aerostatic experiments, which culminated in a balloon ascent with Pilâtre on June 23, 1784, at Versailles, in the presence of the royal court.

In 1786 Proust returned to Spain to teach chemistry, first at Madrid and then in 1788 at the Royal Artillery School in Segovia. The school had been founded in 1764 as part of the program of the government of Charles III to bring Spain abreast of the northern European countries regarding military training. Proust's chair (and an associated school of chemistry and metallurgy) had been proposed in 1784 to introduce artillery cadets to the latest relevant scientific training. Because of Spain's scientific backwardness, expert instructors had to be sought abroad. Proust was recommended by no less than the great French chemist Antoine-Laurent Lavoisier.

Proust did not actually assume his chair until 1792, owing to a combination of bureaucratic inefficiency and his own exacting demands for laboratory equipment. When finally ready, his laboratory was undeniably one of the finest in Europe, and Proust probably did the bulk of his practical and analytical chemistry there. Difficulties with the military authorities, though, resulted in Proust's transfer in 1799 to a chair in chemistry in Madrid.

In 1798 Proust married Anne Rose Chatelain Daubigne, a French resident of Segovia. They returned to France in 1806 under obscure circumstances and settled in Craon, near Angers. Upon the death of his wife in 1817, Proust moved to Angers, where he took over in 1820 the pharmacy of his ailing brother Joachim. Although Proust had returned to France in reduced circumstances, his scientific stature was recognized. He was elected to the French Academy of Sciences to succeed Louis Bernard Guyton de Morveau in 1816, made a chevalier of the Legion of Honour in 1819, and granted a pension by Louis XVIII in 1820.

Proust is best known as an analytical chemist, particularly for his enunciation of the law of definite proportions. The essence of Proust's law is that chemical substances only truly combine to form a small number of compounds, each of which is characterized by components that combine in fixed proportions by weight. Proust's formulation and experimental demonstration of this law was exclusively concerned with inorganic binary compounds, such as metallic oxides, sulfides, and sulfates. He believed that most metals formed two distinct oxides at constant proportions—which he termed the minimum and maximum—and these in turn were capable of producing two separate series of compounds. For sulfides, Proust asserted that there existed only one per metal, with the exception of iron.

Although the statements of the law that attracted the attention of European chemists first appeared in French journals starting in 1797, Proust had formulated the law by 1793 and published it by 1795 in Spanish journals. Proust's law of definite proportion had precursors in 18th-century chemistry and a parallel in 18th-century French mineralogy. Contemporary with Proust's formulation was the doctrine of fixed mineral species in French mineralogy, which was defined in terms of fixed crystal form and constant chemical composition.

Proust's law of definite proportions came under attack in 1803 by the eminent French chemist Claude-Louis Berthollet, who had refined his own chemical affinity theory in 1801 to suggest that chemical combination was not necessarily restricted to definite saturation proportions. The controversy took place in French scientific journals and consisted of a paper or two each year from each protagonist. At the heart of the controversy was the definition of chemical combination. As had been traditional, Berthollet considered solutions to be chemical combinations. Indeed, they were paradigmatic for his concept of a continuum of combining proportions. He had termed some combinations in variable proportions (e.g., metallic sulfides) solutions and considered them to be true compounds. In contrast, Proust distinguished sharply between these and his own true binary compounds at fixed proportions.

What eventually settled the dispute in Proust's favour was the effect of the chemical atomic theory (1801) of the English chemist John Dalton. Dalton's atomic theory provided a simple theoretical underpinning for the law of definite proportions, especially after the Swedish chemist Jöns Jacob Berzelius established the conceptual relationship between Proust's law and Dalton's theory in 1811.

Traditional narratives in the history of chemistry have focused exclusively on Proust's analytical work. However, his career actually was sustained by more practical chemical activities. For example, the context of Proust's earliest assertion that combining substances formed two distinct compounds at maximum and minimum proportions came from his study of the casting of cannon. In particular, it concerned the ratio of tin to copper in two alloys of bronze. In a related area of applied chemistry, Proust published what were then the most comprehensive experimental studies on gunpowder. He also carried out important investigations in nutritional chemistry, suggesting methods for the manufacture of various nutritional supplements.

JOHANNES ROBERT RYDBERG

(b. Nov. 8, 1854, Halmstad, Swed.—d. Dec. 28, 1919, Lund)

Johannes Robert Rydberg was a Swedish physicist for whom the Rydberg constant in spectroscopy is named. Educated at the University of Lund, Rydberg received his bachelor's degree in 1875 and his doctorate in mathematics in 1879. He became lecturer in physics there in 1882 and assistant at the Physics Institute in 1892. He was permanent professor of physics from 1901 until his retirement in 1919.

Rydberg is best known for his theoretical studies of spectral series. Using wave numbers instead of wavelengths in his calculations, he was able to arrive at a relatively simple expression that related the various lines in the spectra of chemical elements. The expression contained a constant term that became known as the Rydberg constant. His principal published work appeared in 1890 as *Recherches sur la constitution des spectres d'émission des éléments chimiques* ("Research on the Constitution of the Spectral Emissions of the Chemical Elements").

20TH CENTURY: RADIATION AND AFTER

Many physicists in the 1880s were saying that their science was coming to an end like an exhausted mine. By

1900, however, only elderly conservatives held this view, and by 1914 a new physics was in existence, which raised more questions than it could answer. The new physics was wildly exciting to those who, lucky enough to be engaged in it, saw its boundless possibilities.

HENRI BECQUEREL

(b. Dec. 15, 1852, Paris, France — d. Aug. 25, 1908, Le Croisic)

French physicist Antoine-Henri Becquerel discovered radio-activity through his investigations of uranium and other substances. In 1903 he shared the Nobel Prize for Physics with Pierre and Marie Curie. He was a member of a scientific family extending through several generations, the most notable being his grandfather Antoine-César Becquerel (1788–1878), his father, Alexandre-Edmond Becquerel (1820–91), and his son Jean Becquerel (1878–1953).

After his early schooling at the Lycée Louis-le-Grand, Henri received his formal scientific education at the École Polytechnique (1872–74) and engineering training at the École des Ponts et Chaussées (Bridges and Highways School; 1874–77). In addition to his teaching and research posts, Becquerel was for many years an engineer in the Department of Bridges and Highways, being appointed chief engineer in 1894. His first academic situation was in 1876 as assistant teacher at the École Polytechnique, where in 1895 he succeeded to the chair of physics. Concurrently, he was assistant naturalist to his father at the museum, where he also assumed the physics professorship upon his father's death.

Electricity, magnetism, optical phenomena, and energy were major areas of physical investigation during the 19th century. For several years the young man's research was concerned with the rotation of plane-polarized light by magnetic fields, a subject opened by Michael Faraday and to which Henri's father had also contributed. Henri then concerned himself with infrared radiation, examining, among other things, the spectra of different phosphorescent crystals under infrared stimulation. Of particular significance, he extended the work of his father by studying the relation between absorption of light and emission of phosphorescence in some uranium compounds.

By 1896 Henri was an accomplished and respected physicist—a member of the Académie des Sciences since 1889—but more important than his research thus far were his expertise with phosphorescent materials, his familiarity with uranium compounds, and his general skill in laboratory techniques, including photography. Together, these were to place the discovery of radioactivity within his reach.

At the end of 1895, Wilhelm Röntgen discovered X-rays. Becquerel learned that the X-rays issued from the area of a glass vacuum tube made fluorescent when struck by a beam of cathode rays. He undertook to investigate whether there was some fundamental connection between this invisible radiation and visible light such that all luminescent materials, however stimulated, would also yield X-rays. To test this hypothesis, he placed phosphorescent crystals upon a photographic plate that had been wrapped in opaque paper so that only a penetrating radiation could reach the emulsion. He exposed his experimental arrangement to sunlight for several hours, thereby exciting the crystals in the customary manner. Upon development, the photographic plate revealed silhouettes of the mineral samples, and, in subsequent experiments, the image of a coin or metal cutout interposed between the crystal and paper wrapping. Becquerel reported this discovery to the Académie des Sciences at its session on Feb. 24, 1896, noting that certain salts of uranium were particularly active.

He thus confirmed his view that something very similar to X-rays was emitted by this luminescent substance at the same time it threw off visible radiation. But the following week Becquerel learned that his uranium salts continued to eject penetrating radiation even when they were not made to phosphoresce by the ultraviolet in sunlight. To account for this novelty he postulated a long-lived form of invisible phosphorescence. When he shortly traced the activity to uranium metal, he interpreted it as a unique case of metallic phosphorescence.

During 1896 Becquerel published seven papers on radioactivity, as Marie Curie later named the phenomenon; in 1897, only two papers; and in 1898, none. This was an index of both his and the scientific world's interest in the subject, for the period saw studies of numerous radiations (e.g., cathode rays, X-rays, Becquerel rays, "discharge rays," canal rays, radio waves, the visible spectrum, rays from glowworms, fireflies, and other luminescent materials), and Becquerel rays seemed not especially significant. The far more popular X-rays could take sharper shadow photographs and faster. It required the extension in 1898 of radioactivity to another known element, thorium (by Gerhard Carl Schmidt and independently by Marie Curie), and the discovery of new radioactive materials, polonium and radium (by Pierre and Marie Curie and their colleague, Gustave Bémont), to awaken the world and Becquerel to the significance of his discovery.

Returning to the field he had created, Becquerel made three more important contributions. One was to measure, in 1899 and 1900, the deflection of beta particles, which are a constituent of the radiation in both electric and magnetic fields. From the charge to mass value thus obtained, he showed that the beta particle was the same as Joseph John Thomson's recently identified electron. Another discovery was the circumstance that the allegedly active substance in uranium, uranium X, lost its radiating ability in time, while the uranium, though inactive when freshly prepared, eventually regained its lost radioactivity. When Ernest Rutherford and Frederick Soddy found similar decay and regeneration in thorium X and thorium, they were led to the transformation theory of radioactivity, which explained the phenomenon as a subatomic chemical change in which one element spontaneously transmutes into another. Becquerel's last major achievement concerned the physiological effect of the radiation. Others may have noticed this before him, but his report in 1901 of the burn caused when he carried an active sample of the Curies' radium in his vest pocket inspired investigation by physicians, leading ultimately to medical use.

For his discovery of radioactivity, Becquerel shared the 1903 Nobel Prize for Physics with the Curies; he was also honoured with other medals and memberships in foreign societies. His own Academy of Sciences elected him its president and one of its permanent secretaries.

Marie Curie

(b. Nov. 7, 1867, Warsaw, Poland, Russian Empire—d. July 4, 1934, near Sallanches, France)

Polish-born French physicist Marie Curie (née Maria Skłodowska) was famous for her work on radioactivity and twice a winner of the Nobel Prize. With Henri Becquerel and her husband, Pierre Curie, she was awarded the 1903 Nobel Prize for Physics. She was the sole winner of the 1911 Nobel Prize for Chemistry. She was the first woman to win a Nobel Prize, and she is the only woman to win the award in two different fields.

From childhood she was remarkable for her prodigious memory, and at the age of 16 she won a gold medal on completion of her secondary education at the Russian lycée. Because her father, a teacher of mathematics and physics, lost his savings through bad investment, she had to take work as a teacher and, at the same time, took part clandestinely in the nationalist "free university," reading in Polish to women workers. At the age of 18 she took a post as governess, where she suffered an unhappy love affair. From her earnings she was able to finance her sister Bronisława's medical studies in Paris, with the understanding that Bronisława would in turn later help her to get an education.

In 1891 Skłodowska went to Paris and, now using the name Marie, began to follow the lectures of physicists at the Sorbonne. Skłodowska worked far into the night in her student-quarters garret and virtually lived on bread and butter and tea. She came first in the *licence* of physical sciences in 1893. She began to work in physicist Gabriel Lippmann's research laboratory and in 1894 was placed second in the *licence* of mathematical sciences. It was in the spring of that year that she met Pierre Curie.

Their marriage on July 25, 1895, marked the start of a partnership that was soon to achieve results of world significance, in particular the discovery of polonium (so called by Marie in honour of her native land) in the summer of 1898 and that of radium a few months later. Following Henri Becquerel's discovery (1896) of a new phenomenon (which she later called "radioactivity"), Marie Curie, looking for a subject for a thesis, decided to find out if the property discovered in uranium was to be found in other matter. She discovered that this was true for thorium at the same time as G.C. Schmidt did.

Turning her attention to minerals, she found her interest drawn to pitchblende, a mineral whose activity, superior to that of pure uranium, could be explained only by the presence in the ore of small quantities of an

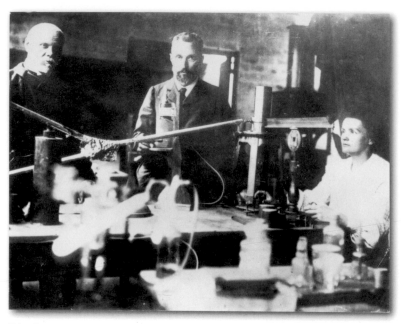

Physicists Marie Curie (right), *Pierre Curie* (centre), *and chemist Gustave Bémont* (left) *in the laboratory.* Photos.com/Jupiterimages

unknown substance of particularly high activity. Pierre Curie then joined her in the work that she had undertaken to resolve this problem and that led to the discovery of the new elements, polonium and radium. While Pierre Curie devoted himself chiefly to the physical study of the new radiations, Marie Curie struggled to obtain pure radium in the metallic state—achieved with the help of the chemist André-Louis Debierne, one of Pierre Curie's pupils. On the results of this research, Marie Curie received her doctorate of science in June 1903 and, with Pierre, was awarded the Davy Medal of the Royal Society. Also in 1903 they shared with Becquerel the Nobel Prize for Physics for the discovery of radioactivity.

The birth of her two daughters, Irène and Ève, in 1897 and 1904 did not interrupt Marie's intensive scientific work. She was appointed lecturer in physics at the École

Normale Supérieure for girls in Sèvres (1900) and introduced there a method of teaching based on experimental demonstrations. In December 1904 she was appointed chief assistant in the laboratory directed by Pierre Curie.

The sudden death of Pierre Curie (April 19, 1906) was a bitter blow to Marie Curie, but it was also a decisive turning point in her career: henceforth she was to devote all her energy to completing alone the scientific work that they had undertaken. On May 13, 1906, she was appointed to the professorship that had been left vacant on her husband's death, becoming the first woman to teach in the Sorbonne. In 1908 she became titular professor, and in 1910 her fundamental treatise on radioactivity was published. In 1911 she was awarded the Nobel Prize for Chemistry, for the isolation of pure radium. In 1914 she saw the completion of the building of the laboratories of the Radium Institute (Institut du Radium) at the University of Paris.

Marie Curie driving a Renault automobile converted into a mobile radiological unit, 1914. Curie used these vehicles, which became known as petites Curies, *to bring X-ray equipment to wounded soldiers at the front during World War I.* © Photos.com/Jupiterimages

Throughout World War I, Marie Curie, with the help of her daughter Irène, devoted herself to the development of the use of X-radiography. In 1918 the Radium Institute, the staff of which Irène had joined, began to operate in earnest, and it was to become a universal centre for nuclear physics and chemistry. Marie Curie, now at the highest point of her fame and, from 1922, a member of the Academy of Medicine, devoted her researches to the study of the chemistry of radioactive substances and the medical applications of these substances.

One of Marie Curie's outstanding achievements was to have understood the need to accumulate intense radioactive sources, not only to treat illness but also to maintain an abundant supply for research in nuclear physics; the resultant stockpile was an unrivaled instrument until the appearance after 1930 of particle accelerators. The existence in Paris at the Radium Institute of a stock of 1.5 grams of radium in which, over a period of several years, radium D and polonium had accumulated made a decisive contribution to the success of the experiments undertaken in the years around 1930 and in particular of those performed by Irène Curie in conjunction with Frédéric Joliot, whom she had married in 1926. This work prepared the way for the discovery of the neutron by Sir James Chadwick and, above all, for the discovery in 1934 by Irène and Frédéric Joliot-Curie of artificial radioactivity. A few months after this discovery, Marie Curie died as a result of leukemia caused by the action of radiation. Her contribution to physics had been immense, not only in her own work, the importance of

Marie Curie, 1931. © Photos.com/ Jupiterimages

which had been demonstrated by the award to her of two Nobel Prizes, but because of her influence on subsequent generations of nuclear physicists and chemists.

PIERRE CURIE
(b. May 15, 1859, Paris, France—d. April 19, 1906, Paris)

French physical chemist Pierre Curie was cowinner of the Nobel Prize for Physics in 1903. He and his wife, Marie Curie, discovered radium and polonium in their investigation of radioactivity. An exceptional physicist, he was one of the main founders of modern physics.

Educated by his father, a doctor, Curie developed a passion for mathematics at the age of 14 and showed a particular aptitude for spatial geometry, which was later to help him in his work on crystallography. Matriculating at the age of 16 and obtaining his *licence ès sciences* at 18, he was in 1878 taken on as laboratory assistant at the Sorbonne. There Curie carried out his first work on the calculation of the wavelength of heat waves. This was followed by crucial studies on crystals, in which he was helped by his elder brother Jacques. The problem of the distribution of crystalline matter according to the laws of symmetry was to become one of his major preoccupations. The Curie brothers associated the phenomenon of pyroelectricity with a change in the volume of the crystal in which it appears, and thus they arrived at the discovery of piezoelectricity. Later Pierre was able to formulate the principle of symmetry, which states the impossibility of bringing about a specific physical process in an environment lacking a certain minimal dissymmetry characteristic of the process. Further, this dissymmetry cannot be found in the effect if it is not preexistent in the cause. He went on to define the symmetry of different physical phenomena.

Appointed supervisor (1882) at the School of Physics and Industrial Chemistry at Paris, Curie resumed his own research and, after a long study of buffered movements, managed to perfect the analytical balance by creating an aperiodic balance with direct reading of the last weights. Then he began his celebrated studies on magnetism. He undertook to write a doctoral thesis with the aim of discovering if there exist any transitions between the three types of magnetism: ferromagnetism, paramagnetism, and diamagnetism. In order to measure the magnetic coefficients, he constructed a torsion balance that measured 0.01 mg, which, in a simplified version, is still used and called the magnetic balance of Curie and Chèneveau. He discovered that the magnetic coefficients of attraction of paramagnetic bodies vary in inverse proportion to the absolute temperature—Curie's law. He then established an analogy between paramagnetic bodies and perfect gases and, as a result of this, between ferromagnetic bodies and condensed fluids.

The totally different character of paramagnetism and diamagnetism demonstrated by Curie was later explained theoretically by Paul Langevin. In 1895 Curie defended his thesis on magnetism and obtained a doctorate of science.

In the spring of 1894 Curie met Marie Skłodowska. Their marriage (July 25, 1895) marked

Physicists Marie and Pierre Curie with their daughter Irène. Photos.com/ Jupiterimages

the beginning of a world-famous scientific achievement, beginning with the discovery (1898) of polonium and then of radium. The phenomenon of radioactivity, discovered (1896) by Henri Becquerel, had attracted Marie Curie's attention, and she and Pierre determined to study a mineral, pitchblende, the specific activity of which is superior to that of pure uranium. While working with Marie to extract pure substances from ores, an undertaking that really required industrial resources but that they achieved in relatively primitive conditions, Pierre himself concentrated on the physical study (including luminous and chemical effects) of the new radiations. Through the action of magnetic fields on the rays given out by the radium, he proved the existence of particles electrically positive, negative, and neutral; these Ernest Rutherford was afterward to call alpha, beta, and gamma rays. Pierre then studied these radiations by calorimetry and also observed the physiological effects of radium, thus opening the way to radium therapy.

Refusing a chair at the University of Geneva so he could continue his joint work with Marie, Pierre Curie was appointed lecturer (1900) and professor (1904) at the Sorbonne. He was elected to the Academy of Sciences (1905), having in 1903 jointly with Marie received the Royal Society's Davy Medal and jointly with her and Becquerel the Nobel Prize for Physics. He was run over by a dray in the rue Dauphine in Paris

Pierre Curie lecturing in a classroom. Photos.com/Jupiterimages

in 1906 and died instantly. His complete works were published in 1908.

OTTO HAHN

(b. March 8, 1879, Frankfurt am Main, Ger.—d. July 28, 1968, Göttingen, W.Ger.)

German chemist Otto Hahn, with the radiochemist Fritz Strassmann, is credited with the discovery of nuclear fission. He was awarded the Nobel Prize for Chemistry in 1944 and shared the Enrico Fermi Award in 1966 with Strassmann and Lise Meitner.

Hahn was the son of a glazier. Although his parents wanted him to become an architect, he eventually decided to study chemistry at the University of Marburg. There Hahn worked hard at chemistry, though he was inclined to absent himself from physics and mathematics lectures in favour of art and philosophy, and he obtained his doctorate in 1901. After a year of military service, he returned to the university as chemistry lecture assistant, hoping to find a post in industry later on.

In 1904 he went to London, primarily to learn English, and worked at University College with Sir William Ramsay, who was interested in radioactivity. While working on a crude radium preparation that Ramsay had given to him to purify, Hahn showed that a new radioactive substance, which he called radiothorium, was present. Fired by this early success and encouraged by Ramsay, who thought highly of him, he decided to continue with research on radioactivity rather than go into industry. With Ramsay's support he obtained a post at the University of Berlin. Before taking it up, he decided to spend several months in Montreal with Ernest Rutherford (later Lord Rutherford of Nelson) to gain further experience with radioactivity. Shortly after returning to Germany in 1906, Hahn was joined by Lise Meitner, an Austrian-born physicist, and five years later they moved to the new Kaiser Wilhelm Institute for Chemistry at Berlin-Dahlen. There Hahn became head of a small but independent department of radiochemistry.

Otto Hahn. Landesbildstelle Berlin

Feeling that his future was more secure, Hahn married Edith Junghans, the daughter of the chairman of Stettin City Council, in 1913. When World War I broke out the next year, Hahn was posted to a regiment. In 1915 he became a chemical-warfare specialist, serving on all the European fronts.

After the war, Hahn and Meitner were among the first to isolate protactinium-231, an isotope of the recently discovered radioactive element protactinium. Because nearly all the natural radioactive elements had then been discovered, he devoted the next 12 years to studies on the application of radioactive methods to chemical problems.

In 1934 Hahn became keenly interested in the work of the Italian physicist Enrico Fermi, who found that when the heaviest natural element, uranium, is bombarded by neutrons, several radioactive products are formed. Fermi supposed these products to be artificial elements similar to uranium. Hahn and Meitner, assisted by the young Strassmann, obtained results that at first seemed in accord with Fermi's interpretation but that became increasingly difficult to understand. Meitner fled from Germany in July 1938 to escape the persecution of Jews by the Nazis, but Hahn and Strassmann continued the work. By the end of 1938, they obtained conclusive evidence, contrary to previous expectation, that one of the products from uranium was a radioactive form of the much lighter element barium, indicating that the uranium atom had split into two lighter atoms. Hahn sent an account of the work to Meitner, who, in cooperation with her nephew Otto Frisch, formulated a plausible explanation of the process, to which they gave the name nuclear fission.

The tremendous implications of this discovery were realized by scientists before the outbreak of World War II, and a group was formed in Germany to study possible military developments. Much to Hahn's relief, he was allowed to continue with his own researches. After the war, he and other German nuclear scientists were taken to England, where he learned that he had been awarded the Nobel Prize for 1944 and was profoundly affected by the announcement of the explosion of the atomic bomb at Hiroshima in 1945. A lifelong mountaineer, even at age 66 he maintained vigorous physical fitness during the enforced stay in England by a daily run.

On his return to Germany he was elected president of the former Kaiser Wilhelm Society (renamed the Max Planck Society for the Advancement of Science) and became a respected public figure, a spokesman for science, and a friend of Theodor Heuss, the first president of the Federal Republic of Germany. He campaigned against further development and testing of nuclear weapons. Honours came to him from all sides. In 1966 he, Meitner, and Strassmann shared the prestigious Enrico Fermi Award. This period of his life was saddened, however, by the loss of his only son, Hanno, and his daughter-in-law, who were killed in an automobile accident in 1960. His wife never recovered from the shock. Hahn died in 1968, after a fall, and his wife survived him by only two weeks.

LISE MEITNER
(b. Nov. 7, 1878, Vienna—d. Oct. 27, 1968, Cambridge, Cambridgeshire, Eng.)

Austrian-born physicist Lise Meitner shared the Enrico Fermi Award (1966) with the chemists Otto Hahn and Fritz Strassmann for their joint research that led to the discovery of uranium fission.

After receiving her doctorate at the University of Vienna (1906), Meitner attended Max Planck's lectures at Berlin in 1907 and joined Hahn in research on radioactivity. During three decades of association, she and Hahn were among the first to isolate the isotope protactinium-231 (which they called protactinium), studied nuclear isomerism and beta decay, and in the 1930s (along with Strassmann) investigated the products of neutron bombardment of uranium. Because she was Jewish, she left Nazi Germany in the summer of 1938 to settle in Sweden. After Hahn and Strassmann had demonstrated that barium appears in neutron-bombarded uranium, Meitner, with her nephew Otto Frisch, elucidated the physical characteristics of this division and in January 1939 proposed the term fission for the process. She retired to England in 1960.

HENRY GWYN JEFFREYS MOSELEY
(b. Nov. 23, 1887, Weymouth, Dorset, Eng.—d. Aug. 10, 1915, Gallipoli, Tur.)

English physicist Henry Gwyn Jeffreys Moseley experimentally demonstrated that the major properties of an element are determined by the atomic number, not by the atomic weight, and firmly established the relationship between atomic number and the charge of the atomic nucleus.

Educated at Trinity College, Oxford, Moseley in 1910 was appointed lecturer in physics at Ernest (later Lord) Rutherford's laboratory at the University of Manchester, where he worked until the outbreak of World War I, when he entered the army. His first researches were concerned with radioactivity and beta radiation in radium. He then turned to the study of the X-ray spectra of the elements. Through a brilliant series of experiments he found a relationship between the frequencies of corresponding lines in the X-ray spectra. In a paper published in 1913, he reported that the frequencies are proportional to the squares of whole numbers that are equal to the atomic number plus a constant.

Known as Moseley's law, this fundamental discovery concerning atomic numbers was a milestone in advancing the knowledge of the atom. In 1914 Moseley published a paper in which he concluded that there were three unknown elements between aluminum and gold (there are, in fact, four). He also concluded correctly that there were only 92 elements up to and including uranium and 14 rare-earth elements.

Moseley's death at the Battle of Suvla Bay (in Turkey) at the age of 27 deprived the world of one of its most promising experimental physicists.

WILHELM RÖNTGEN

(b. March 27, 1845, Lennep, Prussia [now Remscheid, Ger.]—d. Feb. 10, 1923, Munich, Ger.)

German physicist Wilhelm Conrad Röntgen was a recipient of the first Nobel Prize for Physics in 1901 for his discovery of X-rays, which heralded the age of modern physics and revolutionized diagnostic medicine.

Röntgen studied at the Polytechnic in Zürich and then was professor of physics at the universities of Strasbourg

(1876–79), Giessen (1879–88), Würzburg (1888–1900), and Munich (1900–20). His research also included work on elasticity, capillary action of fluids, specific heats of gases, conduction of heat in crystals, absorption of heat by gases, and piezoelectricity.

In 1895, while experimenting with electric current flow in a partially evacuated glass tube (cathode-ray tube), Röntgen observed that a nearby piece of barium platino-cyanide gave off light when the tube was in operation. He theorized that when the cathode rays (electrons) struck the glass wall of the tube, some unknown radiation was formed that traveled across the room, struck the chemical, and caused the fluorescence. Further investigation revealed that paper, wood, and aluminum, among other materials, are transparent to this new form of radiation. He found that it affected photographic plates. And because it did not noticeably exhibit any properties of light, such as reflection or refraction, he mistakenly thought the rays were unrelated to light. In view of its uncertain nature, he called the phenomenon X-radiation, though it also became known as Röntgen radiation. He took the first X-ray photographs, of the interiors of metal objects and of the bones in his wife's hand.

ERNEST RUTHERFORD

(b. Aug. 30, 1871, Spring Grove, N.Z.—d. Oct. 19, 1937, Cambridge, Cambridgeshire, Eng.)

New Zealand-born British physicist Ernest Rutherford was the central figure in the study of radioactivity and nuclear physics.

Ernest Rutherford attended the free state schools in New Zealand through 1886, when he won a scholarship to attend Nelson Collegiate School. He excelled in nearly every subject but especially in mathematics and science.

Another scholarship took Rutherford in 1890 to Canterbury College in Christchurch. He received a bachelor of arts (B.A.) degree and won a scholarship for a postgraduate year of study at Canterbury. He completed this at the end of 1893, earning a master of arts (M.A.) degree with first-class honours. He was encouraged to remain yet another year in Christchurch to conduct independent research.

Ernest Rutherford. Library of Congress, Washington, D.C. (neg. no. 36570u)

Rutherford's investigation of the ability of a high-frequency electrical discharge to magnetize iron earned him a bachelor of science (B.S.) degree in 1894.

In 1895 Rutherford chose to continue his study at the Cavendish Laboratory of the University of Cambridge, which was run by J.J. Thomson, Europe's leading expert on electromagnetic radiation. At Cambridge, Rutherford became the school's first research student. Rutherford looked at radiation emitted by uranium. Placement of uranium near thin foils revealed that the radiation was more complex than previously thought: one type was easily absorbed or blocked by a very thin foil, but another type often penetrated the same thin foils. He named these radiation types alpha and beta, respectively, for simplicity. (It was later determined that the alpha particle is the nucleus of an ordinary helium atom, and the beta particle is the same as an electron.)

Rutherford's research ability won him a professorship at McGill University, Montreal. With Frederick Soddy, Rutherford in 1902–03 developed the transformation theory as an explanation for radioactivity. Atoms were regarded as stable bodies. But Rutherford and Soddy now claimed that the energy of radioactivity came from within the atom, and the spontaneous emission of an alpha or beta particle signified a chemical change from one element into another. They expected this iconoclastic theory to be controversial, but their overwhelming experimental evidence quelled opposition.

Before long it was recognized that the radioelements fell into three families, or decay series, headed by uranium, thorium, and actinium and all ending in inactive lead. Rutherford considered the alpha particle to be key to transformations.

While at McGill, Rutherford became famous. He welcomed increasing numbers of research students to his laboratory, including women at a time when few females studied science. He also wrote the period's leading textbook on radioactivity.

In 1907 Rutherford accepted a chair at the University of Manchester, whose physics laboratory was excelled in England only by Thomson's Cavendish Laboratory. A year later his work in Montreal was honoured by the Nobel Prize for Chemistry.

With the German physicist Hans Geiger, Rutherford developed an electrical counter for ionized particles; when perfected by Geiger, the Geiger counter became the universal tool for measuring radioactivity. Rutherford and his student Thomas Royds were able to isolate some alpha particles and prove that they were helium ions.

Continuing his long-standing interest in the alpha particle, Rutherford studied its slight scattering when it hit a foil. In 1909 when an undergraduate, Ernest Marsden, needed a research project, Rutherford suggested that he look for large-angle scattering. Marsden found that a small number of alphas were turned more than 90 degrees from their original direction, leading Rutherford to exclaim (with later embellishment), "It was almost as incredible as if you fired a 15-inch shell at a piece of tissue paper and it came back and hit you."

Pondering how such a heavy particle as the alpha could be turned through such a large angle, Rutherford conceived in 1911 that the atom could not be a uniform solid but rather consisted mostly of empty space, with its mass concentrated in a tiny nucleus. This insight was Rutherford's greatest scientific contribution, but it received little attention beyond Manchester. In 1913, however, the Danish physicist Niels Bohr showed its importance. Radioactivity, he explained, lies in the nucleus, while chemical properties are due to orbital electrons. His theory wove the new concept of quanta into the electrodynamics of orbits, and he explained spectral lines as the release or absorption of energy by electrons as they jump from orbit to orbit. Thus, a coherent new picture of atomic physics, as well as the field of nuclear physics, was developed.

World War I virtually emptied Rutherford's laboratory, and he himself was involved in antisubmarine research. When he found time to return to his earlier research interests, Rutherford examined the collision of alpha particles with gases. With hydrogen, as expected, nuclei (individual protons) were propelled to the detector. But, surprisingly, protons also appeared when alphas crashed into nitrogen. In 1919 Rutherford explained his third great discovery: he had artificially provoked a nuclear reaction in a stable element.

Such nuclear reactions occupied Rutherford for the remainder of his career, which was spent back at the University of Cambridge, where he succeeded Thomson in

1919 as director of the Cavendish Laboratory. Rutherford and physicist James Chadwick bombarded a number of light elements with alphas and induced transformations. But they could not penetrate to the nuclei of heavier elements, as the alphas were repelled by their mutual charges, nor could they determine whether the alpha bounced off after collision or combined with the target nucleus. More-advanced technology was needed in both cases.

For the former, the higher energies produced in particle accelerators became available by the late 1920s. In 1932 two of Rutherford's students, John D. Cockcroft of England and Ernest T.S. Walton of Ireland, were the first to actually cause a nuclear transformation; with their high-voltage linear accelerator, they bombarded lithium with protons and caused it to split into two alpha particles.

The Cavendish was home to other exciting work. The neutron's existence had been predicted in a speech by Rutherford in 1920. After a long search, Chadwick discovered this neutral particle in 1932. In 1934 Rutherford, Australian physicist Mark Oliphant, and German physical chemist Paul Harteck bombarded deuterium with deuterons, producing tritium in the first fusion reaction.

FREDERICK SODDY

(b. Sept. 2, 1877, Eastbourne, Sussex, Eng.—d. Sept. 22, 1956, Brighton, Sussex)

English chemist Frederick Soddy was the recipient of the 1921 Nobel Prize for Chemistry for investigating radioactive substances and for elaborating the theory of isotopes. He is credited, along with others, with the discovery of the element protactinium in 1917.

Educated in Wales and at the University of Oxford, he worked under the physicist Sir Ernest Rutherford at McGill University, Montreal (1900–02), then under the chemist Sir William Ramsay at University College, London. After teaching at the University of Glasgow, Scotland (1904–14), Soddy became a professor of chemistry at Oxford (1919–37).

Soddy worked with Rutherford on the disintegration of radioactive elements. He was among the first to conclude in 1912 that certain elements might exist in forms that differ in atomic weight while being indistinguishable and inseparable chemically. These, upon a suggestion by Margaret Todd, he called isotopes. In *Science and Life* (1920) he pointed out their value in determining geologic age.

Soddy turned away from the study of radioactivity in 1914 and became involved in social and economic issues. He was highly critical of the inability of the world's economic systems to make full use of scientific and technological advances.

FRITZ STRASSMANN

(b. Feb. 22, 1902, Boppard, Ger.—d. April 22, 1980, Mainz, W.Ger.)

Fritz Strassmann was a German physical chemist who, with Otto Hahn, discovered neutron-induced nuclear fission in uranium (1938) and thereby opened the field of atomic energy.

Strassmann received his Ph.D. from the Technical University in Hannover in 1929. He helped develop the rubidium-strontium method of dating widely used in geochronology. Beginning in 1934 he joined Hahn and Lise Meitner in their investigations of the radioactive products formed when uranium is bombarded by neutrons. Strassmann's mastery of analytic chemistry contributed to the team's recognition of the lighter elements produced from neutron bombardment, which were the result of the splitting of the uranium atom into two lighter atoms.

After serving briefly on the staffs of the Hannover and Kaiser Wilhelm institutes (destroyed in 1944), Strassmann in 1946 became professor of inorganic and nuclear chemistry at the University of Mainz, where he established the Institute of Inorganic Chemistry (later the Institute of Nuclear Chemistry). From 1945 to 1953 he was director of the chemistry department at the Max Planck Institute for Chemistry.

SIR J.J. THOMSON
(b. Dec. 18, 1856, Cheetham Hill, near Manchester, Eng. — d. Aug. 30, 1940, Cambridge, Cambridgeshire)

English physicist Sir Joseph John Thomson helped revolutionize the knowledge of atomic structure by his discovery of the electron (1897). He received the Nobel Prize for Physics in 1906 and was knighted in 1908.

In 1876 Thomson obtained a scholarship at Trinity College, Cambridge, where he remained for the rest of his life. After taking his B.A. degree in mathematics in 1880, the opportunity of doing experimental research drew him to the Cavendish Laboratory.

Thomson's most important line of work, interrupted only for lectures at Princeton University in 1896, was that which led him, in 1897, to the conclusion that all matter, whatever its source, contains particles of the same kind that are much less massive than the atoms of which they form a part. They are now called electrons, although he originally called them corpuscles. His discovery was the result of an attempt to solve a long-standing controversy regarding the nature of cathode rays, which occur when an electric current is driven through a vessel from which most of the air or other gas has been pumped out. Nearly all German physicists of the time held that these visible rays were produced by occurrence in the ether—a weight-less substance then thought to pervade all space—but that they were neither ordinary light nor the recently discovered X-rays. British and French physicists, on the other hand, believed that these rays were electrified particles. By applying an improved vacuum technique, Thomson was able to put forward a convincing argument that these rays were composed of particles. Furthermore, these rays seemed to be composed of the same particles, or corpuscles, regardless of what kind of gas carried the electric discharge or what kinds of metals were used as conductors. Thomson's conclusion that the corpuscles were present in all kinds of matter was strengthened during the next three years, when he found that corpuscles with the same properties could be produced in other ways (e.g., from hot metals). Thomson may be described as "the man who split the atom" for the first time, although "chipped" might be a better word, in view of the size and number of electrons. Although some atoms contain many electrons their total mass is never so much as 1/1000 that of the atom.

By the turn of the century most of the scientific world had fully accepted Thomson's far-reaching discovery. In 1903 he had the opportunity to amplify his views on the behaviour of subatomic particles in natural phenomena when, in his Silliman Lectures at Yale, he suggested a discontinuous theory of light; his hypothesis foreshadowed Einstein's later theory of photons. In 1906 he received the Nobel Prize for Physics for his researches into the electrical conductivity of gases; in 1908 he was knighted; in 1909 he was made president of the British Association for the Advancement of Science; and in 1912 he received the Order of Merit.

Thomson was, however, by no means a scientific recluse. During his most fruitful years as a scientist, he was administrative head of the highly successful Cavendish

Laboratory. (It was there that he met Rose Elizabeth Paget, whom he married in 1890.) He not only administered the research projects but also financed two additions to the laboratory buildings primarily from students' fees, with little support from the university and colleges. Except for its share of a small government grant to the Royal Society to aid all British universities and all branches of science, the Cavendish Laboratory received no other government subsidy, nor were there contributions from charitable corporations or industry. A gift from a devoted staff member made possible the purchase of a small liquid-air machine essential for Thomson's research on positive rays, which greatly increased knowledge of the recently discovered atomic nuclei.

Thomson was, moreover, an outstanding teacher, his importance in physics depending almost as much on the work he inspired in others as on that which he did himself. The group of men he gathered around him between 1895 and 1914 came from all over the world, and after working under him many accepted professorships abroad. Seven Nobel Prizes were awarded to those who worked under him. It was while working with Thomson at the Cavendish Laboratory in 1910, for example, that Ernest Rutherford performed the research that led to the modern understanding of the internal structure of the atom. In the process, the Rutherford atomic model supplanted the so-called plum-pudding model of atomic structure; the latter is known as the Thomson atomic model because of the strong support Thomson gave it for a few years.

Thomson took his teaching duties very seriously: he lectured regularly to elementary classes in the morning and to postgraduates in the afternoon. He considered teaching to be helpful for a researcher, because it required him to reconsider basic ideas that otherwise might have been taken for granted. He never advised a man entering a new research field to begin by reading the work already done. Rather, Thomson thought it wise that he first clarify his own ideas. Then he could safely read the reports of others without having his own views influenced by assumptions that he might find difficult to throw off.

Thomson demonstrated his wide range of interests outside science by his interest in politics, current fiction, drama, university sports, and the nontechnical aspects of science. Although he was not athletic, he was an enthusiastic fan of the Cambridge cricket and rugby teams. But his greatest interest outside physics was in plants. He enjoyed long walks in the countryside, especially in hilly regions near Cambridge, where he searched for rare botanical specimens for his elaborate garden. In 1918 Thomson was made master of Trinity College. This position, in which he remained until his death, gave him the opportunity to meet many young men whose interests lay outside the field of science. He enjoyed these meetings and made many new friends.

angular momentum Property characterizing the rotary inertia of an object or system of objects in motion about an axis that may or may not pass through the object or system.

atom Smallest unit into which matter can be divided and still retain the characteristic properties of an element.

big bang Model of the origin of the universe, which holds that it emerged from a state of extremely high temperature and density in an explosive expansion 13.7 billion years ago.

bremsstrahlung Electromagnetic radiation produced by a sudden slowing down or deflection of charged particles, especially electrons, passing through matter in the vicinity of the strong electric fields of atomic nuclei.

doubly magic nuclei Both the protons and neutrons are magic number amounts. So helium-4 with 2 neutrons and 2 protons is doubly magic.

electron Lightest electrically charged subatomic particle known.

excitation Addition of a discrete amount of energy to a system that changes it usually from a state of lowest energy (ground state) to one of higher energy (excited state).

half-life Interval of time required for one-half of the atomic nuclei of a radioactive sample to decay (change spontaneously into other nuclear species by emitting particles and energy), or the time required for the number of disintegrations per second of a radioactive material to decrease by one-half.

hydrogen bomb Also called thermonuclear bomb. Weapon whose enormous explosive power is generated by the nuclear fusion of hydrogen isotopes.

ion Atom or group of atoms with one or more positive or negative electric charges.

isotope One of two or more species of atoms of a chemical element having nuclei with the same number of protons but different numbers of neutrons.

kinetic theory of gases Theory based on a simple description of a gas as a collection of particles, from which many properties of gases can be derived.

lepton Any member of a class of fermions that respond only to electromagnetic, weak, and gravitational forces and do not take part in strong interactions.

magic number In the shell models of both atomic and nuclear structure, any of a series of numbers of protons or neutrons that denote stable structure. The known magic numbers are 2, 8, 20, 28, 50, 82, and 126.

molecule Smallest identifiable unit into which a pure substance can be divided and retain its composition and chemical properties.

neutrino Fundamental particle with no electric charge, little mass, and a spin value of $\frac{1}{2}$.

neutron One of the constituent particles of every atomic nucleus except ordinary hydrogen.

nuclear fission Division of a heavy atomic nucleus into two fragments of roughly equal mass, accompanied by the release of a large amount of energy, the binding energy of the subatomic particles.

nuclear weapon Bomb or other warhead that derives its force from nuclear fission, nuclear fusion, or both and is delivered by an aircraft, missile, or other system.

nuclide Species of atom as characterized by the number of protons, neutrons, and the energy state of the nucleus.

orbital Mathematical expression, called a wave function, that describes properties characteristic of no more than two electrons near an atomic nucleus or molecule.

photon Minute energy packet of electromagnetic radiation.

plasma Electrically conducting medium in which there are roughly equal numbers of positively and negatively charged particles, produced when the atoms in a gas become ionized (ionization).

prompt neutron In nuclear fission reactions, neutron emitted instantaneously by a nucleus undergoing fission—in contrast to a delayed neutron, which is emitted by an excited nucleus among the fission products at an appreciable time interval (milliseconds to minutes) after fission has occurred.

proton Stable subatomic particle (one of the baryons) with a unit of positive electric charge and a mass 1,836 times that of the electron.

quantum electrodynamics Quantum theory of the interactions of charged particles with the electromagnetic field.

radioactivity Property exhibited by certain types of matter of emitting radiation spontaneously.

scission Division or split in a group or union.

spectral line series Any of the related sequences of wavelengths characterizing the light and other electromagnetic radiation emitted by energized atoms.

spin Amount of angular momentum associated with a subatomic particle or nucleus.

tokamak Device used in nuclear-fusion research for magnetic confinement of plasma.

valence Number of bonds (bonding) an atom can form.

van der Waals forces Relatively weak electrical forces that attract neutral (uncharged) molecules to each other in gases, liquefied and solidified gases, and almost all organic liquids and solids.

BIBLIOGRAPHY

General History

Hans Christian von Baeyer, *Taming the Atom: The Emergence of the Visible Microworld* (1992, reissued 2000), is an engaging and clearly written history of the atom, from the Greeks to modern laboratories. James Trefil, *From Atoms to Quarks* (1980, reissued 1994), is a history of the quest for the ultimate nature of matter. Andrew G. van Melsen, *From Atomos to Atoms: The History of the Concept Atom*, trans. from the Dutch by Henry J. Koren (1952, reissued 2004; originally published 1949), is an exhaustive study of the history of the atom from a philosophical point of view. Steven Weinberg, *The Discovery of Subatomic Particles*, rev. ed. (2003), is a concise historical exposition emphasizing 19th- and early 20th-century discoveries. Helge Kragh, *Quantum Generations: A History of Physics in the Twentieth Century* (1999, reissued 2002), is a detailed one-volume history of physics in the 20th century. Henry A. Boorse and Lloyd Motz (eds.), *The World of the Atom*, 2 vol. (1966), containing reprints of many original papers influential in the development of thought on the atom, is highly recommended for its lively and thorough commentary.

Atomic Components and Properties

Raymond A. Serway, Clement J. Moses, and Curt A. Moyer, *Modern Physics*, 3rd ed. (2005), is a standard introductory textbook. Linus Pauling, *The Nature of the*

Chemical Bond and the Structure of Molecules and Crystals: An Introduction to Modern Structural Chemistry, 3rd ed. (1960, reissued 1993), gives a classic account of the author's valence bond theory. Roger L. DeKock and Harry B. Gray, *Chemical Structure and Bonding*, 2nd ed. (1989), is an excellent introductory textbook for chemistry undergraduates. Robert Eisberg and Robert Resnick, *Quantum Physics of Atoms, Molecules, Solids, Nuclei, and Particles*, 2nd ed. (1985), is for readers with a calculus background but no previous quantum mechanics. Bogdan Povh et al., *Particles and Nuclei: An Introduction to the Physical Concepts*, trans. from the German by Martin Lavelle, 4th ed. (2004), covers nuclear properties, their reactions, and the basics of the Standard Model in more detail, with a minimum of mathematical equations.

Isotope

Useful sources include F.W. Aston, *Mass Spectra and Isotopes*, 2nd ed. (1942), a history of the discovery of radioactive and stable isotopes; Gerhart Friedlander et al., *Nuclear and Radiochemistry*, 3rd ed. (1981); Michael J. Pilling and Paul W. Seakins, *Reaction Kinetics* (1995); Stelio Villani, *Isotope Separation*, trans. from Italian (1967); and James W. Truran, "Nucleosynthesis," *Annual Review of Nuclear and Particle Science*, 34:53–97 (1984).

Radioactivity

Bernard G. Harvey, *Introduction to Nuclear Physics and Chemistry*, 2nd ed. (1969), an excellent introductory text on nuclear phenomena; Aage Bohr and Ben R. Mottelson, *Nuclear Structure*, 2 vol. (1969); C. Michael Lederer and Virginia S. Shirley, *Table of Isotopes*, 7th ed.

(1978), a comprehensive table that lists all the known radioactive and stable isotopes and their properties; and Alfred Romer, *The Restless Atom: The Awakening of Nuclear Physics* (1960, reprinted 1982), a popular account of the discovery of radioactivity and research in that field. Collections of articles and reports are Frederick Soddy, *Radioactivity and Atomic Theory* (1975); and Alfred Romer (ed.), *The Discovery of Radioactivity and Transmutation* (1964). Applications of radiation are discussed in International Atomic Energy Agency, *Industrial Application of Radioisotopes and Radiation Technology* (1982); and Howard J. Glenn (ed.), *Biologic Applications of Radiotracers* (1982), on the use of small animals in radiotracer research.

Nuclear Fission

Louis A. Turner, "Nuclear Fission," *Reviews of Modern Physics*, 12(1):1–29 (January 1940), an excellent review of the early studies on nuclear fission; Henry DeWolf Smyth, *Atomic Energy for Military Purposes: The Official Report on the Development of the Atomic Bomb Under the Auspices of the United States Government, 1940–1945*, new and enlarged ed. (1948, reprinted 1978); and Samuel Glasstone, *Sourcebook on Atomic Energy*, 3rd ed. (1967, reprinted 1979), a comprehensive text on the atom and nuclear energy. For a detailed, authoritative treatment of all aspects of nuclear fission, see Earl K. Hyde, Isadore Perlman, and Glenn T. Seaborg, *The Nuclear Properties of the Heavy Elements*, vol. 3, *Fission Phenomena* (1964, reissued 1971); and Robert Vandenbosch and John R. Huizenga, *Nuclear Fission* (1973). Also useful are Wolf-Udo Schröder (ed.), *Nuclear Fission and Heavy-Ion-Induced Reactions* (1987), papers from a conference;

and a multivolume proceedings series published by the International Atomic Energy Agency, "Physics and Chemistry of Fission." For more popular accounts of nuclear energy and its uses, see Grace Marmor Spruch and Larry Spruch (eds.), *The Ubiquitous Atom* (1974); and Martin Mann, *Peacetime Uses of Atomic Energy*, 3rd rev. ed. (1975), a brief description of nuclear reactors and the uses of radioisotopes in industry, medicine, and scientific research. The story of the atomic bomb is told in William L. Laurence, *Men and Atoms: The Discovery, the Uses, and the Future of Atomic Energy* (1959, reissued 1962); James W. Kunetka, *City of Fire: Los Alamos and the Atomic Age, 1943–1945*, rev. ed. (1978); and Richard Rhodes, *The Making of the Atomic Bomb* (1986).

NUCLEAR FUSION

Further information can be found in Donald D. Clayton, *Principles of Stellar Evolution and Nucleosynthesis* (1968, reprinted 1983), a description of nuclear astrophysics covering energy generation and transport in stars, thermonuclear fusion reactions, and star burning; Francis F. Chen, *Plasma Physics*, 2nd ed. (1984), vol. 1 of *Introduction to Plasma Physics and Controlled Fusion*, a basic introduction; V.E. Golant, A.P. Zhilinsky, and I.E. Sakharov, *Fundamentals of Plasma Physics* (1980; originally published in Russian, 1977), an advanced text; J. Raeder et al., *Controlled Nuclear Fusion: Fundamentals of Its Utilization for Energy Supply* (1986; originally published in German, 1981), an introduction to fusion energy, its technology, and the engineering aspects of conceptual fusion power reactors; Robert W. Conn, "The Engineering of Magnetic Fusion Reactors," *Scientific American*, 249(4):60–71 (October 1983), a descriptive article on the technology of fusion machines and future fusion-energy reactors; and Robert A. Gross, *Fusion Energy* (1984), an introductory text to fusion energy physics and technology, with an emphasis on the magnetic confinement fusion approach.

RADIATION

GENERAL

Historical works include Max Planck, *Introduction to Theoretical Physics*, vol. 4, *Theory of Light* (1932, reprinted 1957; originally published in German, 1927), the classic work on the subject of light and quanta. Other forms of electromagnetic radiation are covered in Otto Glasser, *Wilhelm Conrad Röntgen and the Early History of the Roentgen Rays* (1933; originally published in German, 1931). See also R.W. Ditchburn, *Light*, 3rd ed., 2 vol. (1976), a well-presented text on physical optics that, though not too mathematical, does require understanding of the use of differential equations.

INTERACTION OF RADIATION WITH MATTER

Gerhard K. Rollefson and Milton Burton, *Photochemistry and the Mechanism of Chemical Reactions* (1939, reprinted 1946); William Albert Noyes and Philip Albert Leighton, *The Photochemistry of Gases* (1941, reprinted 1966), are both classic works that include material on internal conversion and predissociation. The language of intersystem crossing is discussed in detail in a comprehensive text, Jack G. Calvert and James N. Pitts, *Photochemistry* (1966). The actual effects of radiation on solids are thoroughly summarized in Hans A. Bethe and Julius Ashkin, "Passage of Radiations Through Matter," in Emilio Segrè (ed.), *Experimental Nuclear Physics*, vol. 1 (1953), pp. 166–357;

G.J. Dienes and G.H. Vineyard, *Radiation Effects in Solids* (1957); and Douglas S. Billington and James H. Crawford, Jr., *Radiation Damage in Solids* (1961). For a survey of radiation effects on aqueous solutions and organic compounds, see J.W.T. Spinks and R.J. Woods, *An Introduction to Radiation Chemistry*, 2nd ed. (1976); *Actions chimiques et biologiques des radiations* (annual 1955–71), the first survey on a large variety of subjects in radiation chemistry written by scientists largely about their own work—some volumes have been translated into English with the title, *The Chemical and Biological Action of Radiations*; and Max S. Matheson and Leon M. Dorfman, *Pulse Radiolysis* (1969), an excellent book on techniques in radiation chemistry. *Advances in Photochemistry* (irregular) is concerned mainly with surveys of advances in the field. See also J.F. Ziegler (ed.), *Ion Implantation: Science and Technology* (1984), a treatment of ion implantation mechanisms, techniques, effects, and practical applications; and Orlando Auciello and Roger Kelly (eds.), *Ion Bombardment Modification of Surfaces: Fundamentals and Applications* (1984), covering surface alteration mechanisms with major emphasis on topographical effects.

RADIOLOGICAL UNITS AND MEASUREMENTS

For descriptions, see Ralph E. Lapp and Howard L. Andrews, *Nuclear Radiation Physics*, 4th ed. (1972); and International Commission on Radiation Units and Measurements, *Radiation Quantities and Units* (1980).

BIOLOGIC EFFECTS OF RADIATION

Ionizing

General information is given in Charles Wesley Shilling (ed.), *Atomic Energy Encyclopedia in the Life Sciences*

(1964). Introductory information on radiation biology is given in J.E. Coggle, *Biological Effects of Radiation*, 2nd ed. (1983); John W. Gofman, *Radiation and Human Health* (1981); Daniel S. Grosch and Larry E. Hopwood, *Biological Effects of Radiations*, 2nd ed. (1979); and Eric J. Hall, *Radiation and Life*, 2nd ed. (1984). More specialized topics are covered in Assembly on Life Sciences (U.S.) Committee on the Biological Effects of Ionizing Radiations, *The Effects on Populations of Exposure to Low Levels of Ionizing Radiation, 1980* (1980); Merrill Eisenbud, *Environmental Radioactivity: From Natural, Industrial, and Military Sources*, 3rd ed. (1987); Donald J. Pizzarello and Richard L. Witcofski, *Medical Radiation Biology*, 2nd ed. (1982); United Nations Scientific Committee on the Effects of Atomic Radiation, *Ionizing Radiation: Sources and Biological Effects* (1982), and *Genetic and Somatic Effects of Ionizing Radiation* (1986); Arthur C. Upton, *Radiation Injury: Effects, Principles, and Perspectives* (1969); and Arthur C. Upton et al. (eds.), *Radiation Carcinogenesis* (1986).

Non-Ionizing

Microwave radiation is treated in National Council of Radiation Protection and Measurements, *Biological Effects of Ultrasound: Mechanisms and Clinical Implications* (1983), and *Biological Effects and Exposure Criteria for Radiofrequency and Electromagnetic Fields* (1986); and R.C. Petersen, "Bioeffects of Microwaves: A Review of Current Knowledge," *Journal of Occupational Medicine*, 25(2):103–110 (February 1983). Visible and ultraviolet radiations are the subject of Walter Harm, *Biological Effects of Ultraviolet Radiation* (1980); A. Jarret (ed.), *The Photobiology of the Skin: Lasers and the Skin* (1984); Kendric C. Smith (ed.), *Topics in Photomedicine* (1984); and Richard

J. Wurtman, Michael J. Baum, and John T. Potts, Jr. (eds.), *The Medical and Biological Effects of Light* (1985).

Nuclear War

Radiation effects of a nuclear war are discussed in Samuel Glasstone and Philip J. Dolan (eds.), *The Effects of Nuclear Weapons*, 3rd ed. (1977); Jean Petersen and Don Hinrichsen (eds.), *Nuclear War: The Aftermath* (1982); Julius London and Gilbert F. White (eds.), *The Environmental Effects of Nuclear War* (1984); and Fredric Solomon and Robert Q. Marston (eds.), *The Medical Implications of Nuclear War* (1986).

Radiation Protection and Safety

Procedures and recommendations for protection are analyzed in International Commission on Radiological Protection, *Recommendations of the International Commission on Radiological Protection* (1977, reprinted with supplements, 1987), and *Nonstochastic Effects of Ionizing Radiation* (1984); National Council on Radiation Protection and Measurements, *Ionizing Radiation Exposure of the Population of the United States* (1987); and Marilyn E. Noz and Gerald Q. Maguire, Jr., *Radiation Protection in the Radiologic and Health Sciences*, 2nd ed. (1985).

APPLICATIONS OF RADIATION

Medical

Radiological imaging techniques are explored in R.P. Clark and M.P. Goff (eds.), *Recent Developments in Medical and Physiological Imaging* (1986); W.-D. Heiss and M.F. Phelps (eds.), *Positron Emission Tomography of the Brain* (1983); Alexander R. Magulis and Charles A. Gooding

(eds.), *Diagnostic Radiology, 1987* (1987); and Albert A.
Moss, Ernest J. Ring, and Charles B. Higgins (eds.),
NMR, CT, and Interventional Radiology (1984). Radiation
therapy is addressed by Gilbert H. Fletcher, *Textbook
of Radiotherapy*, 3rd ed. (1980); and Ernest J. Ring and
Gordon K. McLean, *Interventional Radiology: Principles
and Techniques* (1981). Specific uses of phototherapy are
outlined in Audrey K. Brown and Jane Showacre (eds.),
*Phototherapy for Neonatal Hyperbilirubinemia: Long-Term
Implications* (1977); Wayne F. March (ed.), *Ophthalmic
Lasers: Current Clinical Uses* (1984); and Warwick L.
Morison, *Phototherapy and Photochemotherapy of Skin
Disease* (1983).

Scientific and Industrial

A review of ionizing radiation processing in medicine and
industrial manufacturing is found in Vitomir Markovic,
"Modern Tools of the Trade," *International Atomic Energy
Agency Bulletin*, 27(1):33–39 (Spring 1985). Industrial uses
are explored in Joseph Silverman, "Radiation Processing:
The Industrial Applications of Radiation Chemistry,"
Journal of Chemical Education, 58(2):168–173 (Feb.
1981). International Atomic Energy Agency, *Industrial
Application of Radioisotopes and Radiation Technology* (1982),
is a collection of conference papers.

INDEX

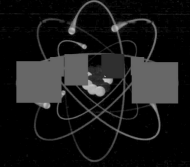